E H Suydam

BOSTON AND THE BOSTON LEGEND

FANEUIL HALL, OLD QUINCY MARKET, AND
THE CUSTOM HOUSE TOWER

BOSTON

and the

BOSTON LEGEND

by

LUCIUS BEEBE

Illustrations by

E. H. SUYDAM

D. APPLETON-CENTURY COMPANY

INCORPORATED

NEW YORK   LONDON

1935

FOR MY FATHER

FOREWORD

THIS is not a history of Boston. There are many of these already in existence and the chronicle of the city is probably as complete in its details as that of any in the world. It was settled in modern times by orderly minded and educated men who were concerned that their actions should be on record, and it has continued into an age when the record is necessary and occupies multiple forms.

Nor is this an essay conceived in the vein that once prompted John Adams, in a singularly unabashed moment, to write of his fellow Bostonians: "The morals of our people are much better; their manners are more polite and agreeable; they are purer English; our language is better; our taste is better; our persons are handsomer; our spirit is greater; our laws are wiser; our religion is superior; our education is better." It is the more pity that Mr. Adams did not touch, too, on the superior modesty of Bostonians.

Far from achieving any Utopian perfection, Boston has

vii

Foreword

always suffered from civic blemishes of greater or less magnitude. It is frequently the faults in any character which, to the perverse human mind, lend it the most flavor.

Rather this is an attempt, through the agency of selected interludes, episodes, personalities and aspects of Boston's past and present, to suggest a character study of the town, neither a portrait of parade nor a caricature, but one implicit, at least, with reality and some vital gusto. Too many among even the friendliest essayists have somehow contrived to invest Boston with all the compelling animation of that favorite English boarding-house dessert, cold shape. And Bostonians themselves have often enough contributed to this sedative legend in a spirit of oblique or indifferent malice, feeling somehow superior for the tolerant suffrage of the rest of the world.

Boston has a past that is not entirely compounded of noble sentiments, heroic sacrifice, and the posturings of oratorical patriots and professional humanitarians, although, heaven knows, it has had its share of such calamities. It has supplied the American scene not only with Peace Jubilees and Browning Societies, but with some of the most gorgeous rioting, hardest drinking, most learned cursing and spectacular high-binding finance on record. The wonder and glory of the American nineties, John L. Sullivan, was known to the world as the Boston Strong Boy, largely, to be sure, because most people had never heard of Roxbury. Boston clipper captains, in many seas, were more representative of the white man's civilization, of order, property and enterprise, than were her Britanic Majesty's viceroys. With the possible exception of first district Cognacs of vintage years and honest Armagnacs there has never been an *aqua vitæ* comparable to the Medford rum that was lightered down the Mystic, although there is a school of thought which cleaves to a similar distillation compounded up the

Foreword

turnpike at Newburyport. Oakes and Oliver Ames, in a
time when such sagacity was universally applauded, inaugurated in Crédit Mobilier a financial scandal that spanned
the American continent with diamond stack locomotives and
was the envy of the world until the time of Kreuger. Make
no mistake, Boston has been as good at uproar as at tatting.

Boston does not represent the quintessential excellence of
all the world's cities synthesised into a paradigm of urban
beauty and virtue, but it is a place at once characteristic, mellow and mature, and possessed of many qualities not entirely
divorced from charm. This portrait-chronicle attempts to
report Boston and its legend in terms of reality: nothing
more. In its preparation the author has been materially
assisted by Mr. Frank Buxton, editor of the Boston
Herald, Mr. Edward Dewey of Harvard University, and
Mr. Gilbert R. Payson, one-time wharfinger of Long
Wharf, and he is in their debt for much of certain chapters.

L. B.

CONTENTS

Contents

ILLUSTRATIONS

Plates

xiii

Illustrations

Headpieces

Illustrations

End-papers

BOSTON AND THE BOSTON LEGEND

Chapter I

AB INITIO

THE prospect from William Blackstone's house was a particularly agreeable one. The broad slope of the hill rolled down to meet the lowlands and the tidewater, and the casual reaches of the Charles River suggested, when the sun was at an appropriate angle, a broad panel of burnished metal stretching far into the West. If he was of a mind Mr. Blackstone could lie abed late of mornings, because the sun did not strike through his windows until some little time after it had risen over Massachusetts Bay, and his evenings were long and peaceful, the only sounds being the animated croakings of frogs in the meadows where Charles Street now runs and the gulls which screamed as they wheeled in search of fish over the edges of the Roxbury Flats. There were, in fact, great numbers of water fowl all the year round, especially geese, which were so easy a mark for gunners that later settlers in Boston town fed their dogs on them and at

3

one man's home it was the inevitable dinner custom "to have every man his duck upon a trencher."

Mr. Blackstone's orchard, with apple cuttings and seckel pears from England, and his gardens where common lilacs and snowballs ran right up to the door, were his particular pride. These and his library. The library too, he had brought from England and that had been a difficult business. All of these, orchard, gardens and library were the first of their sort on the hillslopes of Shawmut and Mr. Blackstone was the first settler to lay out his plantation there. Latterday Bostonians have frequently been fond of the very same things, but, save for the library, there has been increasingly less opportunity to indulge these tastes.

William Blackstone laid down the sills of his house about 1626. He was a retired English clergyman of Episcopalian persuasion with a hanker for none but his own company. He said, later, when he was departing the then growing community that "he had left England because of his dislike for the Lord Bishops and now he did not like the Lord Bretheren." Solitary and scholarly squatter, he was not only Boston's first citizen, but Boston's first "character" as well, and not, it would seem, lacking in a certain sardonic humor. There have been others like him since.

The first record of Mr. Blackstone's occupancy of his Triamount plantation was when he was taxed twelve shillings by the Plymouth Colony on account of the expense incurred by the Colony in capturing and transporting his rowdy neighbor, Thomas Morton of Wollaston. Morton, a hilarious and ribald trader, will be remembered, probably, longer than the Pilgrims who disapproved his conduct. His harem of Indian women were the scandal of Massachusetts Bay and his raffish followers, Morris dancing about his celebrated May-Pole at Merry Mount, can be heard shouting and clogging it down the centuries. The lamentable and

Ab Initio

worthless Morton had a sense of humor and, though the stern Plymouth fathers might wreck his trading colony, he was able to write wittily and disrespectfully about them afterward and the laugh will be on his side forever.

Mr. Blackstone had other neighbors at infrequent intervals. There were little plantations at Weymouth and Hull; and on Noddle's Island, now East Boston, Samuel Maverick, a young gentleman of property and education, had laid out an estate with a fort boasting four mounted pieces. His name was destined, through the agency of a descendant and in the jargon of a then undreamed of empire of cattle and cowboys, to distinguish an individual spirit who traveled apart from the herd. Then on the slope of Bunker Hill, Thomas Walford, a blacksmith, had set up his Charles Town forge, although for what purpose is a debatable question, there being no horses to shoe in the Colony at that time. Mr. Blackstone was not entirely isolated in his frame house on the western slope of Beacon Hill, but the community was far from populous.

There has been a deal of discussion as to just where Mr. Blackstone set up his house, but his orchards, still bearing fruit according to the town records in 1765, became Boston Common, and other parcels of his real estate passed into the hands of the Mount Vernon proprietors years after the first settler had tired of the company of his Puritan neighbors and removed to Rehoboth in the Rhode Island and Providence Plantations, where he lived to the age of eighty. Unhappily his diaries were destroyed when, after his death, the Indians burned his house, so that the store of information that has come down to us about him is meager in the extreme. Mather refers to him in his *Magnalia* in the following terms: "There were also some Godly Episcopalians, among them has been reckoned Mr. Blackstone; who, by happening to speel first in an old hovel upon a point of land

5

there, laid claim to all the ground whereupon now stands the metropolis of English America, until the inhabitants gave him satisfaction." In any event Governor Winthrop recognized his claim and the first settlers bought the peninsula of Shawmut from him for the sum of thirty pounds, assessed upon the inhabitants, some paying six shillings toward the purchase and some more, according to their affluence and means.

When, in the year 1630, Governor John Winthrop and nearly a thousand followers with the charter, heavy with seals, of the Massachusetts Company, set out from "the Cowes," in England the settlement at Salem and the Pilgrim Colony at Plymouth were already established and flourishing communities, Plymouth boasting a population of nearly 3,000. The Massachusetts Company was the fruit of long and tedious details of planning in England, and its existence was due to the growing belief on the part of the English Puritan party that reforms, ecclesiastic or governmental, were impossible in the mother country. Its evolution was predicated upon the removal of an entire unit of society, complete with a government and a church, from one continent to another and it was led by men of very considerable resolution, not, to be sure, quite untempered by religious fervor.

Fortunately for the tradition of Boston and for history, the city came into being, completely emergent, at the fiat of a group of men who were neither adventurers nor mere casual errants. True, the selection of the site of Boston, when a thousand other places offered under the terms of the charter, was not predetermined, but the town came into being in modern times and the record of its evolution and of the men who founded it is reasonably complete. Even in the difficult and disastrous early years there were those who

Ab Initio

concerned themselves for the preservation of an orderly and concise chronicling of their own lives and times.

John Winthrop, even though his stature has grown in proportion to the passing of the centuries, was a man to be reckoned with in his own time. He was born near Ipswich in Suffolk and, despite the circumstance that he was one of the last of the group of leaders to throw in his hand with their venture in the new world, he was a man at once so determined and resolute that he was presently elected governor of the expedition. Weary of the corruption, strife and economic and intellectual complexity of the times in his homeland, he was willing to forego a sure amount of ease and security in the hope of establishing on a distant, yet certain shore a civilization somewhat nearer to the heart's desire. What he sought most of all was a parliamentary government, which had almost entirely disappeared in the England of the first Charles, escape from the crushing taxes necessary to support the British government, and freedom for the special brand of religion conceived as "the true faith" of the Puritan party.

As a preliminary step to their actual removal, under the terms of their charter, twelve men, most of whose names are today to be found in the directory of the twentieth century city of Boston, Winthrop among them, signed the famous Cambridge Agreement, which is the document from which the Boston legend stems. Named for the walls of the university within which it was signed the cartel read as follows:

Upon due consideration of the state of the Plantation now in hand for New England, wherein we whose names are hereunto subscribed, have engaged ourselves, and having weighed the work in regard to the consequence, God's glory and the Church's good, as also in regard to the difficulties and discouragements which in all probabili-

7

ties must be forecast upon the prosecution of this business, considering withal that this whole adventure grows upon the joint confidence we have in each other's fidelity and resolution herein, so as no man of us who have adventured it without the assurance of the rest; now for the better encouragement of ourselves and others who shall join us in this action, and to the end that every man may without scruple dispose of his affairs and estate as may best fit his preparation for this voyage; it is fully and faithfully agreed among us, and every one of us doth hereby freely and sincerely promise and bind himself, in the word of a Christian and in the presence of God, who is the searcher of all hearts, that we will so really endeavor the prosecution of this work, as by God's assistance we will be ready in our persons, and with such of our families as are to go with us, and such provisions as we are able conveniently to furnish ourselves withal, to embark for the said Plantation by the first of March next, at such port as shall be agreed upon by the company, to the end to pass the Seas (under God's protection) to inhabit and continue in New England; provided always that, before the last of September next, the whole Government, together with the patent for the said Plantation, be first by an order of Court, legally transferred and established to remain with us which shall inhabit the said Plantation; and provided also, that if any shall be hindered by such just or inevitable let or other cause, to be allowed by three parts of four of these whose names are hereunto subscribed, then such persons for such times and during such lets, to be discharged of this bond. And we do further promise, every one for himself, that shall fail to be ready by his own default by the day appointed, to pay for every day's default the sum of £3 to the use of the rest of the company who shall be ready by the same date and time.

(Signed)

RICHARD SALTONSTALL	THOMAS SHARPE
THOMAS DUDLEY	INCREASE NOWELL
WILLIAM VASSALL	JOHN WINTHROP
NICHOLAS WEST	WILLIAM PINCHON
ISAAC JOHNSON	KELLAM BROWNE
JOHN HUMPHREY	WILLIAM COLBRON

It was two months after the signing of the Cambridge Agreement that Winthrop was chosen as the leader of the

Ab Initio

group with the title of Governor of the Massachusetts Company.

The group of signatories to this document was by no means unremarkable. William Vassall possessed a trading instinct of the first order; the ancestors of Thomas Dudley had ranked highly in the annals of their country as students of English history well know; Sir Richard Saltonstall had boasted an ancestor who had been Lord Mayor of London; John Humphrey was a son-in-law of the Earl of Lincoln; Increase Nowell boasted powerful ecclesiastical relations, Isaac Johnson was a burgess of very considerable wealth and another son-in-law of the Earl of Lincoln; William Pinchon, Thomas Sharpe, Nicholas West, Kellam Browne and William Colbron were all of them educated gentlemen and each of them of account and standing in his particular countryside.

If one were to seek for a dramatic contrast to the character of Governor Winthrop it would be necessary to go no further than to the person of Thomas Dudley who was associated with him in the Massachusetts Bay Company in the capacity of deputy-governor. Where Winthrop was warm of heart, at times even bordering on the sentimental, actuated by principles conceived in terms of humanity, Dudley was the reverse, a thin-lipped Puritan whose rigid Calvinism was untempered either by humor, affection or tolerance, the actual prototype of generations of sharp-nosed Catos known to legend and caricature as the Yankee witch-burners. Where Winthrop "was expressive of what was finest in the age of Elizabeth, the face of a spiritual brother of Raleigh and Sidney," Dudley, while neither weak nor incompetent, was the lineal ancestor of such mentalities as, three hundred years later, made up the members of the Watch and Ward Society of New England. A cold and bitter man to

9

whom all that was pleasant or amiable in this world smelled suspiciously of the faggot.

The expedition embarked in a fleet of twelve ships led by the *Arbella,* accomplished the trans-Atlantic voyage in 76 days and dropped anchor in the harbor of Salem in June. John Endicott, ruler of the Salem plantation, whose authority was merged with the arrival of Winthrop in the General Government of the Massachusetts Colony, came out to meet the voyagers, and a pleasant account of the occasion was recorded by Winthrop in his diary:

Saturday, 12. About four in the morning we were near our port. We shot off two pieces of ordnance, and sent our skiff to Mr. Peirce his ship (which lay in the harbor, and had been there some days before). About an hour after Mr. Allerton came aboard us in a shallop as he was sailing to Pemaquid. As we stood towards the harbor, we saw another shallop coming to us; so we stood in to meet her, and passed through the narrow strait between Baker's Isle and Little Isle, and came to an anchor a little within the islands.

Afterwards Mr. Peirce came aboard us, and returned to fetch Mr. Endecott, who came to us about two of the clock, and with him Mr. Skelton and Capt. Levett. We that were of the assistants, and some other gentlemen, and some of the women, and our captain, returned with them to Nahumkeck, where we supped with a good venison pasty and good beer, and at night we returned to our ship, but some of the women stayed behind.

In the mean time most of our people went on shore upon the land of Cape Ann, which lay very near us, and gathered store of fine strawberries.

But the little colony at Salem, by reason of its limited resources "pleased not" Governor Winthrop's company, and six weeks after the first discharge of cannon to signal the sighting of a landfall, the entire following removed to the neighborhood of blacksmith Walford's forge in Charles Town and prepared to settle there, across the Charles River from the solitary Mr. Blackstone. Not that the Salem

Ab Initio

Colonists were inhospitable or failed in their Christian duty to urge the recently landed prospectors to settle in their midst, but there was a severe shortage of food in Salem, the inhabitants were weak from illness and poorly sheltered, and it was manifestly impossible for them to give comfort to the voyagers who came ashore from the *Arbella* and her attendant ships.

But at Charles Town, even though a "Great house where the governor and several of the patentees dwelt" was erected and "the multitude set up cottages, booths and tents about the town hill," all was not satisfactory. The worst deficiency of the location was the water supply and it was the matter of potable water that finally determined the settlement upon its permanent site of the town of Boston. Of this second flight of the Colonists and the final selection of a home the following simple account is found in the early records of Charles Town:

In the meantime, Mr. Blackstone, dwelling on the other side Charles River alone, at a place by the Indians called Shawmutt, where he only had a cottage, at or not far off the place called Blackstone's Point, he came and acquainted the Governor of an excellent Spring there; withal inviting him and soliciting him thither. Whereupon, after the death of Mr. Johnson and divers others, the Governor, with Mr. Wilson, and the greatest part of the church removed thither: whither also the frame of the Governor's house, in preparation at this town, was also (to the discontent of some) carried; where people began to build their houses against winter; and this place was called BOSTON.

The order of the Court of Assistants required "That Trimontaine shall be called Boston" for the reason that the name of this town in Lincolnshire, England, was especially dear to the Colonists. Lady Arbella Johnson, for whom the voyagers' ship was named, derived from old Saint Botolph's Town, and John Cotton, who was later to be distinguished

Boston and the Boston Legend

in his own right in New England, as well as by his descendants, was still preaching in the parish church of the old town when new Boston was founded.

The transition from Charles Town across the peaceful river to the Triamount, for all the austerity of purpose and determination of the moment, was not without incident of charm. To this day the Old South Meeting House is the repository of a souvenir of that eventful passage in the form of a contemporary portrait of the first of Boston's woman individualists, Ann Pollard, a spirited part and parcel of the earliest traditions of Boston.

Ann Pollard used to relate that she went over in the first boatload that left Charles Town for Shawmut and that as a little girl she was the first of all that grave company to jump ashore. Doubtless she had her ears boxed for preceding her elders, but, in any event, she lived to be the oldest woman in Boston and died at the mature age of a hundred and five. Time sat easily on the old lady and she insisted on having her portrait painted two years before her death. For years it hung in the rooms of the Massachusetts Historical Society over the Savings Bank in Tremont Street, but now it is at the Old South Meeting House for all to see.

At a time when the domestic status of women had yet to be modified, Goody Pollard was the scandal of the town. The youngest of her numerous offspring was born when she was fifty-eight and at the time of her death she had one hundred and thirteen descendants. Fecundity in early Massachusetts was not confined to the shad of the Connecticut River. She kept the Horse Shoe Tavern at the corner of Beacon and Charles Streets where the chemist shop is to-day, and the Harvard students were fond of coming over and getting hideously boiled on her stone ale and singing "Love at First Sight" or "Ganymede and Helen" which began:

12

Ab Initio

Dardanus et Tyndaris interim feruntur
Atria palatii jam ingrediuntur;
Linquant equos, aureis gradibus nituntur,
Aedes intrant superas, subiti cernuntur,

while the beldame smoked her clay pipe and told about England in the old days. Public prayers were continually being offered in the hope that the old lady would mend her ways, but she went right on burying husbands, serving noggins of stone ale and propelling the scholars into the street among the cows when they started tearing the premises apart or firing their fowling pieces up the chimney. She was a caution.

At long last she died, having been set in her gay ways so long as to have achieved the tolerance accorded an institution, and the whole town, Harvard boys, reverend clergy and all, followed her to the Granary Burying Ground. In a stiff-necked generation, she was the first Bostonian to represent a happy indifference to convention which, from that day to this, has been an integral characteristic of one of the world's most conventional-minded communities.

Had Governor Winthrop and his associates in their adventure in statecraft been able to look into the future and foresee the proportions to which this Boston of theirs was ultimately to emerge they certainly would never have set themselves down on the slopes of Shawmut, for all their need and the pressing hospitality of Mr. Blackstone. The spot was, to be sure, admirably suited to their immediate requirements, if one except the extremes of the New England climate, but its geographic limitations pressed sorely upon subsequent generations when expansion was the order of the day.

Boston in those days was a narrow peninsula the head of which, more than anything else, resembled the head of a club with three protruding knobs. It was surrounded on all sides by water or marshland, save at the neck, and even here,

13

Boston and the Boston Legend

at neap tide and during severe storms, the water frequently overflowed the Roxbury Flats and made the town site an island. It became necessary in later years to fill in large areas of marshland and shallow waters until gradually the head of the club became more nearly round, and the process of reclaiming watery portions of the Back Bay continued well on into the third decade of the twentieth century.

In the center of the peninsula rose three low peaks of glacial origin which lent the locality its original name, Triamount, but subsequent generations of Bostonians quite removed two of these and left only a portion of the third, which is Beacon Hill. The harbor and water-front facilities of the location were, however, admirable and the littoral waters were immediately deep and pleasantly illustrated with low green islands formed by ice-age drumlins.

It has been said of the New England Colonists that, whenever they determined to settle a locality, they first built a church, then the jail, and then set about shooting the Indians, and if this procedure was not quite representative of the founding of Boston, it was not far from it. Governor Winthrop himself settled near one of the fine springs of Mr. Blackstone's discovery near the site of the old Post Office which proved such a barrier to the Great Fire in 1872, where the Federal Building was erected sixty years later. His dwelling was a spacious structure, very free of ornament and characterized by simplicity of the highest order. It must have been reasonably severe to warrant the governor, a few years later, to reprimand Thomas Dudley for the almost Babylonish luxury of ornament on his own house in the form of a wainscoting which actually was nothing more than an extra course of clapboards nailed, for purposes of warmth, in the form of a wainscot. This was one of the earliest Boston feuds and was waged with a bitter-

# Ab Initio

ness of feeling and wealth of repartee characteristic of later and greater municipal uproars.

The governor's gardens, however, were spacious and his fields broad and wide as befitted his station, while down the hillslope from his domain the town's tradesmen erected their structures along the line of the Town Cove in a manner "very agreeable from the water." To the West was the Sentry Field, which was destined shortly to become Boston Common where, both in legend and in fact, the burgesses were accustomed to pasture their cows until fully two centuries later. The entire promontory was covered with growths of shrubbery and blueberries and abounded, as has been suggested, with small forms of game and animal life, but was sadly lacking in wood for fuel or building purposes.

The town's first meeting house was built in King Street, probably in the second year of the founding of Boston and near the first Town House of the community, with walls of mud and a thatched roof. The first houses of the citizens were seldom more than two stories tall, constructed, then and for many years afterward, almost entirely of wood despite disastrous conflagrations, and characterized by the familiar vanes, dormers and cornices of Elizabethan taste. It was a rambling, sprawling town, traces of whose lack of planning are visible to this day, whose only unity derived from an intensity of religious observance and the common cause against the assaults of nature, the Devil, and at a somewhat more mature date, the representatives of the British crown.

Within four years of the anabasis from Charles Town to the slopes of Triamount it became apparent that Boston was there to stay. More than four thousand Englishmen had emigrated to its vicinity and twenty odd villages dotted the bays and islands of its harbor, while a substantial trade in lumber, salted furs and codfish was creating an export market to England. The farms which had come into being were beginning to show a profitable yield despite the late frosts and early New England winters, the stubborn soil and the boulders which every spring worked their way up to the surface of fields before an age of giant powder and blasting and required the invention of that peculiarly Yankee contrivance, the stone boat. Several thousand goats and 15,000 head of fine cattle grazed the fields outside the city or wandered on Boston Common. For several seasons there was so much of a purely utilitarian and economic nature to occupy the attentions of the settlers that there was little time for heresy and the calling of the theologians, and Governor Winthrop was able to look about him on the early Boston scene and find it, with all its limitations, good.

Chapter II

THE PURITAN COMMUNITY

THE early annals of Boston, it must be confessed, possess neither the qualities of edification nor amusement. It was an era at once dolorous, humorless and bitter. Viewed from the security of the twentieth century it is fantastic and unthinkable that people should, in any manner or by any means, have contrived to make the business of living, in a comparatively simple world-scene, so barren of compensation, so fruitless and so determinedly disagreeable.

It is not the purpose of this volume to trace in any detail the religious disputes, the purely theological controversies, the heresies, schisms, revolts and tyrannies of the early years of the Puritan oligarchy in the Massachusetts Bay Colony. Yet these wranglings constitute very largely the history of these years, and it is necessary to realize that behind the frequently gallant impulses of the Revolution, behind the urge to commercial supremacy in the nineteenth century, behind the spirit of abolitionism and the peculiar liberalism of a

Boston and the Boston Legend

later time and behind the whole essential being of Boston of yesterday and today is a record of inspired tyranny and godly brutality the details of which are shocking in the light of modern opinion. In a generation when the formal religious observances of the average individual occupy somewhat less of his time than his attendance at the theater, the extreme preoccupation of the early Colonists with the etiquette of their relations with Divinity can scarcely be comprehended.

It required no more than four years for the settlers of Boston to achieve a state of security from starvation and the elements sufficient, as they considered, to warrant a magnificent debauch in the realm of theology, and for several ensuing decades the record closely parallels that of the years of religious turmoil in England and Europe in snarling, sniveling, blackguarding, witch-burning, exiling and general viciousness and inhumanity over the merest trivia of spiritual existence. For preaching the essential disunity of church and state Roger Williams found it necessary to flee the Massachusetts Bay Colony and seek refuge in the snowbound wigwam of Massasoit before making his way to Narragansett Bay and founding the Providence Plantations. Endicott, Governor of Salem, found himself reprimanded by the General Court in Boston for cutting the red cross of Saint George, which he esteemed an emblem of Popery, out of the royal colors of a little militia company, with his sword. Mrs. Anne Hutchinson was exiled from the Colony for holding that the person of the Holy Ghost dwelt in a justified person and that "no sanctification could help to evidence to us our justification." John Wheelwright, an eloquent preacher, suffered in this same insufferable persecution. Thomas Dudley and John Cotton's assistant, John Wilson, boiled with hatred for all who differed any theological jot with their own envenomed credo. Schism and dis-

18

The Puritan Community

trust and hatred over points of ritual, belief or nomenclature were the order of the day, and the rational and kindly Winthrop was appalled to hear disputants distinguish "being under a covenant of grace or a covenant of works, as in other countries between Protestants and Papists."

By the time Mrs. Hutchinson's Antinomians, as they were called, were setting the Colony by the ears, Winthrop had failed of reëlection as governor and the youthful, personable and distinguished Harry Vane had been elevated in his stead to the office of chief magistrate. He supported the first of New England's lady transcendentalists until her teachings threatened to interfere with raising forces to suppress an Indian attack, when most of the community agreed that things had come to a pretty pass, reëlected Governor Winthrop, and allowed Harry Vane and Mrs. Hutchinson to go into the discard, so far, at least, as the Boston scene was concerned.

To the peril of internal dissension and the ever-present menace of the savages without Boston was added the pressure of the government, a few years later, of the Restoration in London to revoke the terms of the charter of the Massachusetts Bay Colony and so gain absolute control over the principal New England settlements. The struggle for the charter, the rise of the dissenting faiths in the Colony, the war with the Pequots and their subsequent annihilation, the governorship of Andros, all are matters of recorded history and hence not the province of this account save inasmuch as they all contributed to the economic and practical if not the spiritual solidarity of the community.

Boston thrived on hard times and oppression, and when Winthrop died, full of years and honors, in 1649, it had become apparent that the town was destined to become one of the metropolises of America. The tide of immigration from England had abated and the population consisted

Boston and the Boston Legend

mainly of English born who recalled the early hardships of the settlement and of a generation born to the soil and customs of an intensely characteristic and well-defined settlement.

Boston was altogether English in its social usage, but plainer in its observances than London, as befitted a far more provincial setting. A few members of the nobility made their homes there and the title of knight or baronet was essentially familiar, but the average bread and cheese citizens were known as Goodman and Goodwife while Mr. and Mrs. was reserved for ministers and their wives and the higher magistrates. From the first there was a sufficiency of servants, an early writer advising that "tenne or twelve lusty servants being able to manage an estate of two or three thousand pound." To hire Indian servants a special license was required, the dread of the Indians in early Boston being the close equivalent of the dread and distrust of the Romans of Imperial times for the vast numbers of slaves in their midst.

Thursday was market day in Boston Town. Venison, raccoons, moose, beaver, turkeys, geese, wild duck, fish and shell fish were brought in by the Indians, and a Frenchman writing of the mature Colonial period said:

Beef costs twopence the pound; mutton twopence; pork to three-pence, according to the season; flower fourteen shillings the one hundred and ten pound, all bolted; fish is very cheap and vegetables also. Moreover there are quantities of nuts, chestnuts and hazelnuts, wild. They are small but of wonderful flavor. I have been told there are other sorts which we shall see in their season. . . . The rivers are full of fish, and we have so great a quantity of sea and river fish here that no account is made of them. . . . I have been here in season to see a prodigious quantity of apples, from which they make a marvelously good cider. One hundred and twenty pots cost only eight shillings, and at the inn it is sold for twopence the pot; twopence the pot for beer.

20

The Puritan Community

Food the Puritan fathers found it impossible to legislate out of existence, although they did their best to suppress sweets, "it being ordered that no person shall sell any cakes or buns either in the markets or victualling houses or elsewhere upon pain of ten shillings fine; provided that this order shall not extend to such cakes as may be made for burial or marriage, or such like occasions." But strong drink and tobacco outraged them by ameliorating the hard life they esteemed the essence of godliness. The town officers were authorized to join any groups drinking at an ordinary and summarily cut off the supply of drinks. At one time the price of all potations was fixed by law at a penny a quart which made it unprofitable to sell anything but cider. The drinking of healths was characterized as "that abominable practice . . . also an occasion of much waste of the good creatures and of many other sins as drunkenness, quarrelings, bloodshed, uncleanness, mispense of precious time." The authorities tried to popularize cheap beer in the place of strong waters, but the taverners made such fearful home brews "mingled with molasses, coarse sugars and other materials," that none but drink cadgers and the local moochers would touch them. "I'll set you up to a beer," became a standard form of cheap witticism. Boston's neighbors in Plymouth beat the modern blood test for drunkenness by three centuries by defining a souse as "any person who either lisps or faulters in his speech by reason of overmuch drink, or that staggers in his going, or that vomits by reason of excessive drinking, or that cannot follow his calling."

But, as during a later notorious era, folk managed to get themselves stiff, and the elders looked on the flaming younger generation as the source of all contempt for law. Gaffers foretold that this way of life would end in no good, "being sensible of the great increase of profaneness amongst us, especially in the younger sort, taking their opportunity by meeting together in places of public entertainment to corrupt one another by their uncivil and wanton carriage, rudely singing and making a noise, to the disturbance of the family and other guests." The game of shuffleboard was banned by civil decree.

Then there was the disturbing matter of tobacco. Smoking in Boston was viewed with downright suspicion until comparatively recently, puffing in public, save in a designated portion of the Common, being forbidden until the seventies of last century.

New laws forbidding its use were enacted every few years, but a pleasant and aromatic fog hung over the community and seemed to grow thicker the louder the weed was denounced. A variety closely akin to the Connecticut shade-grown leaf of modern times was favored, and pipes were the smoking medium, the seegar and the sinful cigarette being comparatively modern contrivances. From the beginning law-breakers and smokers were classed together, just as lawyers and card sharps were bracketed down to the years immediately before the Revolution.

In matters of dress the times were somewhat less rigorous, due probably to a desire on the part of the authorities to maintain a public decorum of appearance and at the same time preserve the distinctions between the several classes into which society was divided. In general folk were attired according to their means, and the law recorded "its utter detestation and dislike that men or women of mean condition should take upon them the garb of Gentleman, by wearing gold or silver lace, or buttons or points at their knees, or to walk in great boots; or women of the same rank to wear silks, or tiffany hoods, or scarfs, which, though allowable to persons of greater Estates, or more liberal Education,

The Puritan Community

yet we cannot but judge it intolerable in persons of such like condition."

The notion that any sort of pleasure, no matter how innocent according to modern standards, amusement or free leisure should enter into the life of the community was quite apart from the scheme of Calvinist morality. Nagged, bullied, threatened with hell-fire and the stocks by a hierarchy of clergymen with stomach ulcers and too ancient for the pleasures of bed, the early Bostonians were gluttons for punishment.

Such was the dearth of diversion that the prospect of a lecture or religious meeting put the town in a fever of anticipation. Not even the Old World holidays to which hardworking people had looked forward for a little merriment for centuries were allowed to interrupt the course of the Bostonian's religion and toil. No feast days made the rough passage of the Atlantic, and even Christmas was banned. "For preventing disorders," says the record of the General Court of 1659,

arising in several places within this jurisdiction by reason of some still observing such festivals as were surreptitiously kept in other communities to the great dishonor of God and offense of others: it is therefore ordered by this court and the authority thereof that whoso shall be found observing any such day as Christmas or the like, either by forbearing of labor, feasting, or in any other way, upon any such account as aforesaid, every such person so offending shall pay for every such offense five shillings as a fine to the county.

Other offenses against the Calvinist God, in addition to the game of shuffleboard mentioned above, were cards and dice, dancing, bowling and laughter. Football was tolerated if played well away from thoroughfares and residences.

It will be seen from the foregoing and very meager outline of some of the aspects of life in Boston during the early

Boston and the Boston Legend

years of its history that existence was at best hard, exacting, and fairly completely lacking in what modern times would consider compensations for the business of living.

The difficulties and hardships of crossing a lonely ocean and founding a settlement on a not altogether hospitable and certainly not luxuriant coast were surmounted only that other forms of hardship and tyranny should be deliberately and gratuitously devised for the oppression of an already hard-ridden people. Almost everything that might seem desirable in life, repose, a modest degree of creature comfort, the contrivings of human affection, inflamed an insane hatred in the Dudleys and Mathers. Any but a people under the baneful spell of a Calvinist theology would have hanged their priests and magistrates to the most convenient tree and counted it a good job.

It must be counted in considering the qualities of later generations of Bostonians that their forefathers organized the community in hard-bitten and intolerant times. It took an extraordinary amount of courage to be an Ann Pollard or a Mrs. Hutchinson, but the interesting evolutionary circumstance is that their surroundings produced a certain number of persons of pronounced individuality who possessed sufficient assurance to assert themselves in the face of a strictly regimented society. For three hundred years Boston has been the home of individualism, not because there are appreciably more persons of strongly defined characteristics there than elsewhere, but because they have been more clearly and arrestingly outlined against the background of their setting. The birds and the beasts are all there, but the ring-neck pheasant is the more magnificent by reason of the protective coloring of the general run.

Literate and observant travelers in seventeenth century Boston were few and far between. Visitors from the other American Colonies took the town for granted, transacted

24

THE MALL, COMMONWEALTH AVENUE

The Puritan Community

their business and went their ways. There were few of the urban attractions which cause the outlander to linger. Errant commentators from abroad were scarce, and most of those were content to damn the outposts of empire for not being like London or Paris, much as the testy American tourist of the 1920's, purse proud and flown with arrogance, was satisfied to curse the lack of hot showers in English country houses and sneer at the French because they did not serve ham and eggs, country style, for breakfast. That anything save the familiar native institutions to which it was accustomed at home might be amiable or attractive or enjoy any merit at all was as foreign to the time as the notion, which prevailed until the time of Wordsworth and Byron, that beauty might lie in mountain crags or stormy seas or other virile natural manifestations. Boston to the average voyager during the first hundred years of its existence was little more than a catastrophe.

Sam Sewall liked Boston, of course, with almost the intolerant devotion of old John Adams for a latter-day New England in general and wrote fair the scene, but he was a part of it and, presumably, prejudiced. It remained for an English bookseller named John Dunton, who left London shortly after Monmouth's rebellion, to present the first reasonable picture of the Puritan town as it was rapidly growing to assume an importance which was impressing even the British Crown. Dunton wrote a series of letters addressed to his printer back in London and that he was a journalist of perceptions is apparent even after the passage of two and a half centuries. His first impression is of the physical appearance of the town and its structures:

The houses are for the most part raised from the sea-banks [he wrote] and wharfed out with great industry and cost; many of them standing upon piles, close together, on each side the streets, as in London, and furnished with many fair Shops; where all sorts of

Boston and the Boston Legend

commodities are sold. Their streets are many and large, paved with Pebbles; the Materials of their Houses are Brick, Stone, Lime, handsomely contrived, and when any New Houses are built, they are made conformable to our New Buildings in London since the fire. Mr. Shrimpton has a very stately house there, with a Brass Kettle atop, to shew his Father was not ashamed of his Original [he had been a brazier]: Mr. John Usher (to the honour of our Trade) is judg'd to be worth above 20,000 pounds, and hath one of the best Houses in Boston; They have Three Fair and Large Meeting-Houses or Churches, [the First Church, which stood on the south side of what is now State Street on Washington Street; the second church or North Meeting-House which stood at the head of North Square; and the Third or Old South Church] commodiously built in several parts of the Town, which yet are hardly sufficient to receive the Inhabitants, and strangers that come in from all Parts.

Their Town-House [which stood from 1657 to 1711 on the site of the present Old State House] is built upon Pillars in the middle of the Town, where their merchants meet and confer every day. In the Chambers above they keep their Monthly Courts. The South-side of the Town is adorned with Gardens and Orchards. The Town is rich and very populous, much frequented by strangers. Here is the dwelling of Mr. Bradstreet, Esq. their present Gouvernour. On the North-west and North-east two constant Fairs are kept, for daily Traffick thereunto. On the South there is a small but pleasant Common, where the Gallants a little before sunset walk with their Marmalet Madams, as we do in Moorfield &c till the Nine-a Clock Bell rings them home; after which the Constables walk their Rounds to see good order kept, and to take up loose people. In the high-street towards the Common, there are very fair Buildings, some of which are of stone.

As was inevitable the inquisitive Dunton attended divine services shortly after his arrival and sent back to London the following account of church ritual and the moral measures of the time in Boston:

On Sundays in the After-noon, after Sermon is ended, the People in the Galleries come down and march two a Brest, up one Isle and down the other, until they come before the Desk, for Pulpit they have none: Before the Desk is a long Pew, where the Elders and

26

The Puritan Community

Deacons sit, one of them with a Money-box in his hand, into which the People, as they pass put their Offerings, some a shilling, some two shillings, and some half a Crown or five shillings, according to the Ability or Liberality of the Person giving. This I look upon to be a Praise-worthy Practice. This money is distributed to supply the Necessities of the Poor, according to their several wants, for they have no Beggars there. Every Church (for so they call their particular Congregations) have one Pastor, one Teacher, Ruling Elders and Deacons.

Their Laws for Reformation of Manners are very severe [he now goes on to say], yet but little regarded by the People, so at least to make 'em better or cause 'em to mend their manners. For being drunk, they either Whip or impose a Fine of Five shillings: And yet notwithstanding this Law, there are several of them so addicted to it, that they begin to doubt whether it be a Sin or no; and seldom go to Bed without Muddy Brains. For Cursing and Swearing they bore through the Tongue with a hot Iron. For kissing a woman in the Street, though but in way of Civil Salute, Whipping or a Fine. . . . For adultry they are put to Death, and so for Witchcraft; For that they are a great many Witches in this Country the late Tryals of 20 New England Witches is a sufficient Proof. . . . An English Woman suffering an Indian to have carnal knowledge of her had an Indian cut out exactly in red cloth, and sewed upon her right Arm, and enjoyned to wear it Twelve Months. Scolds they gag, and set them at their own Doors, for certain hours together, for all comers and goers to gaze at. Stealing is punished with Restoring fourfold, if able; if not, they are sold for some years, and so are poor Debtors. I have not heard of many Criminals of this sort. . . . For I say again you must make a Distinction: For amongst all this Dross, there runs here and there a vein of pure Gold: And though the Generality are what I have describ'd 'em, yet is there as sincere a Pious and truly Religious People among them, as is any where in the Whole World to be found.

The next thing I have to do is to proceed to give you some account of the Visits I made: For having gotten a Warehouse and my Books ready for sale, (for you know mine was a Learned Venture) 'twas my Business next to seek out the Buyers: So I made my first Visit to that Reverend and Learned Divine, Mr. Increase Mather: He's the Present Rector of Harvard College: He is deservedly called, The Metropolitan Clergy-Man of the Kingdom. And the

Boston and the Boston Legend

next to him in Fame (whom I likewise visited at the same time) is his son, Mr. Cotton Mather, an Excellent Preacher, a great Writer; He has very lately finish'd the Church-History of New England, which I'm going to print; And which is more than all, He lives the Doctrine he Preaches. After an hour spent in his company (which I took for Heaven) he shew'd me his Study: And I do think he has one of the best (for a Private Library) that I ever knew. . . . I am sure it was the best sight I had in Boston.

Resolved as he was to experience all that contributed to life in Boston, Dunton also insinuated himself into the exercises of a military nature which were held from time to time on the Common. Probably he was not liable for ordinary service, but he wanted to miss no fun and trailed a pike to the drill "as best for a young Souldier—there was another reason for it too, and that was that I knew not how to shoot off a Musquet. Twas the first time I was even in arms."

Being come into the Field the Captain call'd us all into Close Order, in order to go to Prayer, and then Pray'd himself: And when our Exercise was done, the Captain likewise concluded with Prayer. I have heard that Gustavus Adolphus, the warlike King of Sweden would, before the beginning of a Battel, kneel down devoutly at the head of his Army, and pray to God (the Giver of Victories) to give them Success against their Enemies, which commonly was the Event; and that he was as Careful also to return thanks to God for the Victory. But solemn Prayer in the Field upon a Day of Training, I never knew but in New England, where it seems it is a common Custom. About three of the Clock both our Exercise and Prayers being over, We had a very Noble Dinner, to which all the Clergy were invited.

Not only did Dunton find good copy in Boston for his letters home, but an admirable market for the volumes which were his stock in trade. The Rev. John Cotton, then librarian at Harvard, showed him over the college, as distinguished visitors have been often enough since, and was

28

The Puritan Community

so fetched with his personality that he urged the students to purchase their textbooks of him. This was perhaps the earliest instance in America of a later and widely observed academic practice by the terms of which eminent savants foregather at learned conferences to mutter, "You make your classes use my text on the Doura-Euphrates inscriptions and I'll make mine buy yours."

Almost Dunton was persuaded to reside in Boston, but a wide world beckoned him and he was off to Holland and the Rhine. Historians, however, are in his debt for some colorful observations of a scene too little of the color of which has survived, and Puritan Boston is the more real to us for his wanderings in Queen Street and the Cornhill and over the drill grounds of the Common.

Chapter III

THE PROVINCIAL CAPITAL

THE Boston that Sam Adams knew, the provincial capital, was a very much more urban and urbane vicinage than it had been at the time of the death of Governor Winthrop. It was in every sense the capital of English America, the seat of the representatives of the British Crown and the principal township of New England. Even in a time when unrest against transatlantic authority was smoldering and within a few decades of the revolt which should dissolve British rule in America for all time, Boston took pride in being the viceregal seat, and pleasure in the presence, the opulence and the dignity of the representatives of the English king.

The word urban can only apply to Boston in the provincial period in a comparative sense, for in the middle of the eighteenth century there were only about eighteen thousand inhabitants of the town, twelve hundred of whom, the register points out, were widows, and therefore of scant account

The Provincial Capital

and classified with the negroes and the poor. The fields and pastures bordered on what is today the downtown business section of the city and the whole scene, more than anything else, resembled that of a prosperous English market-town.

But already, both in the growing shipping of Boston and in the pride and independence of the burgesses, were visible antecedent traces of the city it was to be in another hundred years, when the house flags of its merchants were to be known from the Orkneys to Java Head and its merchants were to represent the most solid generation of "warm men" ever to dominate a social scene in modern times.

In Sam Adams's time the life of the town, as in any maritime community, centered around the water-front. An average of more than five hundred vessels a year cleared the port and almost as many entered, not counting coastwise shipping, the discrepancy being accounted for by the circumstance that it was customary for merchants to build, outfit and load ships sailing from the port and dispose of them, complete, cargo and all, when they could advantageously do so abroad. There were sixty-odd commercial warehouses along the water-front, and the harbor itself was protected from raiders, pirates and the possibility of hostile invasion by an extraordinarily powerful battery at Castle William, secure in its island fastness in the harbor. A hundred guns commanded the channel, which at that point was narrow enough for a musket shot to be effective, and twenty of these pieces were laid at the water level itself, an armament heavy enough to have cut into neat upper and lower slices any man-o'-war known to the time. On an adjacent promontory there was the first lighthouse of the harbor, "an exceeding fine" one, according to a traveler, from which signals could be relayed to the beacon atop Triamount in the event of the approach of an enemy. The flaming basket of faggots swung from a tall mast lent Beacon Hill its later name, and in the event of an alarm, cannon were fired and the town flocked to the water-front, armed with firelocks, pitchforks and billhooks, ready to worry and mangle any foes who might survive the batteries of Castle William.

Pirates in Boston were what horse thieves were in the settling of the West, public enemies of the worst order and thoroughly unpopular citizens. The open season on them lasted the year round. A half century previous, the famous Captain Kidd had run foul of the Earl of Bellomont, then royal governor, and in Sam Adams's time a popular and mournful ballad based on his hanging, with the words, "I murdered William Moore, as I sailed as I sailed," was sung by urchins gathering firewood in the neighborhood of Long Wharf. A few years later John Quelch and five of his crew were hanged in chains in Boston Harbor, the execution providing a happy holiday for the town, who flocked to the scene in barges and shallops, bringing their lunches and bottled noggins and making dismal hurrah as the prisoners were treated to a lengthy sermon on the tropic resort to which their souls were unquestionably bound as soon as they might be strangled. Another pirate, William Fly, was gibbeted at Nix's Mate, a forlorn rock in the outer harbor near Long Island, where his bones remained on view in a cage for months to come. This lonely reef was itself named for a Captain Nix, likewise alleged to have sailed with the brethren "on the account," who was hanged there protesting his innocence and declaring that in proof of it the ledge would eventually be swept away by the tide. Surveys made three centuries later by the Coastal Survey, when Nix's Mate is visible at low tide alone, would seem to indicate, belatedly, the rover's innocence.

Perhaps the most romantic pirate tale of Massachusetts Bay, however, was that of Captain Samuel Bellamy of the ship *Whidah* which was wrecked near Wellfleet on Cape

THE OLD STATE HOUSE IN STATE STREET

The Provincial Capital

Cod. A hundred of his crew were drowned in the hurricane and he and five associates who contrived to escape were brought to Boston and hanged with ceremonies of impressive proportions. "And to this day," wrote an early historian of Wellfleet, "there are King William and Mary coppers picked up, and pieces of silver called cob money. The violence of the seas moves the sands on the outer bar, so that at times the iron caboose of the ship at low ebb is seen." And in "The Highland Light" Thoreau recalls that "for many years after this shipwreck a man of very singular and frightful aspect used every spring and autumn to be seen traveling on the Cape, who was supposed to have been one of Bellamy's crew. The presumption is that he went to some place where money had been secreted by the pirate, to get such a supply as his exigencies required. When he died many pieces of gold were found in a girdle which he constantly wore."

Just as, in remote New England towns, the arrival of the evening train with the mail and the Boston papers is still the event of the day, the great excitement at Boston in the middle of the eighteenth century was the advent of overseas letters. The post from England and the other colonies all came by water and its arrival and delivery were a matter of public excitement and general participation. There had been, to be sure, a postmaster appointed for the purpose of overseeing the mail as early as 1677, but his function seems to have been taken over by a large and interested body of assistants recruited from wharf loungers, tavern hangers-on, and the many townspeople who gathered at the water-front whenever a sail was lifted. The postmaster, as he had access to whatever mail was not immediately claimed by its owners, was accustomed to get out the town's first journal under the name of the *Boston News-Letter,* and it was popularly supposed to be a digest of everybody's personal correspond-

33

ence. A querulous notice appeared in one issue of this feuilleton which would indicate that his duties were ruining the postmaster's digestion: "These are to give notice to all persons concerned that the postoffice in Boston is opened every Monday morning from the middle of March to the middle of September, at seven of the clock to deliver out all letters that do come by the post till twelve a'clock; from twelve to one a'clock, being dinner-time, no office kept, and from two a'clock in the afternoon until six a'clock. . . ."

The general rate of postage across the Atlantic was a shilling, a charge which stood until the first Cunarders began carrying the royal mails, but the postmaster a century before this complained that thrifty folk were in the habit of commissioning captains and officers to take their mails abroad at reduced charges. This Yankee habit of using the common carriers without sanction of postoffice still stands in many parts of New England, and conductors and trainmen of the New Haven Railroad for many years have delivered messages and parcels for friends of the line, ferrying lost galoshes, overcoats, and business documents between Boston and New York aboard the crack expresses, the Yankee Clipper and the Knickerbocker Limited, as they did for a century previous on less luxurious trains.

Boston was an extraordinarily dressy town, or, as it was known at the time, elegant, and both men and women who could afford it waited breathlessly upon the latest word on what was being worn at promenade hour in Saint James's Park in order that they might, at the earliest possible moment, reproduce the mode for the edification of strollers in the Common Mall after supper. The best record of the attire of the times is, perhaps, in the portraits of John Singleton Copley, most famous of all portrait painters in Boston's history. Copley himself was fond of making a handsome appearance, preferring generally a maroon dress with large, solid gold buttons. His subjects are invariably luxuriously dressed in an era before Beau Brummel had decreed that the attire of a gentleman should be in black and white, a judgment which has left its mortmain on masculine dress ever since. "The subject is dressed in crimson morning dress with white small clothes, stockings and wearing a dark velvet cap," recites the catalogue of his portraits, and again: "a distinguished merchant of Boston: a cocked hat . . . a gold laced coat and waistcoat, with a white wig and silk stockings. . . ." And still again: "He wears a long, very dark green velvet waistcoat, trimmed with narrow gilt braid. The sleeves of the coat reach about three-fourths the length of the arms, with buttons at the tops of the cuffs, a small portion of the shirt sleeves are seen below, fastened with gold sleeve buttons."

Sam Sewall, the Pepys of Boston, spent a good deal of time and energy battling the abomination, as he considered it, of perukes, which appendages he considered of a highly unbiblical nature. He had small support, however, and Farnham, the peruke-king of Boston, did a land office trade, while all the wig-wearing clergy of Massachusetts looked upon him with the respect and admiration accorded an artist.

Transportation through the lower city of Boston has progressed little so far as speed is concerned since Sam Adams knew the town, for all the introduction of automotive conveyances. The first hackney coach, the licensing records indicate, was for hire from Jonathan Wardell who, in 1711, opened the first cab stand in town outside the Orange Tree Inn, near the head of Hanover Street. Without doubt the last hackman in Boston was an ancient gaffer called Freddy (his last name history will probably never discover) who used to patrol the streets outside the South Station in the late twenties of the current century. Freddy was a favorite with the youths of Harvard who, silk hats waving, used to

Boston and the Boston Legend

perch in incredible numbers atop his ancient herdic to be ferried across the river after late dances in Boston. He invariably wore rubber boots and a frock coat, was entirely amenable to taking his fee in strong waters, and boasted of having taught Theodore Roosevelt to box. Doubtless Freddy and the antecedent Jonathan are honored elders in the ghostly council of Elysian Fields licensed coach drivers.

In mid-century there were more than four hundred coach horses in Boston, and Bennett, in his *Manuscript History of New England,* says:

There are several families that keep a coach and pair of horses, and some few drive with four horses; but for chaises and saddle horses, considering the bulk of the place, they outdo London. They have some very nimble, lively horses for the coach, but not any of that beautiful black breed so common in London. Their saddle horses all pace naturally and are counted sure-footed, but are not kept in that fine order as in England. . . . Their roads, though they have no turnpikes, are exceeding good in summer; and it is safe traveling night or day, for they have no highway robbers to interrupt them. It is pleasant riding through the woods, and the country is pleasantly interspersed with farmhouses, cottages, and some few gentlemen's seats between the towns.

It seems safe to say that neither coach dogs nor stag hounds accompanied the horseback riders as they went afield, since the butchers, driven out of their wits by the depredations of the town's Fidos and Towsers, had an order passed against dogs over ten inches high. Evidently this was the maximum size against which their hung meat was safe.

The principal municipal scandal of the times was the service of the Charles Town ferry, a matter which provided material for impassioned editorial writers all through the nineteenth century as well. There were complaints to the council that the ferrymen were either drunk or asleep or

36

both a large portion of the time; that they missed their slips and were a peril to navigation, and that their language was the equivalent of that of cab drivers at a later era. There were supposed to be three ferries in attendance all the time, one on the water and two in their berths, but there was a deal of muttering and threatening to write to the governor about the service, and old-timers demanded to know whatever were things coming to in these slovenly times?

Public virtue was as much of a concern as ever although the theologians ruled with less of a high hand. But people were forever encouraging each other to do good, and one society of virgins even went so far as to put on a spinning wheel contest in the interest of promoting industry and frugality.

"In the afternoon," wrote a contemporary, "about three hundred young female spinsters, decently dressed, appeared upon the Common with their spinning wheels. The wheels were placed regularly in three rows, and a female was seated at each wheel. The weavers also appeared, cleanly dressed in garments of their own weaving. One of them working at a loom on a stage was carried on men's shoulders attended with music. An immense number of spectators were present."

Brave doings, my masters, and £453 was collected!

Boston has always been a funeral-going town, and a service of importance at Trinity or Emmanuel is sure to find the first citizens out in force with wide bands on their top hats, happy in an impenetrable, but for all that thoroughly enjoyable, atmosphere of gloom. The custom is rooted in respectable antiquity and the gentlemen of the town once counted the number of times they had participated in such pomps as most young men today take pleasure in the number of times they have served their friends as best man or usher.

Judge Sewall was the town's most prominent funeral-goer

at the period under consideration and his diary records the following incident, one which evidently tempted him sorely, for he hated to miss such an occasion:

This day John Ive, fishing in Great Spie-pond, is arrested with mortal sickness which renders him in a manner speechless and senseless. Dies next day; buried at Charlestown on Wednesday. Was a very debauched, atheistical man. I was not at his funeral. Had gloves sent me, but the knowledge of his notoriously wicked life made me sick of going; and Mr. Mather, the President, came in just as I was ready to step out and so I staid at home, and by that means lost a Ring, but I hope had no loss.

It was customary for pallbearers in funerals to receive gloves and a ring as souvenirs of service and it must have hurt the good old man cruelly to miss these souvenirs. A later occasion was far happier, however, and the Judge wrote in his day book:

Our neighbor, Gamaliel Wait, eating his breakfast well, went to do something in his Orchard, where Serg. Pell dwells; there found himself not so well, and went to Pell's, his Tenant's House, and there dyed extream suddenly about noon and then was carried home in a chair, and means used to fetch him again, but in vain. To the children startled about him he said Here is a sudden change; or, There will be a great change, to that purpose. Was about 87 years old, yet strong and hearty and had lately several new Teeth. People in the Street much startled by this good man's sudden Death. Governor Hinckley sent for me to Mr. Rawson's just as they were sending a great chair to carry him home. Satterday—Father Wait buried: Magistrates and Ministers had Gloves. There heard of the death of Capt. Hutchinson's child by Convulsions and so pass to the Funeral of little Samuel Hutchinson, about six weeks old, where also had a pair of Funeral Gloves. May 2—Artillery day and Mr. Higginson dead, I put on my mourning rapier; and put a black ribbon into my little cane.

There were, however, other diversions. Bowling was tolerated by the provincial divines about this period,

The Provincial Capital

although frowned upon by the more sober members of the community and shortly afterward, although it amounted to an open scandal, a dancing school for children was opened, thus paving the way for Lorenzo Papanti's celebrated salons in the nineteenth century. Papanti, like the Boston Museum, was a household word during the sixties and for a generation thereafter, and his dancing academy, with its wonderful spring floor was, to the young Bostonians of the time a souvenir of childhood which had a parallel only for a later generation of youths and maidens whose hair was inevitably cut in the upright plush and mahogany chairs of the Vendome's haircutting salon in Commonwealth Avenue. All good Boston children went to Papanti's, where his lean figure, glossy wig and elegant patent leather dancing pumps, and above all his pointed fiddle-bow, used both as an instrument of correction and harmony, struck terror to all juvenile hearts.

Laura E. Richards, who is a daughter of Julia Ward Howe, recalls winter afternoons there long ago. " 'Point your toe, Mees Howe!' [Papanti would exhort her] 'So!' And if the toe were not pointed right it was smartly rapped by the fiddle-bow. We learned not only the waltz and polka, quadrille—plain and Lancers—but also the Scottische, the Varsovienne, the Spanish Dance, all graceful and charming. Even more so were the gavotte and the Shawl Dance, attained by specially proficient pupils. . . ."

In Provincial times, however, and long before Papanti, the celebration of Guy Fawkes Day and the suppression of the gunpowder treason was a universal custom and gave the law officers all the trouble the Fourth of July was to promise later. The demolition of outhouses with charges of blasting powder on November Fifth became fashionable with the younger generation and was destined to continue, a proud and patriotic tradition of liberty, for years.

Chapter IV

TAVERN REVOLUTION

IN his romantic and moving novel of life in post-revolutionary Tidewater Virginia, *Balisand,* Joseph Herge-sheimer causes his leading character, a Federalist of heroic integrities, to remark that "when he had occasion to spend a night in a Virginia tavern he would know that Thomas Jefferson had been elected president," and, by implication, that all sound things had perished. But Tidewater Virginia was by no means as populous as New England in far earlier times and in that hospitable land travelers of any importance whatsoever were expected to stop at the great houses of gentlefolk and share their terrapin and Antigua rum, wild-fowl and Madeira and, doubtless, their political opinions.

Even Richard Bale frequented the local tavern for the *viva voce* elections of the time, to drop fabulous sums at hazard, and to place his bets on cockfights of note and horse-

Tavern Revolution

races, and the function of the New England tavern, while along more austere lines, perhaps, was still closely parallel to this community office of business and merriment.

If it was divorced from the enterprises of dice-rolling, horse bragging and the dancing of congos, reels and jigs on festival occasions, the Boston inn of early times, in addition to performing the functions universally associated with such establishments, was inseparably associated with politics and not altogether divorced from religion. There the burgesses resorted to prime themselves against the interminable sermons of divines; the duels which, until the times of professional assassins and shady political colonels were the accepted hallmark of honor, had their origin, largely, in taprooms. The American Revolution was actually hatched over the pewter and crystal of Boston ordinaries, and along the middle of the eighteenth century it was a generally accepted scandal that certain decks of painted cards were to be had in the upper rooms for the diversion of gentlemen.

The clergy of the town foretold that this way of life would come to nothing good, but the local men of fashion hastened every evening to their favorite resort where they slammed down full hands on the deal tables and absorbed phenomenal quantities of assorted noggins until they fell out of their seats and were left by the surviving chivalry to roll on the floor among the kittens and the cuspidors. Boston mornings after, it is reported by contemporary authorities, were somewhat worse than the universal product elsewhere by reason of the quantities of overproof trade rum which were absorbed along with all other beverages from slings to sangaree.

In Puritan times, however, things were different. The first taverns in and around Boston followed close upon the settlement of the town, and it was the duty of the town constable to see that nobody was served more than, as the ambiguous phrase has it, "was good for him." A compelling penchant for minding other folks' business was, in point of fact, a dominant characteristic in those times, and has not entirely faded from the New England scene to this day. *Vide* the activities of the Watch and Ward Society of our own twentieth century.

But despite the distrust of the snitfaces and the distressingly pious among the founding fathers, the innkeeper was even then widely regarded as a pillar of society, a heart of oak, a stout fellow and everybody's friend. There were a few who regarded his high calling as a snare, and it was commonly agreed that to be seen about his premises before noon (save, of course, for medicinal purposes and in the event of snakebite or parenthood) was a sign of depravity, but by and large the taverner was a substantial citizen and the repository of more confidences than all the members of the council put together.

The ordinary of Samuel Cole, located near where the Old Corner Book Store stands today, is first recorded in 1634, although there are few enough colorful details to keep alive its remembrance, and by 1647 the number of applicants for tavern licenses was so great that the General Court delegated the licensing power to the "county courts of the shire" so that it might have time for more pressing business. The King's Arms, the Anchor, the Ship, the Red Lion; how pleasantly the homely names ring down across almost three centuries of good cheer and sound table fare!

Of all the pre-revolutionary taverns of the town, however, the Royal Exchange commands the greatest interest. After the General Court had been turned into the street by a fire in 1747 it met in the taproom of Luke Vardy, its proprietor, and it may be supposed that during this amiable interregnum its deliberations were of a less austere and pontifical nature. The only duel ever to be fought on Boston Common orig-

Tavern Revolution

inated upon its premises. The Boston Massacre of 1770 took place before its grave brick façade, and its sign hangs out in the midst of the black-powder smoke of Revere's famous picture of this historic violence.

But it was in revolutionary times that the Boston tavern achieved its full florescence as a public institution. It was within its premises that the Revolution itself came into being and was sheltered until sturdy enough to stalk the open streets of the old town, hurl defiance at the king's men as they stood with grounded muskets waiting the command of hesitant officers, and send frightened Tories in full flight in the general direction of Canada, so that "Go to Halifax" is to this day the Boston equivalent of a more common brimstone exhortation.

The most colorful and prominent of Revolutionary taverns was, without doubt, the Green Dragon, located in the present-day business maze of the North End near Hanover Street. It was chiefly notable because it seems to have been a middle ground or meeting place for several of the groups or juntos which furnished the initial impetus of the struggle. Samuel Adams, Dr. Warren, James Otis, William Molineaux and other lawyers, intellectuals and what might be described as the cabinet of the protestants against British rule were generally accustomed to meeting in private dwellings, usually at the Brattle Square residence of William Cooper. The mechanics, tradesmen and artisans foregathered at the Sons of Liberty and other resorts of a less pretentious sort. But the Green Dragon was a focal point for seditious endeavor. There John Hancock and Paul Revere, Dr. Warren, Thomas Boylston, John Scollay, Timothy Newell, Oliver Wendell and Josiah Quincy, Jr., met the representatives of the coopers and wainwrights, harbor workers and smiths, to foster the Whig cause and, doubtless, to drink deep and repeated damnation to his majesty over the Atlantic. There is no good reason for believing that these posses of patriots, meeting in clandestine conclave in Green Dragon Lane, did not combine a certain amount of gaiety with more urgent pursuits.

At the southeast corner of State and Kilby Streets stood one of the most notable Boston taverns of all times, the Bunch of Grapes. It was famous for its punch, notable for its hearty table fare, and in 1733 was the scene of the founding, with Paul Revere as its first master, of the first lodge of Masons in America by the special authority of Lord Montague, Grand Master of England. To this day it is known as Revere Lodge. But in Revolutionary times it became so notorious a resort of patriots as to become as well known as Whig Tavern as by its proper designation. After the evacuation of the town by British troops General Washington was entertained there by his officers and a group of prominent townsfolk, and if a later celebration, a description of which is chronicled by Samuel Adams Drake in his *Old Boston Taverns* may be taken as an index, it should have been a major feast day.

In consequence of the news (of the victory at Bennington) we kept it up in high taste, wrote a participant in the celebration. About sundown a hundred of the first gentlemen of the town, with all the strangers then in Boston, met at the Bunch of Grapes, where good liquors and a side table were provided. In the street were two brass field pieces with a detachment of Colonel Craft's regiment. In the balcony of the Town House all the fifes and drums of my regiment were stationed. The ball opened with a discharge of thirteen cannon, and at every toast given three rounds were fired and a flight of rockets sent up. About nine oclock two barrels of grog were brought into the street for the people that had collected there. It was all conducted with the greatest propriety, and by ten oclock every man was at his home.

In the light of very similar present-day assurances, not unaccompanied by morning calls for cracked ice and restoratives, it is, perhaps, permissible to close a knowing eye in the direction of this penultimate declaration of virtue.

In a time when gentlemen's clubs, as they exist today, were unknown and when the common boozing kennels of the town had yet to be designated "poor men's clubs," the tavern played a very appreciable part in the common social and political life of Boston, and as the resort of every condition of townsmen and, until differences of creed became so bitter that Whig and Loyalist might not amicably drink together, of every party, it may not be amiss to consider, from the pot-boys' point of view, perhaps, the men who met in them and at length set alight the powder train of rebellion.

It has been widely written and almost equally widely accepted as established historic circumstance, not by chroniclers of Anglophile cast so much as by those to whose neat minds absolute generalities are essential, that Boston colonists were sharply demarked in their political allegiance by the terms of their social and economic condition. The supposition has been that persons of influence and property, in short the established men of the community were, without exception, king's men, and that revolt flourished only in the ranks of an irresponsible and footless rabble that had nothing to lose.

As a matter of record, and like so many precisely conceived theses, this is far removed from the facts of the case. For one thing, Boston in 1774 contained an almost negligible element that could by modern standards be termed a rabble, and by every modern standard the cause of the rebellion was agitated and encouraged by men of property, cultivation and high character.

That many who remained loyal to the lion and unicorn of England suffered cruelly, as did Thomas Ward and Nicholas Boylston and Benjamin Hallowell, who were subjected to vilification, pillage and banishment, and the three

Boston and the Boston Legend

hundred odd others who were never permitted to return after embarking for Halifax, is undeniable. But much of the motivating power of the American Revolution derived from Boston citizens who stood in the way of no material gain from their defection, but rather endangered by it everything they possessed. Nor were the men who met over the pewter mugs of the Bunch of Grapes the flyblown intellectuals and insufficient class renegades familiar to the scenes of so many other revolutions, but rather they were substantial merchants, kindly burgesses, urbane and polished men from many walks of life. While the artisans and less pretentious townsmen who were associated in their endeavors were men of English descent and temperament to whom property and law were nothing to be held in disrespect until profoundly moved in their grievances.

Boston in 1774 was a town of very considerable prosperity. While no impressive fortunes had been made, there was surprisingly little poverty. More than a thousand ships cleared its port annually; a distinguishing old-world comfort was characteristic of the general tone of its existence, and, despite the turbulence of the times and the subsequent provocations of a common enemy, "throughout this whole period of ferment and revolution, not a single human life was taken by the inhabitants, either by assassination, popular tumult or execution."

As the issues between England and her American Colonies became more and more clearly cut, the Whig spirit of the times became increasingly representative of several score secret organizations known as caucuses, to one of which a reference is found as early as February 1, 1763, in the diary of John Adams:

This day learned that the Caucus Club meets at certain times in the garret of Tom Dawes, the adjutant of the Boston regiment. He has a large house and he has a movable partition in the garret

46

Tavern Revolution

which he takes down, and the whole club meet in one room. There they smoke tobacco till you cannot see from one end of the garret to the other. There they drink flip, I suppose, and there they choose a moderator, etc., . . . They send committees to wait on the Merchants Club and to propose and join in the choice of men and measures.

Three years later Mr. Adams spent the evening with the Sons of Liberty in their room "in Chase and Speakman's distillery," in company with John Avery, a liquor merchant, John Smith, the brazier, Thomas Crafts, the painter, Edes, the printer, Joseph Field, the master of a vessel, and George Trott, the jeweler. The names and trades will give some notion of the men who comprised the "rabble" of the casual historian.

It was this type of unpretentious patriot who formed the backbone and core of the Revolutionary party, but associated with him were affluence and prestige, learning and the cloth. There was John Hancock whose merchantile connections and social position made him one of the first citizens of the community; James Bowdoin, a member of the General Court; Benjamin Church, a physician with the most conservative practice in town; James Lovel, a scholar and instructor of wide accomplishments; William Phillips, the merchant prince and Deacon of Old South Church; David Jeffries, the town treasurer and Timothy Newell, Deacon of the Brattle Street Church. And the list continues impressively through Dr. Warren of imperishable glory at Bunker Hill; William Cooper, for half a century the town clerk; Samuel Adams of Puritan pride and probity; Paul Revere, the silversmith; the wealthy and amiable Henry Hill. The American Revolution, so far as Boston was concerned, probably had more people of quality associated with it than any similar revolt before or since.

Neither the satisfaction with which Bostonians may view

47

the absence of fatal popular violence in the years preceding the Revolution nor the high character of its guiding spirits can, however, hide the circumstance that the Boston mob, when incited by these respectable citizens, was, like all other mobs, cruel, cowardly and dedicated to loot and insult more emphatically than ever it was concerned for the cause of liberty or other high aspirations. Riotous vandalism which was not to have its parallel until the destruction of the Ursuline Convent in Somerville nearly three quarters of a century later was the work of a mob that could have been composed of nothing but Boston tradesmen and mechanics and had its origin in these same amiable taverns where harmless enough pleasures and more generous patriotic discussion were the usual rule.

The news of the passage of the despised Stamp Act arrived in Boston in the end of May, 1765, but it was three months before a mob gathered from the boozing cans of the town demonstrated that then, as during a twentieth century police strike, Boston rioters could afford an obscene spectacle of gratuitous destruction and determined pillage. Arthur Oliver was the king's stamp distributor and it was he, not unnaturally although equally unfairly, against whom popular hatred was directed.

Late one hot August evening Oliver came to town from Milton, and just as the port and walnuts were being set out after dinner word reached him from loungers about the Bunch of Grapes and the Royal Exchange that radicals were setting up drinks and urging outrage against the persons of Paxton Hallowell of the customs house and the admiralty officers and that, should their money hold out, it was not impossible that sufficient trade rum would be absorbed to make it hot for any unguarded men in the king's service. At about this time, too, a confused roaring became audible down the side of Fort Hill, upon whose summit Oliver's

WORCESTER SQUARE AND CITY HOSPITAL

house was located, which the alarmed gentleman correctly construed to be a mob engaged in the pious work of wrecking his stamp office. The thorough nature of the destruction of this building may be gauged by the fact that Drake records that during its course no one "received any hurt, except one of the spectators, who happened to be rather too nigh the brick wall when it fell."

With admirable discretion Oliver and his family retreated to the house of a neighbor, and none too soon either, for his son, just clearing the kitchen offices, heard a leader shout as the front door came down, "Damn him; he's upstairs. We'll have him."

Messages came soon, one after another, to another house where I was [the unfortunate man wrote later] to inform me that the mob were coming in pursuit of me, and I was obliged to retire through yards and gardens to a house more remote where I remained until four oclock, by which time one of the best finished houses in the Province had nothing remaining but bare walls and floors. Not content with tearing off the wainscot and hangings, and splitting the doors to pieces, they beat down the partition walls; and though that alone cost them near two hours they cut down the cupola or lanthorn, and they began to take up the boards and slate from the roof, and were prevented only by the approaching daylight from a total demolition of the building. The garden house was laid flat and all my trees, etc., broke down to the ground.

Such ruin was never seen in America. Besides my plate and family pictures, household furniture of every kind, my own children's and servants' apparel, they carried off about nine hundred pounds in money, and emptied the house of everything whatsoever, except a part of the kitchen furniture, not leaving a single book or paper in it, and have scattered and destroyed all the manuscripts and other papers I have been collecting for thirty years together, besides a great number of public papers in my custody.

One other tavern figured more or less prominently in the heated times of the schism between the Colonies and England, and that was The Cromwell Head, located on the north

Boston and the Boston Legend

side of School Street and conducted, probably in a manner just a thought less puritanical than that suggested by its name, by Mine Host Joshua Brackett. It was a wooden house of three stories and, according to the town records, thirty windows; and a something less than flattering likeness of the Lord Protector hung out over the footway. Despite the good fare of the house and the hospitable entertainment offered all comers by Brackett and his wife, Abigail, there were ultra Royalists, especially among the military, who would not enter its portal. The very name, they said, cried out against the memory of the martyred Charles, and some even went so far as to cross the street in order not to pass under the ill-omened Puritan visage of the sign. No great political movements had their origin there, but at the time of the British occupancy Brackett found it more discreet to stow his sign away in the garret rather than risk the smashing of his precious glass windows by "the British hirelings." And to this day there exists a bill from the Cromwell Head to General Israel Putnam for lodging there in December, 1785. The charges are two pounds, eight shillings, for board; sixteen shillings for liquors, and ninepence for washing.

Boston's part in the American Revolution had its origin in its taverns, much of its wartime strategy was evolved there, and afterward, and for several decades, it was in the town's taverns that the heroes of the time were lodged and honored.

Chapter V

TEA PARTY

THAT happy infamy and most picturesque of outrages, the Boston Tea Party, as the events of the night of December 16, 1773, have come to be known, was just one more example of the town's taste for masquerades. In the previous century a mob, "disguised as clergymen," had quaintly taken the old market to pieces, distributing its internal economy in minute portions from Copp's Hill to the Roxbury Flats, and when it came time for the next costume party the committee in charge of arrangements decreed that nobody could attend unless attired in war paint, feathers and fringed buckskins. Everybody agreed later that the rout had been an unprecedented success and that it might be a good thing if it were perpetuated annually.

That so entirely amiable and comforting a commodity as Ceylon tea should prove the fulminate which detonated the

Boston and the Boston Legend

blasting charge of a revolution was a mere circumstance of fate. It might have been something much more spectacular—like the supply of giant powder, smooth-bore bronze field guns and heavy flintlock muskets secreted at Concord, which occasioned the epic of Paul Revere—but Clotho had a whim that it should be breakfast tea, and so it was.

The tax on tea, threepence a pound, was not in itself a crushing burden but it did produce a substantial revenue. Tea and molasses, as a matter of fact, paid the only import taxes of any account, and more of these were used in Massachusetts than in all the other British Colonies in America put together. Tea was as universal and respectable a beverage as was New England rum and it represented no small sacrifice on the part of householders when they decided that rather than pay the unpopular tax to the home government they would go without the drink to which they were three times a day accustomed. Thomas Hutchinson, the royal governor of the time, was entirely correct when he said that "the poor people in America drank the same tea in quality at three shillings a pound which people in England drank at six shillings," but, strangely enough, it was a matter of principle and not parsimony which dictated that the right people should not drink tea in the 1770's. The East India Company got into a state of mind over it, the officers of the Crown were vexed, and London merchants were of the opinion that perhaps Bostonians should be fed tea forcibly as a method of persuasion. Tea, in oceans, continued not to be served in Massachusetts.

So things stood until the spring of 1773 when the East India Company, whose wharves and warehouses in London and whose godowns and factories in the East were overflowing with a vast surplus of tea by reason of the falling off of the American trade, applied to Parliament and received permission to export their product without paying the usual

FANEUIL HALL

Tea Party

export duty in Great Britain. This enabled them to put tea
on the market in the Colonies at such a low price that they
felt Yankee thrift would get the better of Yankee principles,
and shiploads were sent to consignees in Charleston, Philadelphia, New York and Boston in an ingenuous effort to
restore the trade. The brigs *Dartmouth, Eleanor* and *Beaver*
sailed up Boston Harbor and were warped alongside Griffin's Wharf at the foot of Pearl Street where one watchman
could keep an eye on the three. Under the revenue regulations they could not be cleared in the Port of Boston with
the cargo still aboard, nor could they be entered in England,
and twenty days after their arrival they were liable to
seizure. The more level-headed Boston patriots were anxious
for them to depart quietly, while Governor Hutchinson was
equally determined they should never sail without discharging, and took the precaution of double shotting the guns at
the Castle and stationing two war-ships in the channel. Everyone concerned in this historic difference of opinion had his
mind made up on the subject, and the whole affair promised
closely to resemble the logicians' engaging hypothesis of the
irresistible force and the immovable body. Then, as later,
a paradigm of correct procedure, Boston was watched by
the other tea ports in an effort to determine the proper
etiquette of such a situation. It put on a good show.

There had been a number of meetings of citizens' committees before the *Dartmouth,* Captain Hall, had berthed.
There had been oratory and resolutions and communications
with patriotic bodies elsewhere, all of which were considered
the essential curtain raiser to any notable drama, and the
Thursday after the ship arrived a monster mass meeting
was called at the Old South Meeting House. Horsemen rode
in in troops from Brookline. The Charlestown ferry was
perilously overcrowded all day. A number of gouty old citizens who hadn't been seen out of their gardens in years de-

53

Boston and the Boston Legend

scended from hackney coaches and shook their walking sticks in the general direction of the water-front before they went up to sit on the platform with Sam Adams, Rowe and Young. There were seven thousand people gathered outside and the jam that swelled against the rail of the balcony and sat on the stairs inside would have frightened a fireman, had there been one present, out of his wits.

Everyone was angry and having an extremely enjoyable time getting more so. Governor Hutchinson had prudently removed to his country house at Milton, and Francis Rotch, owner of the *Dartmouth,* had hurried out to attempt to get a pass for his ship. Sensing the temper of the town he was anxious to get to sea, cargo or no cargo. It was late in the afternoon when Adams started haranguing the crowd and it was necessary to light the candles in the meeting house. When he finished, Josiah Quincy, Jr., who hadn't been able to get up front at all, managed to make his way to the front of the gallery and everyone turned around to look up and cheer while he denounced the Government of England, the King, the East India Company, Governor Hutchinson, Parliament and the consignees, all categorically, specifically, personally and with a wealth of flavor, anecdote and oratorical resource not entirely unaware of the Anglo-Saxon monosyllables and the opportunities offered by genealogical reference. There was no mistaking that, generally and individually, Mr. Quincy disapproved of them all. The distinguished but conservative Harrison Gray responded from the floor and warned "the young gentleman in the gallery" against immoderate abuse and language which would outrage the ears of a hackney driver. Mr. Quincy struck a posture as well as he could with the rail of the balcony pressing into his coffee-colored breeches just above the knee and replied that "if the old gentleman on the floor intended by his warning to the young gentleman in the gallery to utter only a friendly voice in the spirit of paternal advice, he thanked him. If, on the other hand, his object was but to terrify and intimidate, he despised him." Everyone was fascinated. There hadn't been such oratory since the funeral of the victims of the "massacre" three years before.

It was at this point that Rotch arrived from Milton with word that the governor would not allow his ship to sail. There was an intense silence. The few candles burning in the almost dark chamber flickered in a draft from the front door. An old gentleman in the back row polished his glasses more carefully and stared over his shoulder. "I'm perfectly sober, but I see Indians," he said to his neighbor. There were a number of Indians in the back of the hall. Quincy was speaking again. "I see the clouds which now rise thick and fast upon our horizon," he said. "The thunders roll and the lightnings play, and to the God who rides on the whirl-wind and directs the storm I commit my country."

"This meeting can do nothing to save the country," said Samuel Adams from the platform. The Indians had disap-peared, but suddenly there were loud war-whoops from Milk Street outside. Nobody knew what was up, but there was an angry muttering about mixing tea and water and there were the footsteps of a mob pounding off in the direc-tion of the harbor-front.

As a matter of fact, while the mass meeting had been in progress at the Old South another meeting had been under way over in the south side of Court Street in the Long Room which was the back office of Edes and Gill's printing house. Edes and Gill were patriots; had printed a twenty-four page feuilleton called "The Stamp Act," and were the publishers of the *Boston Gazette and Country Journal*. Sam Adams was moderator of the Long Room Club. Hancock, Otis, Samuel Dexter, Paul Revere, William Cooper, the town clerk, Quincy, Royal Tyler, Thomas Fleet and Sam Phillips were among the members. There were seventy or eighty of them and all those who were not attending the mass meeting had spent the afternoon at the Long Room. They had been shouting with laughter and sticking feathers in each other's hair and cutting up the furniture with trade tomahawks got from an old warehouse that had supplied them as far back as King Philip's wars. On the deal table there had been a five-gallon punchbowl and nobody had neglected it. The Massachusetts Historical Society later collected a considerable literature about the bowl, but neglected the detail of what had been in it. Bostonians familiar with the legend, however, assert that it was an arrangement very like modern fish-house punch with a base of Medford rum, arrack, lime and brandy, probably in this case apple brandy rather than Cognac or Charente spirits, since they were very costly then as now. By six-thirty everybody was looking and acting precisely like Mohawks.

It had been the intention of the Long Room members to attend the mass meeting at the Old South but, heartened with oratory, mutual encouragement and fish-house punch, they started straight for Griffin's Wharf with the overflow crowd from Milk Street at their heels. The wharf watchman was told it would be to his advantage to go somewhere else and, whooping and screaming, the mob of Mohawks descended upon the three tea ships. They rolled back the tarpaulins from the hatches, sprung the battens, and in ten minutes there was a cascade of lead foil cases of tea going over the ships' sides and into the harbor. The crowd on the pier cheered and slapped each other on the back. The Mohawks brandished their trade axes and dared the King of England to stop their tea party. Sometimes the Indians missed their footing and fell to the deck with cries of surprise and indignation, scattering tea leaves under foot. Sometimes they mistook the water side of the vessel and tossed the cases down on the heads of the crowd on the dock. Now and then they stopped to give their attention to the supply of punch which had been brought along from the Long Room in case of emergency. They disposed of three hundred and forty-two chests of tea valued at £18,000 in a little under three hours, and the tide carried it out, past Wing's shipyard and the South Battery, past Gibbs' Wharf and Wind Mill Point, and the next day the Dorchester shore was covered with it. There is still some of it in a phial in the possession of the Massachusetts Historical Society.

But for all the ruin they caused in the cargo holds of the tea ships, the whole party was accomplished "without the least injury to the vessels or any other property." Nobody was hurt and nothing was stolen. There was a general observance of the proprieties even about the gesture that was about to shake an empire.

The Mohawk disguises were, of course, to make it impossible for the authorities to identify the participants in the raid, and their names were not revealed until after the Revolution. Captain Henry Purkitt, the last survivor, died at the age of ninety-one in 1846, a garrulous old gaffer to the end and proud of his participation in the Tea Party.

The next morning Paul Revere started on horseback for New York and Philadelphia with news of the night's work. All the church bells of Boston were rung and cannon were fired along his route in salutation. For, while the passage of time may make the Tea Party seem more of a gesture of protest than an act bordering on open revolt, it was a momentous business at the time and, for all that it was executed in a manner not totally devoid of comedy, it was a valiant undertaking. As long as they lived the members of the Mohawks were held in high esteem in Boston, first citizens in a time when citizenship was held in more regard than perhaps a later generation can understand. More than any single incident the Tea Party brought home to all the British Colonists in America the thought that total independence from England rather than a mere patching up of relationships might be the order of the day. People came to talk openly of independence and there began to be some sort of unity of sympathy and opinion from Arundel to North Carolina. The pot was simmering fiercely and would shortly boil.

Today, in Atlantic Avenue, near the South Station, where the tides of commerce roar unceasingly over the stone pavements, there is a bronze tablet set into the wall of a modern building. It shows a full-rigged ship above and the text reminds passers-by that there once stood Griffith's Wharf where, "to defeat King George's trivial but tyrannical tax of threepence a pound," the citizens of Boston one night held the most famous tea party in history.

Chapter VI

AND TWO IF BY SEA

IMMORTALITY did not come to Paul Revere, posthumously, as some believe, through the galloping strophes of Henry Wadsworth Longfellow's heroic poem. He was one of the first citizens of Boston during his lifetime, an artisan of distinction, and high in the circles of patriots who foresaw and prepared for the inevitable struggle with England. He would have been known to history as an integral part of the Boston legend without the agency of the *Tales of a Wayside Inn*, even though there can be no doubt that his ride on the fateful eve of the Battle of Lexington was perpetuated by the lines of the poem. But he was no waif or stray of history brought into being through the casual agency of verse.

In an age when specialization in any field of endeavor was, happily, rare, Revere turned his hand to a number of achievements. He was a copperplate engraver of some skill

59

and his two harbor-front views of the city may still be seen. He built false teeth "in such a manner that they were not only an Ornament, but of real Use in Speaking and Eating," which was an enterprise of humanitarian proportions at the time. He roofed the dome of the new State House in copper before its historic gold-leaf was laid on and, at the request of General Washington, he devised a new form of field gun-carriage much like the spaded tail piece of modern quick firing rifles. He manufactured all the copper trim for the frigate *Constitution*, was proprietor of a goldsmith's shop and bell foundry, engraved the first great seal of the Commonwealth of Massachusetts, and was official courier of the rebellious Colonists. These activities were not so potentially dramatic as his ride to Lexington, but they were substantially useful.

As relations between the Colonies and England became increasingly strained, it was voted by the Continental Congress that, should military force be summoned to enforce the alteration of the Massachusetts charter commanded by Parliament, all British America should support the inhabitants of Massachusetts. Militia was organized and widely drilled in secret. A Committee of Public Safety was organized with executive authority. A store of munitions, comprising muskets, bayonets, pistols and light field pieces, was accumulated and cached at Concord, and it was apparent to most thoughtful persons that the time was not far distant when they would be handy things to have around.

The ride of Paul Revere on the night of the eighteenth of April in 1775 was occasioned by the presence of these stores. The Committee of Safety was concerned for them. It was widely rumored that the British troops under the command of General Gage in Boston would one night sally forth and seize them, and Joseph Warren, Revere and John Hancock thought it would be a good idea to keep a close watch

THE OLD STATE HOUSE AND
DEVONSHIRE STREET

And Two if by Sea

on military headquarters with an eye to knowing in advance if the move were actually contemplated. John Hancock, as a matter of fact, was in hiding from the British authorities with Sam Adams in Lexington, but almost daily messages passed between Boston and the Middlesex countryside and they were frequently carried by Paul Revere.

Tuesday April eighteenth had been a warm, clear day and the evening found the Committee of Safety around the table in an upper room of a tavern in Menotomy, now Arlington, a pleasant two hours' drive in a chaise from the town and free from the attentions of the king's men. Elbridge Gerry was present as were Abraham Watson, Richard Devans and several other gentlemen, and there had been Madeira and oysters and some grilled guinea-fowl after the business of the day had been transacted. A little after sunset Devans and Watson had a stirrup cup of Circeal, climbed comfortably into their carriage and started home by way of Charlestown.

They were almost into Cambridge when suddenly, around a curve in the dusty turnpike, appeared a small group of horsemen. The dying light gleamed on the gold facing of their tunics and epaulettes, their cordovans were mellow and freshly soaped, and it was apparent that they were a group of British staff officers and their servants riding out into the country. They were no sooner out of sight than Devans and Watson turned their chaise and, by way of a devious route and a deal of galloping over uneven byways, got back to the Menotomy tavern ahead of them and just in time to send a courier post-haste to Lexington to warn Sam Adams and John Hancock that troops were abroad in the countryside and that they had better not stand on the order of their going but get away as quickly as possible. Then they retraced their route and reached Charlestown well after dark.

Boston and the Boston Legend

Charlestown and across the river, Boston, were tense with expectation when they arrived. The evening was sultry and history hung impending in the atmosphere. Eight hundred British grenadiers had been commanded to fall in at their barracks and General Gage had taken what he considered was every precaution to keep their movement secret. But Dr. Warren had been informed of their assembly almost before the sergeants had finished dressing their ranks. His first thought, too, had been for Adams and Hancock and he had dispatched William Dawes to Lexington by way of Roxbury to warn them. Paul Revere had already been summoned by Warren who desired him to start for Lexington, also, to make doubly certain that the patriots in hiding should escape. All roads led to Lexington that night.

Revere had made arrangements with friends in Charlestown that, should the British set out to take Concord by stealth at night, he would have a lantern hung out in the steeple of the North Church on the Boston side. Should they be coming by way of Charlestown itself there were to be two lights, if by way of the Neck and Roxbury, one. Word came that the regiment had marched to the bay at the foot of the Common and that boats were meeting them there in the shallow water where now the Public Garden stands. Warren and Revere received the news in the library of Warren's house. It was eleven o'clock. Warren and Revere were standing. The lamplight shone on the soft calf tones of the bindings around them and on the face of the messenger, panting from running up Beacon Hill. In the street outside two belated pedestrians were making their unhurried way home. Warren's library clock ticked the even flow of time. It was the eleventh hour and the curtain was up on the drama of a nation's freedom.

Revere picked up a pair of jack-boots and strapped them securely just below each knee. He was protected from the

And Two if by Sea

chill of the night, which had come with darkness, by a heavy dark blue cloak with little capes over the shoulders. Everything was moving as it should. Two lanterns gleamed from the wooden belfry in North Square and Devens was busy borrowing a horse from Deacon Larkin across the quiet Charles. Six bells rang out from the deck of the *Somerset*, man-o'-war, anchored in the stream and were followed by the singsong voice of the man on watch. In fifteen minutes Revere was in a boat which he kept at the water-front and was rowing across the river over a nearly high tide on which a full moon showed yellow and new risen. If the watch on the *Somerset* saw the shadow of his caravel they were not concerned enough to hail or challenge it. From his place, braced on the rower's thwarts, Revere could see the twin lanterns above the silhouetted rooftops of the town. Nearly a thousand years before, the galley of Leif Ericson had shifted slowly up the Charles, crossing the place of his present passage as the rowers behind their shields ranked along the gunwales had leaned on their oars and scanned the hills of a new world. He turned to look over his shoulder. The Charlestown shore was close.

A masked lantern flashed a hundred yards downstream, and Revere altered his course to be pulled ashore by Devens and a group of Charlestown patriots who were leading Deacon Larkin's horse, saddled and bridled and outraged from interrupted slumber. The barges filled with soldiers were just coming around Barton's Point under the riggings of Barry's shipyard. He was in good time. They couldn't land and reassemble their ranks for almost an hour.

There is no schoolboy who does not know the rest of the legend, how Revere rode through the length of the moonlit night, through Cambridge to the peaceful green of Medford on the banks of the Mystic, and from Medford on to Lexington and Concord, beating against the doors of farmsteads and taverns and turning out the sleeping Minute Men. It was history and it was drama. Behind him he left turmoil and the ringing of church bells. On village greens bronze field pieces exploded in a white florescence of powder smoke in the darkness. At Woburn and Winchester and Stoneham they had their echoing counterparts. In Reading the bell of the Congregational Meeting House rang out across the placid water of Lake Quannapowit to South Reading, where the meeting house didn't boast a bell, but awakened citizens leaned out of their bedroom windows and fired off muskets and shouted with excitement. The clamor swelled to cross the open meadowlands where Lynnfield now stands, and in Saugus there was a great tumult and scurrying as hard-bitten farmers filled powder horns, keeping them carefully away from the candle for fear of being blown into the barnyard. The fields and roads of Middlesex were alive with figures calling to each other and heading westward. Most of them got there in time for the running fight under the noontide sun that day that history knows as the Battle of Lexington.

A few years later the Old North Church with its steeple window facing toward Charlestown was pulled down and burned for firewood by the British, but it achieved the position of the foremost of Boston churches through the events of that night, and to this day, every year, the ride of Paul Revere is celebrated by a horseman who gallops his way over the old route on the nineteenth of April to warn the Minute Men that "the British are coming." And in Lexington there still stands the house where a wounded Middlesex farmer sought refuge after he had fallen before a volley fired from the Brown Bess muskets of the English king on the town Common of Lexington.

BUNKER HILL FROM THE TRAINING FIELD

Chapter VII

THE WHITES OF THEIR EYES

THE military engagement at Charlestown, somewhat pretentiously known to history as the Battle of Bunker Hill, was scarcely a battle in the sense that the word applies to Marathon, Hastings or Gettysburg. The dead of both sides totaled fewer than three hundred and seventy and the wounded but eleven hundred. But it was a momentous occasion in the conduct of the War for American Independence because it demonstrated in a shockingly abrupt manner to the British officers charged with keeping order in the Colonies that they were faced with something more than disorganized skirmishes such as Lexington, and that provincial countrymen, fired with a cold and Yankee fury, could outshoot, withstand and outfight British regulars trained to fear nothing in this world but an enemy between them and their base of supplies. Lexington had been characterized by sniping guer-

65

rilla tactics and the presence of a body of independent and undisciplined Minute Men upon whom it was impossible to train field guns or advance in solid company formation, and the Middlesex farmers had picked off Percy's men at a reasonably safe distance from behind stone walls and outhouses. But at Bunker Hill there was a more formal observance of the proprieties of warfare, and General Howe's officers had less with which to excuse themselves over their Port in subsequent regimental messes.

In the middle of June, 1775, the summit of Bunker Hill in Charlestown had been fortified in accordance with the recommendations of the Colonists' Committee of Safety. The profile of Charlestown, as seen from the shore of Boston across the Charles River, was that of a gently undulating countryside, rising in three successively higher hillslopes, Moulton's Point, Breed's Hill and Bunker Hill. The town itself was at the harbor level, directly opposite the shipyards and Mill Pond of Boston which, of course, was entirely in the hands of the British military under General William Howe. Breed's Hill, too, had been fortified with a redoubt and a sequence of six-foot trenches in order that the British forces, when the time should come for the attack on Bunker Hill, might not form their lines in the shelter of the lesser elevation.

It was a still moonlit night when Colonel William Prescott and his colonial militia set out for Charlestown and the business of entrenching on the two hilltops. There were twelve hundred troops, and Captain Nutting and a substantial company of Connecticut riflemen were stationed in the lower town to guard against a surprise landing party from the British fleet in the harbor. Breed's was to be fortified first, and then Bunker Hill, and at Charlestown Neck they were met by General Israel Putnam and a group of other officers whose names, before the next sundown, were to be part of the American saga.

The Whites of Their Eyes

The moon glinted silver on the vanes and slate roofs of Boston town. The American vedettes, their mounts tied in the shadows of the water-front streets of Charlestown, could hear the sentries on the piers of Hunt and White's shipyard assuring each other at regular intervals that the night was fine and all was well. The anchor chains of the *Lively,* man-o'-war, rasped against her catheads as she swung on her moorings off Moulton's Point. Aboard the *Falcon* Captain John Linzee, whose granddaughter was to marry William H. Prescott, the historian, tossed aside a copy of Pope's "Essay on Man" of which he was inordinately fond, un-bottoned his mess jacket, and went to bed. A cock crowed the false dawn in Deacon Larkin's stable on the Charlestown side and a youth with brown wavy hair and a slow country-man's smile who was to be blown into a cloud of bloody mist by a short-time shell the next day pounded his bootheels in the shadow of a warehouse and wished he were home in Saugus with a tot of blackstrap to keep him warm. It was a cool night for June.

The seventeenth dawned clear over Boston Harbor and bos'n's pipes summoned the watches on deck to brighten the brass-work of the *Cerberus, Somerset* and *Glasgow.* Captain Linzee was awakened by a midshipman who announced breathlessly that the officer of the day requested his presence on deck at his most prompt convenience. He climbed the companionway without waiting for his wig, his head swathed in a generous bandanna, and in half a minute was survey-ing through a glass the fortifications thrown up during the night atop Breed's and Bunker Hills. Linzee was a man of action and what he saw convinced him that instant action against the enemy was not only justified but requisite. A spring was put on the cable of the *Falcon,* the starboard battery was shotted, linstocks poised above the quills of priming powder, and the opening broadside of the Battle of Bunker Hill

Boston and the Boston Legend

flashed and banged in a dense mist of white smoke which rolled slowly up the river on the morning sea breeze. Showers of earth sprang up on the hillside of Breed's as the solid shot, tossed at a high trajectory over the steeples of Charlestown, fell wide of their mark, and the gun-layers of the *Falcon* eased their pieces into better aim on paraffined trunions. There was swift activity aboard the other men-o'-war. People in Boston ran for the water-front to see what was up, and across the harbor they could hear the sarcastic cheering of the militiamen behind their barricades. Admiral Graves, after the first broadside, ordered the firing temporarily to cease, but in a few moments sent his authority to Captain Linzee and other ship's captains for its resumption at their discretion.

General Gage and his staff appeared shortly afterwards at the water-front, scanning the breastworks which had been thrown up while they slept. It was apparent to the British officers that the American forces were becoming more perilously secure in their positions with every hour and, after a brief council, it was decided to attack the two hills from the front, where the infantry advance could be conducted under the fire of the war-ships and floating batteries in the upper harbor as well as by the heavy guns mounted at a suitable elevation on top of Copp's Hill in Boston itself. A flood-tide in the early forenoon aided in swinging the floating batteries into place. The fire from the men-o'-war continued as fast as was practicable without heating the guns. Dragoons galloped through the streets of Boston carrying dispatches to company and battalion commanders, and artillery carriages were driven toward the ferry slips at a dead gallop. The king's men were going into action with the glittering precision of tattoo or guard mount.

Noon was the hour for landing on the Charlestown shore and the maneuver was brilliantly accomplished under a

The Whites of Their Eyes

terrific barrage from the guns on ship and shore. The *Falcon* and *Lively* swept the low ground below Breed's with a hurricane of grape and time-shells which rolled the Connecticut infantry back to the shelter of the breastworks as a high pressure hose would mop up a brush fire. The *Glasgow* and the *Symmetry,* transports, elevated their pieces by shifting ballast until they dropped shells by mortar fire into the trenches on Bunker Hill itself. The floating batteries thundered and shook under the recoil of the bronze guns mounted on their flat decks, and at one o'clock with scarlet uniforms blazing and battle flags flying, the British troops landed at Moulton's Point without the slightest molestation. While General Howe was reconnoitering the American works his men and officers made a light luncheon in the pastures that ran down to the water.

The Battle of Bunker Hill was fought in the afternoon. All morning volunteers from Cambridge and Arlington had been streaming in across the Neck with extra horns of powder slung about their tunics, their muskets primed and shotted. A few men had been struck by the barrage laid down to cover Gage's landing, and when one volunteer had been cut in two by a six-pound shot that whistled in from the *Lively* there had been something of an indignation meeting among the Americans because he was buried then and there without benefit of church service. The men in the firing steps on Bunker Hill had never had much war experience. Colonel Prescott had found their nerves at such a pitch that he thought it expedient to walk around the breastworks in full view of the enemy, twirling a little Sunday cane and humming airs from light opera as the falling shot showered him with débris.

At three o'clock the king's troops moved forward to the attack. The Tenth Corps Grenadiers, the Tenth Light Infantry, and four other regiments had fallen in where they had landed at Moulton's Point and been addressed by General Howe who had spoken very evenly, as to men of whose valor and experience he had no faintest doubt.

"I am very happy to have the honor of commanding so fine a body of men," he said against the smashing of the twelve pounders in the harbor. "I do not in the least doubt that you will behave like Englishmen and as becometh good soldiers. If the enemy will not come out from behind their entrenchments we must drive them out for remember, gentlemen, we have no recourse to any resources if we lose Boston, but to go on board our ships, which will be very disagreeable to all of us. I will not desire any of you to go a step further than where I shall go myself at your head."

The grenadiers and light infantry moved on Bunker Hill slowly, burdened as they were with full marching equipment, hindered by tall grass and inconvenienced by the blazing sun which, after the chill of the night, streamed down with the full heat of June. Solid shot, grape and time-shells rattled and whisked over their heads from the fleet and kept the American riflemen below the top of their parapets. Powder, too, was scarce among the Colonials, and officers had run along the trenches briskly knocking up the pieces of riflemen who, tempted by the target offered, were preparing to fire. "Aim at the handsome coats; those are officers," ran the word. "Pick off the commanders, then we'll see them run. Don't fire till you see the color of their eyes." The famous line had been first spoken by Prince Charles in 1745 when, in retiring from Jagendorf, he had cut through the center of the Austrian army. Twelve years later at the Battle of Prague, the Prussians had remembered the order and the word was "By push of bayonets; no firing till you see the whites of their eyes." Prescott, unarmed at the moment save for his little stick, passed up and down the lines slapping the men on their behinds as they stood to the firing steps. "Show the bastards,"

The Whites of Their Eyes

he said. "You show them." History waited as the five companies of His Britannic Majesty's Marines under Major Pitcairn forged up the gentle slope of Bunker Hill.

The crash of gun-fire flared in streaks of red and orange in the faces of the attackers. The whole rim of the redoubt above them blossomed into one concerted, level blaze of flame and shocking explosions. The heavy flintlocks jerked sharply upward and back against the men who held them, the back flash of the priming fire in the pan blackening their right cheekbones, and the recoil slapping familiarly into the pectorals just below the collar-bone. After the last vision of crimson coats and black spatterdashes over the foresights the enemy were blotted from view in a rolling cloud of smoke which clung to the grass and clover and tasted cloyingly of burnt sulphur. The gunwaddings started tiny fires in the dead grass close to the earth. For several moments there were only a few scattered shots and the clatter of ramrods sliding down the muzzles of hot muskets.

The first discharge had stopped the advancing lines of troops in their tracks, almost as though a tangible barrier had been raised against their progress. The fire had been deadly accurate and scores of killed and wounded had fallen out of the ranks, but battle was nothing new to British regulars and they waited where they stood until the smoke should clear and they could catch the American gunners in the act of reloading. The engagement became general, and the warships in the harbor ceased firing altogether because of the involved nature of the fighting. On the right General Howe was leading his wing against the barricade of rail fences packed with green hay which the Americans had erected on that side of the hill. The barriers were too stout to be overturned so that considerable delay was experienced in climbing over them, and the next day the wooden bars were found to be pierced with gunshot less than a handsbreadth apart.

71

On both fronts the defenders were aiming at the bright uniforms of officers. Lieutenant Abercrombie of the grenadiers was shot at the foot of the breastworks, and, as his friends were bearing him from the field, he begged them to spare the life of his old friend, Putnam. "If you take him alive, don't hang him," he said, "for he's a brave man." Major Pitcairn was killed outright in the thick of the engagement. He had been wounded twice and placing himself at the head of his men he was rallying them with a cry of "For the glory of the Marines" when he was struck in four places at once. Major Spendlove, an officer of distinguished gallantry who had served with the Forty-third Regiment for forty years and fought with Wolfe on the Plains of Abraham, was killed by rifle fire. Howe's aide-de-camp and Captain Addison, who was related to the author of the *Spectator,* fell under the setting sun late that afternoon. The loss among officers was staggering. In hotness of fire, British witnesses afterwards said, Bunker Hill exceeded Minden.

In the meanwhile the town of Charlestown had been fired by incendiary shot from the *Lively* and the Copp's Hill battery where sweating gunner's assistants trotted back and forth from the shot furnaces with glowing cannonballs carried in metal cradles. Men from the *Somerset* landed and started conflagrations at the east end of the town, and by teatime a huge mushroom of black smoke was rising into the still air to a height of several thousand feet and flames were running along the ridge-poles of a score of homes, churches and wharves. The batteries had opened fire again, this time on the Breed's Hill fortifications; at moments the alarm bells of Cambridge could be heard above the sounds of battle; a nest of mortars had been set up beyond the burning town and was dropping shells in plunging fire onto the summit of Bunker Hill itself, and the neighboring fields and steeples were black with spectators.

The Whites of Their Eyes

The British had twice been held in their advance on the redoubt and Colonel Prescott assured his men that if they could be driven back once more they could not be rallied again that day. But his worst fears for the supply of ammunition appeared to be all too well grounded. As the English were being reassembled for a third assault it was discovered that only a few cannon cartridges remained, and these were broken open and the precious powder rationed among the men. The third attack was characterized by new tactics. Instead of advancing in close ranks the British marched up the hill in columns, offering a far more difficult target than before. Instead of stopping to fire, they prepared for a bayonet assault, and a battery of field pieces was brought up to enfilade the American redoubt with its fire. The attack came from three sides at once and, weakened by their losses, harassed by artillery fire on their flank, and betrayed by a shortage of ammunition, it was apparent to the Americans that the day was finally lost.

Unaccustomed to military discipline as they were, the retiring forces more nearly approximated a rout than an orderly retreat. The dust cloud that arose from their going was impenetrable and brought some measure of safety from the British who were swarming over the barricades and bayoneting the stragglers. General Putnam rode in the rear of his troops, urging them to stand, and at one point paused to serve an abandoned field piece which he laid and fired with his own hand to cover the retreat of his men. He only mounted his horse and galloped away when the ranging advance files were almost on him. Prescott refused to leave until he was surrounded by British who made passes at him with bayonets. These he parried with his sword and "did not run, but stepped long with his sword up." His banyan and waistcoat were so pierced and tattered with gunshot as to resemble nothing so much as a mosquito netting. It was during the last unhappy

73

moments of the retreat that Dr. Warren was struck and left dead on the field he had so courageously defended.

The results of Bunker Hill were of more moral and political importance than military. It was the first engagement of consequence between the Colonists and the forces of England. It established the existence of open war and it demonstrated the effectiveness of Colonial militia against the trained troops of the king. By every obvious standard it was a military triumph for the British who, in any similar engagement, must have lost more men than their opponents by reason of the nature of the disputed terrain, but the fact that the American forces had actually stood up against veterans of the great Canadian campaigns and wars of the Continent and held their own against them while their ammunition lasted was of incalculable moral value to the cause of the Revolution. It was not long before the Colonists began to view Bunker Hill as a veritable victory over the British and, by the same optimistic and oblique reasoning, it has so been regarded ever since and the anniversary is celebrated in Massachusetts as a holiday of fair omen. It is also the date upon which good Bostonians who possess their own gardens invariably serve the first home-grown green peas of the season, and the seventeenth of June has acquired a significance at once patriotic and horticultural.

Probably Bunker Hill Monument is more familiar to visitors to the historic scenes of New England than to Bostonians themselves. It is, at best, a fearful climb unmitigated by the presence of lifts or other convenient latter-day contrivings. Amateurs of the florid forensics of the nineteenth century will linger fondly over Daniel Webster's dedicatory address.

"It is a plain shaft," said the orator. "It bears no inscriptions, fronting to the rising sun, from which future antiquarians shall wipe the dust. Nor does the rising sun cause

The Whites of Their Eyes

tones of music to issue from its summit. But at the rising of the sun and at the setting of the sun, in the blaze of noon-day and beneath the milder effulgence of lunar light, it looks, it speaks, it acts, to the full comprehension of every American mind, and the awakening of glowing enthusiasm in every American heart."

A more realistic generation would be content to say that at Bunker Hill was fought the first engagement of consequence of the War for American Independence, and that it was a hot and dusty and bitter set-to between determined and courageous men whose character gave neither side a monopoly of gallantry or brave endeavor.

75

Chapter VIII

BEACON HILL MAGNIFICO

TRAFFIC stops in Beacon Street when the Governor of the Commonwealth, surrounded by a hundred horsemen in crimson tunics with lances and Uhlans' helmets tipped with gold, sets out for Commencement at Harvard. The horses shy as the motorcycle police clear the road, the guard of honor wheels into a double lane with pennons dipped; staff officers in their fourrageres and decorations snap buckskin gloves to salute; the High Sheriff of Middlesex County flashes his court sword in a graceful arc, and the black and ermine of learning and the lawn of the church bow gravely. It is a good show of state when Massachusetts is on parade, but John Hancock was accustomed to even greater trappings of circumstance.

For John Hancock, President of the Provincial Congress, President of the Continental Congress, first signer of the Declaration of Independence and first Governor of the

Beacon Hill Magnifico

Commonwealth of Massachusetts, was a person of exquisite taste, a connoisseur of the fine art of living and a gentleman of means in an age when the phrase was unimpeached by sentimentality and the envy of the shiftless. He lived well, and he believed that the office of chief executive of a sovereign state required glamour and stateliness. He had the imagination and the resources to supply them, and post-revolutionary Boston was the more magnificent for him.

Hancock was at all times a man of aristocratic intelligence and, like Washington, possessed a strong sense of property values and loyalties to an ordered scheme of things. But he did not hesitate, when he felt that the struggle with England was not only inevitable, but justified, to throw in his lot with the Colonists while other rich King Street merchants took passage to Halifax and, proscribed and outlawed, he added his signature to the Declaration of Independence so boldly that his name has been synonymous with an expansive gesture of self-identification ever since. "John Bull can read that without spectacles," he remarked as the quill flourished over the parchment. "Now let him double his reward for me!" His patrician contempt was sufficient both for the suffrage of his inferiors and the insolence of those in high office.

Probably the average Bostonian of post-revolutionary times vaguely resented the magnificence of Hancock, but he looked up to him as a foremost and able citizen and failed in no show of respect when the governor's carriage turned out from his Beacon Street house toward the summit of the hill to take the governor and Dorothy Quincy out for the air. The Hancock house has since vanished from its site, but its legend, as the focal point of Boston's entertaining, elegance and brave show, has long survived it.

There was substantial luxury in Boston toward the close of the eighteenth century. It was not the immediate tangible opulence, say, of the plantations of tidewater Virginia, with their broad fields and terrapin pounds, their numbers of house and field servants, shooting lodges, stables and gardens, the rich resources of a self-sufficient countryside independent of the outer world save for its silk knee-breeches, Madeira and its gold plate. Nor was it the heavy, almost oppressive richness of New Orleans, where the blacks in the Louisiana cotton fields and Mississippi packets, freighted with goods for the Europe of a waxing Napoleon, brought scented and dangerous ways of life to the Faubourg Ste. Marie, pistols with set triggers to the *salles d'escrime* of the town's exquisite masters of arms, and every distinguished foreign traveler to North America to the Creole balls. Rather it was a cleanly defined abundance deriving from the wealth of commerce and represented by Heppelwhite chairs, family portraits by Copley, fine music in ball-rooms austere with crystal but mellow with manners and associations, and a hospitality of table fare and entertainment which was at once reserved but generous with the open-handedness of a town not yet wholly divorced from the country resources of New England while aware of the use of luxuries from other lands.

The Hancock mansion, almost at the top of Beacon Hill, had been built by Thomas Hancock and dated from 1737. Thomas was an uncle of the first governor, and the estate was given him by his aunt Lydia. The site of the State House was the pasture of these princely acres, and the gardens and promenades and orchards covered a generous extent of the hillslope today occupied by private residences. It was one of the show places of New England, massively built with an ornamental balcony of Braintree stone and a tiled roof surmounted by a white railed "widow's walk" similar to those still visible on top of the homes of Folgers, Starbucks, Coffins and other old families on the island of

78

Beacon Hill Magnifico

Nantucket. A stone wall protected it from the Common and tall shade trees, including the two traditional elms of old New England homesteads on either side of the door, lent it graciousness and repose. A contemporary wrote:

> As you entered the governor's mansion, to the right was the drawing or reception room, with furniture of bird's-eye-maple covered with rich damask. Out of this opened the dining hall in which Hancock gave his famous breakfast to Admirable D'Estaign and his officers. Opposite this was a smaller apartment, the usual dining hall of the family; next adjoining were the china-room and offices, with coach house and barn behind.
>
> At the left of the entrance hall was a second saloon, or family drawing room, with the walls covered with crimson paper. The upper and lower halls were hung with pictures of game, hunting scenes and other subjects. Passing through this hall, another flight of steps led to the garden and a small summer house close to Mount Vernon Street. The grounds were laid out with ornamental flower beds bordered with box; box trees of large size, with a great variety of fruit, among which were several immense mulberry trees, dotted the garden.

There were not many estates in revolutionary Boston as pretentious as Governor Hancock's, but it was representative of what was generally conceived as the ideal gentleman's home of the time.

When Hancock was in hiding at the time of the Battle of Lexington the British soldiers broke open and pillaged the house and carried away the fence rails for firewood until the selectmen gathered in righteous fury and demanded that General Gage send officers to occupy it. The English gentlemen detailed for this purpose carefully preserved the furniture and pictures even after the house and stables were filled with the wounded from Bunker Hill, and it returned to the hands of its owner unharmed, so that in 1781 he was able to entertain there in his accustomed style in honor of Lafayette and a few years later to furnish forth a magnificent banquet for President Washington. So stately was the latter occasion that Madam Hancock subsequently reported that "the Common was bedizened with lace."

"King Hancock," as he came to be known, spared no magnificence suitable to his time and situation in his manner of living. He seldom appeared in public save in his superb coach which bristled with peruked lackeys in the white and blue livery of the family and was drawn by three span of fastidiously matched bays. Half a hundred outriders went ahead, and gentlemen of his household in cocked hats fringed with gold lace rode behind.

> The Governor came, with his light horse troop,
> And his mounted truckmen, all cock-a-hoop;
> Halberds glinted and colors flew,
> French horns whinnied and trumpets blew,
> The yellow fifes whistled between their teeth
> And the bumble-bee bass drums boomed beneath.

A grave and learned amateur of fine wines, whose Boals and Malmseys were the admiration of his guests and the envy of other Boston merchants, a gourmet whose cook understood the true magnificence of shad when this glory of American rivers was so common in the Connecticut that farm boys returned them alive to the stream, it is only natural that Hancock should have had a flair for brave attire. His famous coat of crimson velvet, worn with a gold fringed waistcoat of sky blue watered silk and white small clothes that fitted as though they had been shrunk to his person, was the envy of the gilded youth of the town. At levees he affected a skirted coat of claret shade, lined with white silk and faced with gold braid and frogs, which was complemented by a white satin waistcoat with solid gold buttons and a three-cornered hat with heavy fringes of cloth of pure gold. His pumps were silver buckled and his stockings of sheerest French silk. In his portrait by Copley he

EH Suydam
Park Street & the State house. Boston

PARK STREET TO THE STATE HOUSE

Beacon Hill Magnifico

is dressed with less ostentation, the only apparent richness of his attire showing itself in the fine lawn ruffles at the wrists as he turns the pages of the account book which, for all time, will show him the Boston merchant that he was.

Nor was the first governor without his lighter moments. His closest companion was Nathaniel Balch, a well-known hatter whose wit was most highly esteemed after the ladies had left the table and the cloth had given way to Port and walnuts. Of a quiet spring evening good Bostonians would sometimes hear immoderate howls of laughter echoing through the open windows and across the Common and know that Balch was recounting a Colonial anecdote of the sort which began "it appears there were two traveling bagmen. . . ." Whenever the governor traveled the shutters were sure to be up at Balch's shop, as the first citizen could scarcely journey a stage overland without his valiant raconteur for company. His swaying phaeton was said to be audible two miles away on the Newbury pike, what with the delighted yells of the governor and his staff, and Hatter Balch served as well as any postilion with a horn to have the change of horses waiting at the inn yard when they drew up. Their arrival at Portsmouth, New Hampshire, was once chronicled in the public prints to the effect that "On Thursday last arrived in this town Nathaniel Balch, Esq., accompanied by His Excellency John Hancock and the Hon. Azor Orne." Everyone was secondary to the wag of the chief executive's entourage.

Almost as though he designed purposely to round out a full self-portrait, Hancock's life had, in addition to adventure and battle, public office and the refinements of urbanity, a dash of romance thrown in for good measure. He was engaged to Dorothy Quincy, quaintly known to tradition as "Dorothy Q.," when he was proscribed and forced to flee for his life to her home in Lexington where, with Sam

Boston and the Boston Legend

Adams, he was specifically exempted from the offers of pardon extended by the royal governor to the other rebels against the authority of the crown. The exciting events of the night of the eighteenth of April which culminated in the rides of Revere and Dawes were partly occasioned by the apprehension felt for their safety by the conspirators still in Boston. Hancock, it must be admitted, had no stomach for facing the British officers at that moment nor had he means of knowing the extent of the resistance about to be offered their progress by the embattled farmers of Middlesex, and he fled the scene in a fever of apprehension which barely permitted him to send word of his going to Mistress Quincy with instructions to follow with a fresh caught salmon designed for breakfast the next day. At a more distant farmhouse she caught up with the fugitive, but just as the precious salmon was done to perfection and the famished Hancock was tucking a napkin in his stock, another courier dashed up with the mistaken information that the British were searching the premises of the next farm down the road, and the future governor of the sovereign Commonwealth started dodging behind hedgerows again. It was all very painful remembering, and Dorothy later wrote, "The Governor's hobby is his dinner-table and I suppose it is mine." Salmon never appeared there.

Hancock married Dorothy Q., during the height of the war, in Thaddeus Burr's farmhouse at Fairfield, Connecticut, where to this day the name of Dorothy is popular when a girl child is to be christened.

The Hancock mansion-house on Beacon Hill has long since given way to other buildings. The State House dome rises above what was once its cow pasture, and the traffic of Beacon Street flows endlessly by the site of its garden gate. The first governor's dress clothes are in the museum cases of the Old State House and his Chippendale chairs

Beacon Hill Magnifico

and Copley portraits, his silver and crystal glasses and Heppelwhite settees are in half a hundred museums and collections where people do not live and where no useful or beautiful thing should ever be. But once in republican times Boston saluted the clattering outriders and proud coach of a magnifico and that, at least, is a legend that can never be diminished nor dissolved.

Chapter IX

SHIPS AND CAPTAINS OF THE OCEAN SEA

THE spacious years of Boston's commercial dominance of the American scene were to have their inception in the decade following the close of the War of 1812 and, like all the fortunes that had come to the community during the past two centuries, they were to come from the sea.

The times were changing and mutation, social, political and scientific, was in the air. In the affairs of national state the Federalist party had already faded from the American horizon, and in the year 1822 after a heated but decorous debate, the old town government of Boston was voted into the discard and the city's first mayor, a compromise candidate named John Phillips, was elected to office. The great foreign immigrations which, a few decades later, were in many places to replace native American labor with the less costly hands of Ireland and Germany had not yet begun, and of such orderly homogeneity was the populace that but

Captains of the Ocean Sea

twenty-four policemen were required to maintain order among sixty thousand in the Puritan city. And Dr. Nathaniel Bowditch's *Practical Navigator,* published some twenty years previously, had established itself as the standard work of navigation of every shipmaster of the English speaking nations. These seemingly unrelated circumstances were to combine, together with the genius of Donald McKay and the great revival of world trade which followed peace in Europe, to achieve for Boston the realization of her economic destiny.

So firm a hold upon the general imagination has been secured by the tradition of the Yankee clippers of last century that only those informed in marine history are apt to recall that the clippers which carried the house flags of Boston merchants over half the known oceans of the world were the mature and crowning wonder of many years of maritime endeavor carried on through the agency of less exploited vessels.

Before the clipper came the packet, just as before it there were many generations of pinks and snows, frigates and luggers, but it was the packet that laid the foundations for Boston's empire of commerce and it was from the lines and rigging of the packet that there sprang, full blown, McKay's dream and devising of the clipper.

The first authentic characteristics of the clipper ship, a maritime paleontologist would find, date from the period of the second war with England, when certain swift vessels, patterned after the French luggers of the time, were launched to thwart the British blockade and known as Baltimore clippers. But the true California clipper from which stems the tradition of speed and daring in navigation unabated to this day came into being with the launching of the *Stag Hound* in 1850, and for three decades previous to that the packet ship had dominated the shipping

85

Boston and the Boston Legend

lanes of the world and had been more instrumental than any other concrete factor in the growth and prosperity of America and Great Britain. The effects upon the life and history of Boston and the nation of these two types of ship are today visible at every turn of the social, cultural and economic chronicle of an era, although the last of the younger race of clippers has long since been relegated to the Alaska salmon trade or a yearly voyage deep laden with Australian wheat. They were to establish the names of Merchant's Row Yankees in the hongs of the Orient, to bring occupation and wealth to two generations of New Englanders, and in their holds they bore the seeds of an urban culture which has been Boston's essential characteristic from the time when Captain Samuel Shaw made his first voyage to Canton aboard the *Empress of China* until today.

In the early days of the packets the China trade was what engaged the attention of every Boston trader from Summer Street to Topliff's Reading Rooms. All the great firms had correspondents in China and their own hongs, as the Canton factories were known, the first contacts in the opium and tea trade having been established by Captain Shaw about the time of the close of the Revolution.

No foreigner, in those days, was allowed in the Canton customs house and none might remain in the city the year round, so that the factors, as soon as the ships were loaded and they had settled their accounts with the Chinese, returned to Macao, where the various trading nations maintained headquarters, until the ships returned for next year's cargo.

It became the established custom for the sons of Boston merchants, as soon as they graduated from Harvard, and in many cases without benefit of an interlude among the groves of the academe, to embark upon one of the family vessels, outbound, in order to learn the details of the China trade from personal observation and experience. Russell Sturgis, of the great firm of Sturgis and Company, served his apprenticeship in this manner, as did his son Julian afterward. Thomas Handasyd Perkins first viewed the Whampoa anchorage filled with the spars of tall ships at an age when most youths of today are in high school. Augustus Hemenway, who was to become one of the city's most influential merchants, worked for Benjamin Bangs and Co., at the age of fifteen, receiving as supercargo a salary of sixty dollars a year. Captain Robert Forbes, having been captured by the British three times before he was nine years old, went to sea as an apprentice at thirteen and commanded the *Canton Packet* at the age of twenty. A Boston trader, it will be apparent, knew his business at first-hand even though a large measure of its transactions were carried on upon the other side of the world.

The rapidly expanding China trade brought enormous wealth to Boston in the thirties and forties. The residential scheme of the town was different then, and the more affluent merchants' families lived either on the Hill or in what is now the retail section of downtown, along Summer and Washington Streets and in Temple Place. Usually the merchants themselves, in black or white beaver hats, black stocks and blue tailcoats with gold buttons, walked to and from their counting houses and warehouses adjoining the waterfront, devoting, as a matter of course, a considerable portion of each day to business conversation with colleagues at the Merchants' Exchange or at Topliff's Rooms. In 1829 these premises were located beside the United States Post Office in an old structure at Congress and Water Streets and here, "where most they do congregate," the ship-owners were supplied with the latest marine intelligence, dispatches, sail and arrive notices, and reports of vessels spoken on the far-off oceans of the world. A semaphore at Nantasket relayed the names of incoming packets to an observation station on top of Constitution Wharf, and thus a merchant might learn of the arrival of his cargo and make arrangements for its sale or storage several hours before it was tied up in India Wharf.

Two of the most extraordinary trades in the history of world shipping came into being in the era of the packets and were largely the product of Boston inventive genius. One was the carriage, during the gold rush days—when, as a matter of fact, packets and clippers sailed around the Horn together—of California laundry, all the way across the Pacific, to be scrubbed and starched at Manila or Canton; and the other was the establishment by Frederick Tudor of the ice monopoly of the Orient out of the Port of Boston.

The transoceanic trade in *blanchissage,* which flourished while Californians were too busy washing gold to be bothered with details of their toilet, and which took their ruffed shirts and cambric handkerchiefs out one year and returned them the next, is actually more a part of the glamorous history of the times of the young West, but the ice trade is a purely New England affair.

In the year 1805 Bostonians laughed heartily when Tudor, hearing of the ravages of yellow fever in the West Indies and knowing that the plague could be curbed with ice, planned to ship three hundred tons of the stuff from his Saugus pond to the Island of Martinique aboard his brig *Favorite.* The public merriment at his expense communicated itself to the newspapers, and there were editorial sneezes and jeers on every hand. "We hope the venture may not prove a slippery one," remarked a newspaper wag. "We fear his assets will perceptibly melt away," punned another, and it became difficult to enlist a crew, as sailors the length of the water-front unanimously subscribed to the theory

88

Captains of the Ocean Sea

that the entire cargo would melt and founder the vessel.

But the load arrived in Tudor's Martinique ice-house in precisely the gelid condition in which it had left Saugus for the Charlestown wharf, and from that time forth the merchant found himself the ice king of the world. Thirty years later the trade in Massachusetts ice, "those crystal blocks of Yankee coldness," as a newspaper called them in an era when reporters were prone to refer to fish as "the finny tribe," had extended itself to Calcutta, where it paid for itself handsomely. "Indeed, the ice trade gave Boston a long mastery of the general Calcutta traffic," wrote Winthrop L. Marvin, chronicler of the American merchant marine. "The originality and audacity of the ice export business were vividly American. No man who was not sure of himself could have sent such a perishable freight out upon a four or five months' voyage, which involved crossing the fiery equator, doubling da Gama's stormy Cape, and steering through the furnace heat of the Indian Ocean." Nobody save, perhaps, Lord Timothy Dexter, Tudor's contemporary and the celebrated shipper of warming pans to the tropics.

One man who left a lasting impression upon Boston business in its teeming years was no Yankee at all, but the celebrated Chinese merchant, Houqua. The most powerful of all Canton shippers, he was the personal friend of scores of American traders and merchants and their captains, and his honesty and generosity became a household word in two hemispheres. Houqua was agent for Russell and Company and Perkins and Co., and many captains and factors had orders from their home offices to deal with no one else.

All trading on the Island of Shameen in the Canton River in the early days of the tea trade was conducted through the agency of a go-between or comprador, who was at once interpreter and the licensed representative of the Chinese merchants. It was through these that the transactions in

89

incoming opium, cotton goods, quicksilver, lumber and gin-seng were negotiated and tea, silk and matting for the Port of Boston was purchased. Upon one occasion it was discovered that a Canton comprador was $5,000 short in his account with Russell and Co., and although not legally obligated for the amount, Houqua was so anxious to retain the esteem of Boston shippers that the sum in full was sent that same evening to the office of the American firm.

In later years Russell Sturgis, when he was the head of Baring Brothers, the British bankers, was asked if the tradition were true that no written agreements had ever passed between Houqua and the American firm for which he had so long worked. Mr. Sturgis unearthed a yellowed slip of rice paper a few inches long on which were inscribed the words: "Forty thousand dollars. Houqua." It was the only memorandum of agreement he could recall having seen written by the Chinese.

During the dull season between shipments in 1837 a group of English and American residents at the hongs founded for their amusement the Canton Regatta Club. The orientals, to whose minds the idea of sport for sport's sake seemed simple insanity, were greatly upset by the nautical activity that followed, and three local merchants, headed by Houqua, made a protest in the following lyric terms:

On the river boats are mysteriously abundant; everywhere they congregate in vast numbers; like a stream they advance and retire unceasingly. Thus the chances of contact are many; so are accidents even to the breaking of one another's boats, to the injury of men's bodies, while even more serious consequences might ensue.

Houqua translated this for the benefit of Julian Sturgis, who had been active in the founding of the boating society. "More better no go," he explained.

Captains of the Ocean Sea

When Houqua died his estate was estimated at $26,000,-
000, but this was by no means as much as he had assisted his
correspondents in salting away in various Boston banks,
and there are Beacon Street families where to this day his
name is as familiar as that of any ancestor who ever drove
his ship into the teeth of the northeast monsoon or un-
masked a swivel gun in the face of China Sea pirates. It
ranks in the annals of commercial enterprise with those of
Russell and Ammidon, Delano, Dana and Coolidge.

The genius of Donald McKay became allied to the resources of Enoch Train, Boston's leading shipping merchant, in the middle forties. McKay, a product of Nova
Scotia, had behind him, by the time he had achieved the
age of thirty-four, a notable record as a marine designer
and builder. Apprenticed to a New York shipwright, he
had shown an extraordinary aptitude for his calling, and
by 1832 he was a free-lance ship builder of established
reputation in Manhattan's East River shipping community.
A visit to Wiscasset in Maine opened his eyes to the opportunities that offered for a man of his abilities in New
England, and for several years he was located at Newburyport on the broad Merrimac. It was here that his achievements were called to the attention of Train who, in the
imperial manner which rested so easily on the merchant
princes of the era, grasped his hand and said, "Come to
Boston. We need you."

At one time in his mercantile career Train owned the
largest number of ships of any man in New England. In
1844 when McKay built for him his first packet, the *Joshua
Bates,* he was, as the English of the period would have
said, a "warm" man. His fortunes and prestige were steadily
on the ascendant, and to receive a "good morning" salutation as he passed down Commercial Street on the way to his
counting rooms was a Boston accolade. McKay was in good

company, and he knew that the highroad to success stretched before him under such auspices.

Train's celebrated fleet of Liverpool packets flying the White Diamond house flag was inaugurated with McKay's *Washington Irving,* a ship which attracted widespread attention in professional shipping circles by reason of her strength and simplicity of design and her performance on the Atlantic run. This vessel was followed in close succession by the *Anglo Saxon* for the same line, the *New World* for Moses H. Grinnell of New York and many other beautiful and swift packets culminating in the magnificent *Star of Empire* and *Chariot of Fame* in 1853.

But coincidentally with the perfection of the packet ship came the evolution of the clipper. McKay's first contribution to the Cape Horn fleet, the *Stag Hound,* lengthened the lines of the packet, lent an extreme sharpness to bow and stern, and proportionally increased the propelling power: mast, yards and canvas.

The launching of the *Stag Hound* in 1850 was an event with dramatic implications for the entire world of seafaring. It was a bitter December day when a crowd of over ten thousand gathered at the East Boston shipyards, and so low was the level of the mercury that it was feared the tallow would freeze on the ways. The finely carved and gilded stag hound that was her figurehead towered above the workmen who were laying plugs of tobacco on the question of whether she would budge or not. A group of calkers led by a foreman thought no. McKay thought yes but was not betting. Representatives of Sampson and Tappan, the East India merchants who had bought her, pulled their mufflers over their ears, canted their top hats against the wind that whistled up from Noddle's Island and the channel, and wished (qualifiedly) that they were back by the cannonball stove in their counting house.

Captains of the Ocean Sea

Suddenly and without any warning the ship above them began to move. A workman had tentatively struck a dog shore or so in the interest of getting on the right side of a plug of Farmer's Favorite, and, before he could lay his bet, his curiosity had its answer. Smoke curled from the ways. A cheer rose from the no-freeze faction on the shore, and the yard foreman who at the moment was in the fore peak hastily seized a square bottle of Medford rum and shouted *"Stag Hound—Stag Hound,"* as he leaned over the bulwarks to smash it on her forefoot. The record shows that he lost his hat in the excitement.

When the *Stag Hound* was laden for California at her New York berth she filled to the decks with freight at a dollar forty per cubic foot, and her first cost was paid before she cleared the Narrows for the open ocean. When she returned with a cargo of tea it was found that the earnings of her first voyage, on which she had been gone less than eleven months, had paid for herself and netted in addition the sum of $80,000 for her owners.

McKay's next achievement, the immortal *Flying Cloud,* made the trip around the Horn to the Golden Gate in eighty-nine days, twenty-one hours, and three years later she beat her own record by thirteen hours. She was bought on the stocks by Grinnell, Minturn and Co., and Enoch Train in after years repeatedly asserted that he regretted nothing in his life so much as not having been her proprietor.

When McKay, still at East Boston although his yard had been moved to allow for the lengthening of Border Street, launched his *Sovereign of the Seas* the vessel was of such unprecedented proportions that no merchant would buy her and her designer was forced to go into shipping on his own account. Commercial Street shook its conservative head and allowed that perhaps he had over-reached himself, trying to run flour to 'Frisco with no assurance that some other

93

Boston and the Boston Legend

ship would not have glutted the market the day before his arrival. But McKay played in luck. Flour was selling for $44 a barrel when he anchored off the Embarcadero, and the *Sovereign's* freight and passage money topped $80,000. Later, on the Liverpool run, this remarkable ship beat the Cunard steamer *Canada* to Queenstown, and before her time was up, made many brilliant passages in the Australian trade.

One of the longest-lived sources of prosperity to Boston shippers was trade with the Port of Fayal in the Azores, which continued an unabated marine tradition from the opening of the nineteenth century until nearly to its close, when steam was universally replacing canvas and strong spars. The principal trade with these islands was that in whale oil deposited there by long voyage whalers for re-shipment to Boston and New Bedford, but at other seasons there was a considerable traffic in fruit and island wines and passenger travel was continuous.

The ships *Swiftsure, Sarah, Harbinger, Azor, Hortense* and *Azorean* were built for Charles W. Dabney of Boston —one of the Dabney family which distinguished itself by supplying three generations of American consuls at the Azores—and they achieved an almost personal significance for the people of Fayal. The bark *Azor* brought prosperity and news of the world across the Atlantic for many years, and upon one occasion when she was posted as overdue the entire island offered prayers for several days for her safe arrival.

Captain Edmund Burke of the *Azor* enjoyed among Bostonians of the fifties and sixties very much the same esteem and prestige associated in the present century with Captain Alfred W. V. Trant of the *Devonian* (Boston people sailed with Captain Trant as unquestioningly as they traded with Pierce, the grocer, or summered on Buzzard's

Captains of the Ocean Sea

Bay) and on the islands Burke's beaver hat and mutton-chop whiskers were received with a veneration otherwise reserved for Divinity alone. On one occasion he rescued some three hundred passengers from the *Gratitude* in mid-Atlantic when that vessel was foundering, and in order to accommodate them it was necessary to jettison an entire cargo of fruit consigned to Boston fruiterers. The insurance firms refused to indemnify the shippers, but the value of the oranges was raised by popular subscription and presented to Captain Burke with suitable ceremonies. Upon another occasion, when an epidemic of smallpox had broken out at Fayal, Boston ships were specially exempted from quarantine, but the port was strictly closed to ships from New York, Philadelphia, *Chicago and Cincinnati!*

Throughout the forties and fifties, the sea and the ships that sailed it were the breath of life to commercial Boston. After the war New England manufactories and a new sort of less daring commercialism were to come into flower, but for many years salt water and the bearded captains of the ocean-sea brought Boston close to the hongs of Canton, the assay office of San Francisco and the perfumed islands of the hither and the farther Indies.

Contest was the order of the day and betting was a universal fever. Ship-owners shook fists under each other's chin whiskers in front of Merchants' Exchange in State Street and wagered the earnings of their house flags for the next six months over whose packet out of Lintin would be spoken first at Topliff's. Clerks from H. C. Thacher's office would lay the customary beaver hat against the judgment of clerks from the tall stools of E. Atkins and Co., and together they would race to the office of A. & C. Cunningham over Rowe's Wharf, where there was a loophole and old-fashioned spy-glass scanning the harbor, for vindication in disputes nautical. Longshoremen and roustabouts

95

fought like draft rioters in Atlantic Avenue over the relative merits of clippers, and sailors who fell into water-front gutters with happy roarings were known as "bounty" drunk, signifying that they had just been paid off from a successful voyage. The sea as completely overflowed the consciousness of the town as cotton engulfed all other concerns at Natchez or tobacco at Havana.

Speed was the word. When Daniel Draper, a fruit merchant, commanded the building of his *Jehu,* it was reported that he told the builder he must have a vessel that could carry canvas even if she had room for only a single crate of oranges. American shippers were so famous for their achievements that in 1852 the American Navigation Club, of which Daniel Bacon of Boston was president, challenged British ship-builders to a race from China to England in duplicate ships for the sum of £10,000. Captain Philip Dumaresq was to have sailed the American craft, but, despite the baiting and encouragement of rivals and friends, no Englishman would take the challenge. Later the Americans raised the stake to £20,000 and a two weeks' handicap, but there were no takers.

The Civil War and the newly perfected fixed ammunition of Captain Raphael Semmes of the *Alabama,* changing times and the steam triple-expansion engine put an end to the saga of sail, and lean-faced men who traded in rail shares in the shadow of Wall Street's Trinity Church sent the shipping of the world to the East and North Rivers. But once there was a glory over Boston Harbor, before Canada's wheat went down the Saint Lawrence and before luxury liners nosed their way up the splendid Hudson. A glory of sail and a kingdom and a power of ships.

STATE STREET TODAY

Chapter X

GOLDEN AGE OF LETTERS

THE literary great of Boston in the nineteenth century present a solid and unassailable front. Many of them were neighbors, almost all of them were friends. They shared mutual enthusiasms, went transcendental or abolitionist in groups, and set up Utopias in the pleasant fields of neighboring villages. The magnificence which sentimental literary critics attribute to the Golden Age of Boston literature is largely mythical, but New England belles lettres produced a few memorable works and several distinctive personalities.

It is well to remember that after 1850 the center of literary activity passed from the South to the North. The freak genius of Poe had worn out, Irving and Cooper were established and continued to write sedate and mediocre fiction. Whatever new life, then, was to come, must come from a fresh invigoration. Yankee Boston and Yankee New England gave American letters that invigoration. The writers of this renaissance had the bluest blood in their veins. They also had the inheritance of the Puritan which made them question conscience and attach moral significance to much of what they wrote. They were never entirely free from the New England conscience which "does not prevent you from doing things, but prevents you from enjoying them." Essentially pious, they denounced the flesh and the Devil. Their new aristocracy was one of culture rather than breeding. They were touched, almost all of them, by the heady fog of transcendentalism, which led them to set down as inspiration a multitude of half-formed thoughts and repressed fancies. They dined well and wined little. They kept the air pure.

Ralph Waldo Emerson was literary dictator of the age. Born into a religious family, he grew up in Boston schools and found his way to Harvard, as—so a Harvard man will say—every New Englander of account has done. He traveled, lectured, and preached. He wore somber black suits and ties to match, and his boots usually needed polishing. Yet there was something about this provincial New Englander that brought Indian dignitaries, German scholars, English historians and essayists, exponents of free love, and country yokels to his feet. This attraction was due to the two essences of his teaching: intellectual independence and the application of common sense to living. In his essay "Self-Reliance" he wrote: "Act singly, and what you have already done will justify you now." But to reach Emerson's essences and to find the way to such simple maxims as this is not always easy. When he writes of friendship, nature, heroism, or love he can be followed. It is when he writes cryptically of the "over-soul" and transcends the transcendentalists that he is murky and foreign.

Although he is best known as an essayist, his verse has

its own charm. "Days" and "The Rhodora" are common-places of American poetry. To him a bumblebee was a "yellow-breeched philosopher," the rhodora a microcosm. He preferred to wander through the Concord fields ponder-ing on things deeper than the Eleusinian mysteries than to mount the lecture platform; he would rather have the com-pany of cabbages than kings.

Although all Boston worshiped him, he seldom came to Boston. Occasionally he visited the Athenaeum, accompanied by his daughter Ellen, who, as his factotum, carried his books and papers in her satchel. He could never remember where he put things.

Walt Whitman kept him walking up and down Boston Common for half a day when the two first met to discuss the advisability of publishing *Leaves of Grass,* and when Emerson finally gave the "revolutionary document" his divine sanction, they both retired to the American House for what Emerson described as a "bully good dinner." The menu has, unhappily, perished.

The "curious, sociable, cheerful public funeral," as Henry James describes him, was a mixture of Buddha, Sweden-borg, and rustic peasant, but at heart he was a Puritan. It is these strange elements that make him fascinating and baffling and obscure.

It is perhaps unfair to call Thoreau a Bostonian, since he was really a Concord hermit and hated cities. Yet his name must be linked to Emerson's and *The Dial,* and right-fully he belongs to the Boston group. Born poor and brought up poorer, he went through Harvard on scholar-ships and made lead pencils for a living. Since he "did not need a post-office," he built himself a shanty on the edge of Walden Pond in Concord where he lived intermittently for several years. He was famously untidy and eloquently blunt in speech. He was as ill at ease in Boston parlors as an untrained sheep-dog. And yet he is the best example of the stoical attitude which characterizes the Puritan. Like his friend Emerson, he is a paradox. He loved the country he lived in and yet he refused to pay taxes because it kept slaves. He envisioned Utopias where all men would live together like brothers, yet always preferred his own company. He traveled frequently alone, and his best-known works *A Week on the Concord and Merrimac Rivers* and *Walden* are adventures in solitude. He was an exceptional naturalist and his *Journal* is full of accurate and enthusiastic observations of plants and animals. His style is highly individual, crossed by puns and picturesque observations. He was more the farmer and less the dreamer than was Emerson. What he bequeathed to the literature of his time might equally well belong to any time. Yet his shrewdness, his frequent wit, and his vigorous independence make him New England's own. His verse, much overpraised, is largely schoolboy posturing in prosody. In one of his most admired poems occur the lines:

> The waves slowly beat
> Just to keep the noon sweet.

Such lines are hardly compensated by his rare flashes of poetical insight.

He was constantly surprising himself that he wrote at all, or that he should be taking part in the controversies of his day. There is no statement more typically Thoreau than one in a letter to Emerson when, after commenting on a recent election for governor, he wrote: "Ain't I a brave boy to know so much of politics for the nonce?"

The maternal grandfather of the author, while a professor of mathematics at Harvard, was more or less closely associated both with Emerson and Thoreau, but the sole remaining fragment of his own something less than pious verses which has survived for posterity runs:

> Qui semper sobrius in cubiculo sedat
> In mensis Octobris cum foliis cedat.

For all its handsome Latinity it is doubtful if the temperate Sage of Concord would have endorsed the sentiment.

Next door to Emerson and Thoreau lived Bronson Alcott, temple priest of the transcendental school. He is less important as a writer than as a leader of thought, and what he wrote will not be long remembered. But he well represents the "new spirit" that was inundating New England. With two English friends he established the georgic "Fruitlands" where he set up some quaint rituals. Vegetables that grew down were taboo because they did not aspire. Worms and insects were to be allowed their right to life. Meat must not be eaten, and the earth must not be profaned with manure.

When Alcott was not busy with his Eden garden, he was agitating for dress reform, temperance, and the water cure. He became Dean of the Concord School of New Thought, and held seminars in the higher mysteries of the psyche and the radiations of Divine Eminence. He also delivered a series of very philosophic conversations for which he charged a handsome fee. He never understood why "Fruitlands" was a failure.

His more famous daughter, Louisa May Alcott, grew up in this atmosphere of sweetness and light. It touched her novels and made at least one of them, *Little Women,* an immortal book for children. When she was a little girl she used to be allowed to come into the parlor and be dandled on the knee of the "Concord Pan," as her father called Thoreau, and her exposure to the Concord literary lights filled her with high ambitions. If one can wade through the sentiment of her best novels, one will discover an accurate and pleasantly mellow picture of New England small town life. But most of her fiction is a sentimental journey through a highly improbable New England.

For the novel in the mid-century, one must go to Hawthorne. Although the best of his books were written about early New England, he is characteristic of the struggle between reticence and independence that brought so many of his contemporaries so low. Born and brought up in Salem, he, like Longfellow, committed the unpardonable indiscretion of going to Bowdoin College. After a few lean years as weigher in the Boston Customs House, he joined the Brook Farm movement. This settlement was not quite as mad as "Fruitlands." It was started by George Ripley and Charles A. Dana, and was an experiment in coöperative living. Everyone was to work with his hands, and work hard. Labor was to pay for board and the school set up on the farm.

Hawthorne's first assignment was to play chambermaid, as he expressed it, to a cow. He quickly named this cow Margaret Fuller because of her "cussed stubbornness." He joined whole-heartedly with the movement, murmuring protests only on such occasions as the junket (or dance orgy—they were always dancing at Brook Farm) when George William Curtis appeared as première ballerina in a short green skirt. But they were not always frolicking at the Farm. There was much metaphysical discussion. Even at dinner it was common to say, "Is the butter within the sphere of your influence?" This noble experiment died a sudden death after a severe fire in 1846, and Hawthorne returned, after a few years' residence in Concord, to Salem.

The Scarlet Letter made Hawthorne famous. It was the most daring book to come from a New England pen, because it actually created sympathy for its heroine—a

Golden Age of Letters

woman of Sin and Shame. In all of Hawthorne's novels his talk is unnatural and as graceless as the talk of the present-day Yankee farmer, but his scenes glow, and his sense of the Puritan qualities is astounding. In spite of the shyness and delicacy which some of his most charming stories reveal, he was "a tall, shapely figure rendered military by a thick mustache," and how he loved to follow a band! Lowell in his "Fable for Critics" describes him as possessing:

> A frame so robust, with a nature so sweet,
> So earnest so graceful, so lithe, and so fleet,

that he was:

> . . . worth a descent from Olympus to meet.

It is perhaps fair to say that indeed Hawthorne was of all New Englanders the first and the last Olympian.

It has been said that almost every Boston family in the nineteenth century boasted either a potted palm or an author. One might add that then and now almost every Boston family of account boasts somewhere in it a Lowell. And every Lowell boasts a sense of humor. James Russell Lowell was the gayest of the Boston Parnassians. In Harvard he was lamentably irresponsible and frivolous. In later life he had the same gaiety and, in fact, perpetuated a *jeunesse dorée* to a seasonable age. His interests were catholic: he edited the *Atlantic Monthly,* the Bible of New England letters; he went as ambassador to the Court of St. James's and later became minister to Spain; he was a prominent abolitionist. His Cambridge home, Elmwood, was as much a fashion as it was a literary center. Men modeled their clothes after his, and women came in droves to his open teas. He was, moreover, the best literary critic in America before 1900.

103

Boston and the Boston Legend

He was both a Yankee and a cosmopolite. In his *Bigelow Papers,* written originally as a verse satire in dialect on the Mexican war, he captures the full flavor of Yankee wit: crude, forceful, pungent. Lines like:

> An' you've gut to git up airly
> Ef you want to take in God . . .

may not be literature, but they are admirably expressive of the New Englander's Anglo-Saxon directness. Of his verse the "Fable for Critics" is the best, in that it has shrewd appraisals and buoyant humor.

A critic unfamiliar with the social background of Boston literature would be led to think (with the exception of Howells and Henry James) that the Boston literateurs had no drawing-rooms. There is a lack of urbanity in Boston letters, even in such a man as Lowell, that bespeaks the frontier. The most bucolic poet of the time was John Greenleaf Whittier, like Lowell a vigorous abolitionist. His literary career began with the editorship of the *American Manufacturer,* published in Boston. Here he became a marked man because of his refusal to drink beer at Parker's in School Street and his substitution of cider, a New England beverage which upon occasion has been known to achieve a commendably high degree of alcoholic content. He compensated for this social deficiency, however, by a profane vocabulary which was the wonder and glory of the town. His resource and imagination in this field of endeavor were the envy of hackmen and would have corrupted the ears of a fishwife. As a man of letters he was milder, and the bulk of his early work concerned itself with abolitionism.

Better as a poet was Henry Wadsworth Longfellow. At his funeral Emerson (who was losing his memory) found that this man, whose name he could not remember, had a nice face. This remark characterizes Longfellow. Everything about him was nice: his manners, his taste, his Brattle Street home, and most of his verse. Craigie House was the most sacred of all the houses on Brattle Street, Cambridge's *Via Sacra*. When Longfellow entertained, which was not often, he bade his guests arrive on the dot, and if they failed to do so, they were rebuked by a stony stare from the bluest and coldest eyes in New England. He wrote too much, and of what he wrote, only a little attains excellence. He did restore the dignity of the sonnet to American verse. He made a respectable translation of Dante, a task he entered upon to divert himself after his wife had perished in a holocaust in their library. His ballads have a good swing, and the *Tales of a Wayside Inn* brought fame to the tavern of the same name in Wayland—until Henry Ford bought it for a museum piece. Longfellow wrote for a sentimental public. His best-known poems, *Evangeline* and *Hiawatha,* are cloying and infantile. His most touted prose works, *Hyperion* and *Outre-Mer,* have cluttered up the second-hand bookshops on Cornhill for so long they are not even welcome on the nickel counter. Longfellow is the epitome of excellence to the Watch and Ward Society, that self-appointed body of censors who have rather ineffectively tried to keep Boston uncontaminated from Sin these many years. He was a good man—good and frequently dull with the dullness of too abundant virtue.

Oliver Wendell Holmes, less popular than Longfellow, but a far more astute writer, was proud his life long that he had been born the same year as Lincoln. He was a Brahmin among Brahmins, tracing his lineage to Anne Bradstreet of Puritan days. Throughout his life he showed the facility with his hands of which every true New Englander is proud. He photographed, and invented a clumsy stereoscope; he was one of the fathers of the safety razor and one of the few beardless men in a school of hirsute

Boston and the Boston Legend

Athenians. He was proud that no Harvard graduate had read less than he. He described himself as "omniverbivorous by nature and training" to which a great diversity of interests ably attests. His *Autocrat at the Breakfast Table* is a rambling series of conversations and monologues touching hundreds of subjects from puns to poetic composition. He also wrote "medicated novels," of which the most diverting is *Elsie Venner*. In this novel, the heroine's mother is bitten by a rattlesnake before Elsie's birth, and thus a strangely evil nature is transmuted to Elsie. He dallied in verse, but was no poetaster. Like many New Englanders, he did a great deal with competence and little with distinction.

No account of Boston letters would be complete without the garland of ladies who added, if not to the stature of Boston literature, at least to its color. First among these was Margaret Fuller, famous for her nasal voice, her trick of opening and shutting her eyelids rapidly as she talked, and her ever-present diamond necklace. She danced her first quadrille at a ball given for President Adams, and was so near-sighted she kept bumping into her partner. She was arrogant, truculent, and apparently strangely alluring. She was transcendentalist, mystic, editor, traveler, confidante of George Sand and Mazzini, and managed, with everything else, to carry on an abortive courtship with a wealthy Jewish merchant in New York. Her brochure, *Women in the Nineteenth Century*, heralded feminism in America. She spurned the niceties of Beacon Hill literary salons for the fresh air of "Fruitlands," and had the restless, errant spirit that characterizes the modern clubwoman. She confessed that she was in love with everyone who was in love with her, man, woman, or child, and that love—to quote from one of her poems—made her cry out, "I am immortal! I know it! I feel it!" Her mannish mind enabled her to battle with wits like Holmes and Emerson. She was New England's Lysistrata.

At 241 Beacon Street lived Julia Ward Howe, whose fame resides in "The Battle Hymn of the Republic." Witty, animated, she, like Margaret Fuller, had the independence of mind more nearly masculine than feminine. She founded the New England Women's Club and bossed it with an iron hand for several decades. She was the Emily Post of her day, and her *Social Customs* and *The Correct Thing* made her arbiter elegantiarum without rival. Her house was stuffed with curio-cabinets, what-nots, marbles, and rubber-plants. Her company was fastidious. In the summers she moved her salon to Newport, where there was much discussion about what should be written, and little writing.

There were other salons in Boston. Mrs. Harrison Gray Otis opened her spacious house to the Elect and made midnight suppers of cake and non-alcoholic punch fashionable. She danced the first waltz in America. In 1842 Dickens dined at her house and commented on the "two mighty bowls of hot stewed oysters, in any one of which a half-grown Duke of Clarence might be smothered easily." Oysters were the fashion. Thackeray, eating his first one at the Parker House, remarked that he felt as if he had swallowed a baby.

Mrs. James T. Fields dispensed less food and better talk. In her plush-lined library with its sputtering gas globes and uncomfortable chairs, Dickens and Thackeray were frequent callers. It was here that Dickens and Fields cooked up the famous walking match. Dickens said that Doldy, his agent, could outwalk Osgood, Fields's partner. After a six and a half mile walk with only a few oranges and bottles of beer for stimulants, Osgood won. Fields and Dickens followed comfortably in a hired coach.

Boston and the Boston Legend

The Fields also discovered Sarah Orne Jewett. Although Miss Jewett was a resident of Boston for many years, she was, in her own words, "never prouder . . . than when some old resident of Berwick [Maine] meets me and says, 'You're one of the Doctor's girls, ain't ye?' " She published her first story in the *Atlantic* before she was twenty; at thirty she was, in New England, famous. Today *The Country of the Pointed Firs* is still an eminently respectable, charming, unexciting book. She, together with Mary E. Wilkins Freeman, discovered how to use local color in the novel and story. Neither pretended to write about anything more than they knew or were, which was decidedly middle-class.

It is this lack of aristocracy which surprises in a literature written by self-styled Brahmins. The fiction written in and around Boston during the nineteenth century abounds in gigs, home-made bread, poor farms, mendicants, and country doctors. Poetry runs either to the bucolic or the derivative ballad and narrative type of Victorian England. Tennyson dominated poetical taste. Frivolity remained the province of the theater.

For the sober-minded there were lectures at the Athenaeum, presided over by Tabby the Wise, a cat who lived out nine long lives in the dusty stacks. It was here that a most scandalous occurrence shocked Boston: Hannah Adams, the first professional literary woman in America, was given the freedom of the library. Several trustees wanted to resign immediately. Then there were lectures in the winter at the College. Cutters bore solemn ladies and Port-braced men across the river to hear Matthew Arnold intone on the beauties of poetry.

There were two drawing-room writers of the period. One, William Dean Howells, was a middle-westerner and had a newspaper man's training. He joined the ranks of

Golden Age of Letters

the *Atlantic* and began to write Boston novels. Of these *A Modern Instance* and *The Rise of Silas Lapham* are justly the only ones to be remembered. Lapham begins life in the middle-class, and slowly achieves Back Bay. Howells makes his characters more credible than do most of his contemporaries. He is not sentimental, he is often dull, but there is a certain accurate recording of talk and manners in his novels that gives him the right to be called a father of American realism.

Henry James, on the other hand, was to the manor born. William, the philosopher-brother, wrote the better of the two—wrote so well, in fact, that it was said of the James brothers that the "novelist wrote like a philosopher, and the philosopher like a novelist." Henry spent the better part of his years abroad, an expatriate by choice. Wealthy, precious, snobbish, he gently despised Americans. An unknown woman admirer once wrote him a gushing letter which he described as "tawdry." He did not like to mingle in the Beacon Hill world. On one of his return visits to Boston, he was given a series of soirées, so that for weeks, as he said, Boston had made him "jump through pink paper hoops." This was characteristic of James. The *mot juste,* the exquisitely phrased, are everywhere in his writings. Nothing ever really happens in a James novel. A hero may be left standing against a mantel for thirty pages or a heroine left on the steps of a library for an entire story. But James's conversations and the observations that lie back of them are subdued and dramatic.

Some say that the Götterdämmerung has come upon Boston. Some will belittle and many will overpraise its homely contribution to American letters. The fact remains that, since Boston's Golden Age, nowhere else in the country has there been a time when there was the same unity, the same outspoken independence among writers.

Chapter XI

BROADCLOTH MOB

THE greatest single catastrophe in the history of the United States—a civil war regarded by many realistic historians to have been a gratuitous engagement, the principal objective of which would have been accomplished without its agency in a few decades of normal economic evolution—had its origin in Boston. The conventional record of the Abolitionist movement is a legend of disinterested altruism, an epic of lofty striving in the vineyards of humanitarian endeavor. No economic considerations are allowed to intrude upon the chronicle of the movement which reached its dramatic climax when the first Parrott rifle fired across Charleston Harbor on Sumter and its justification with the emancipation proclamation. But the fact stands that the destruction of vast resources of treasure and manpower, the ruin of the South, and the erection of a barrier of lasting memories between two societies accomplished, not only a humanitarian reform of dubious timeliness, but assured the eco-

Broadcloth Mob

nomic supremacy of New England in the middle morning of
the industrial era. It is vastly improbable that William
Lloyd Garrison or Wendell Phillips foresaw the full amount
of their own usefulness, but it remains that sentimental
humanitarianism in the shadow of Beacon Hill paid dividends of which the entrepreneurs, a few years later, of
Credit Mobilier need not have been ashamed.

The fulfillment of the cause of Abolitionism was accomplished in thirty years, a single generation of time, and it
was evolved, championed and exploited by a militant group
of self-consecrated right thinkers whose posturings and
pirouettings and fancied martyrdoms were not, in retrospect, altogether divorced from the humorous. The era of
the Abolitionists from the thirties to the sixties was characterized by such pious oratory, such tub-thumping, such
cloak swirling, invocations of divine lightnings and general
rhodomontade as may never again be vouchsafed for the
scandal of the sedate and the edification of the irreverent.
The whirling dervishes of the Lord, their eyes lifted on
high and their feet treading the mazes of emotional sara-
bands which would interest strangely modern students of
psychologic urges, clamored from the lectern and embraced
the cause of the reluctant and terrified serfs with the enlightened fury of fanatics. It was for all the world a thirty
years war of tracts, the holy lunacy of a revival meeting
lasting for three delighted decades.

Boston in the early thirties was not an altogether urban
community. True, the form of municipal government had
been altered from that of a town to a chartered city, and a
notably distinguished succession of mayors, beginning with
John Phillips and continuing through the terms of Josiah
Quincy, Harrison Gray Otis and Theodore Lyman, Jr.,
promised a high level of office-holders for some time to
come. The outstanding metropolitan achievement of the

Boston and the Boston Legend

middle twenties, and it will serve as an index to the tranquillity of the times, was the establishment of Quincy Market adjacent to Faneuil Hall, and a vital topic of conversational interest was whether or not members of fire brigades should be exempt from militia duty. At the solicitation of the Society for the Suppression of Intemperance, a brass band was installed on the Common on Sunday afternoons in the hope of abating the Sabbath tumult and pub crawling so popular with the uninhibited classes. The denizens of Copp's Hill and the jungles of Noddle's Island were enchanted, and became hideously barreled to martial music which, it was discovered, stirred them to hitherto unimagined riot and abandon. The Marquis of Lafayette was welcomed back to Boston amid fanfaronades, firing of maroons and other noises of hospitality. Knee-breeches had almost disappeared from the streets, save among elderly gaffers and upon the more formal evening occasions. The ringing of the church bells was changed from eleven o'clock in the morning to one, or, as was said at the time, from the hour of drinking to that of eating. The principal residents of Park Street were Abbott Lawrence, the merchant and ambassador, Jonathan Amory, Governor Gore and Dr. John C. Warren. The house at the corner of Beacon Street was not yet notable for the occupancy of George Ticknor and his celebrated library. Such was the almost pastoral community which was shortly to be set by the ears by a flaming controversy over freeing the negroes of the South, the nearest of whom were two full days distant by Long Island Sound packet and overland train brigade.

The two outstanding figures of the anti-slavery movement in Boston were Wendell Phillips and William Lloyd Garrison. Stemming from different backgrounds, but each thrilling to the joys of a cause which enabled its partisans to deliver interminable addresses and harass their fellows

HARRISON GRAY OTIS HOUSE, 1795, AND
THE OLD WEST CHURCH, 1805

Broadcloth Mob

with, presumably, the indulgence and even the approval of heaven, they emerged upon the unwilling consciousness of the city in the early thirties and have never been entirely erased from it since. In the course of time they associated with themselves such persons as Samuel E. Sewell, Samuel May, Lucy Stone, Ralph Waldo Emerson, William Ellery Channing and Edmund Quincy, the last of whom was by no means the least influential since, of all the embattled legions of liberation, he alone possessed an acute sense of the ridiculous and could laugh at the absurdities, self dramatization and martyr fixations of his fellow Abolitionists.

The initial fulminations of the reformers and of their periodical, the *Liberator,* and the proposal that the entire body of possessed negroes of the land should be freed for purely humanitarian reasons provoked little more than the tolerant tut-tuts of bored auditors. There followed a period during which the pretensions and consequence with which they invested their dreary gestures of righteousness were savored with appreciative gusto by a limited but fastidious group of connoisseurs of the preposterous. When Dr. Channing and Garrison were reconciled, with suitably dramatic gestures, in the name of the cause, a spectator of the affecting scene wrote that "Righteousness and Peace had kissed each other." "A million females in this country," thundered Garrison—himself with an eye to what a later journalism would call "the woman's angle" in the news, "are recognized and held as property—liable to be sold or used for the gratification of the lust or avarice or convenience of unprincipled speculators without the least protection to their chastity. Have these no claims upon our sympathies— prayers—charities?

> "When woman's heart is bleeding
> Shall woman's voice be hushed?"

Boston and the Boston Legend

When such gay reading was chronicled daily in the public prints it is easy to understand why the Abolitionists were accorded the same fascinated and reverent attention as the end-of-the-world gospelers and flat earth prophets who today claim the west side of the Common on Sunday afternoons. In a few years, however, it was apparent that the South failed to see the point of this comedy. The *Liberator* was causing friction and unrest, and Southern purchasers were taking their business away from Boston to the New York market. The Abolitionists were gaining converts among women and churchgoers and were becoming more outrageous and unrestrained in their demands. The vein of burlesque was running thin.

By 1835 almost all classes in the community were definitely tired of the entertainment and regarded the anti-slavery cause as a proven nuisance and a real potential menace. The Abolitionists were condemned by the merchant in his home in Summer Street and by the teamster in the Bell in Hand tap-room as reckless fanatics inciting the slaves to rebellion and willing to divide North and South in civil war. Such, of course, was actually the case, although a later generation has inclined to view the circumstance with more tolerance than scorn, a sentiment which only the cynical will connect with seven intervening decades of New England dividends from mills, railroads and manufactories. Elsewhere the Abolitionists were being taken care of. A school for colored girls in Canterbury, Connecticut, was arbitrarily closed down; mobs sacked the home of a New Yorker who had once bailed Garrison out of a Baltimore jail, and in Vermont Sam May was mobbed five times in a month. Conservative Bostonians decided it was time to clean house.

The circumstances leading to what has become known to history as "the mob of well-dressed gentlemen" were: the

114

Broadcloth Mob

growing feeling in Boston that, blinded by its fanaticism, the anti-slavery element was becoming oblivious to every other aspect of the public peace and welfare; and the presence at the time of a British Abolitionist orator named George Thompson. It had been highly impolitic of the Anti-Slavery Society to secure Thompson as a speaker and it was only natural that, with a generation still living which recalled both wars with England, he should have been denounced as "a British emissary," "a vagabond," and a "scoundrel who should be thrown overboard if he dared speak again." Harrison Gray Otis, Peleg Sprague, and other first citizens were incensed, and for once a united public opinion was shared by the gentlemen of Merchant's Row and the shiftless and disorderly element of the city's stews and backwashes. The town seethed with feeling, the rival factions assuring themselves they were doing the Lord's work and conjuring up unprecedented flowers of oratory to prove it. The Bible and the Constitution were quoted on every street corner, and Abolitionists thriftily wore their second best top-hats when they went abroad after dark.

It was in October, 1835, that a meeting of the Boston Female Anti-Slavery Society was announced in the building at 46 Washington Street in which the *Liberator* was published, with Thompson as the speaker. The same day a placard was issued at the office of the *Commercial Gazette* to the effect that "the infamous foreign scoundrel, Thompson, will hold forth this afternoon. The present is a fair opportunity for friends of the Union to snake Thompson out." A hundred dollar purse was raised to be paid the first man to lay hands on the reformer "that he might be brought to the tar kettle before dark." A hundred dollars was a powerful inducement in those days, and, added to the incentive of patriotic endeavor, was practically irresistible. Double orders of high-proof courage were being rushed across the bar in every tavern and it was apparent that the patriotism of the populace would never abate so long as the supply of Medford held out.

Thompson was not at the meeting, however, and whether it was his own discretion which prompted his absence, or the solicitude of his friends, is lost in the blast and counter-blast of accusations, recriminations and catcalls which followed hard on the events of the afternoon. The mob of several thousand people which assembled at the head of State Street didn't know he wasn't present and probably wouldn't have cared one way or the other. Abolitionists, whether imported or native, were of much the same color in its opinion.

Garrison was busy in the *Liberator* editorial rooms penning a letter to a friend, in which he was describing the doings in the street outside, when violence, in a more or less conservative Bostonian manner, burst into flame. A sudden and tremendous outbreak of cheering in Washington Street brought him to the window long enough to recognize a number of the town's first citizens, hats on the back of their heads and their stocks under one ear, passing brown bottles to one another with cries of mutual encouragement. Some ill-favored fellows whom he was able briefly to identify as teamsters were uprooting paving blocks in front of the old State House, and almost immediately a loud smashing noise followed by rowdy huzzahs indicated that someone had tossed a dornick through the window of the ladies' meeting across the hall. Garrison had no further time to devote to his observations, however, for at that moment there was a splintering sound behind him and a number of determined persons came through the door without the formality of unlatching it. Shrill cries and a flutter of protesting black-mitted hands behind them indicated that the ladies' meeting was being adjourned *sine die*.

TOWARDS BOWDOIN SQUARE

Broadcloth Mob

The leaders were disappointed not to find Thompson present as advertised and, while they realized there were limits to what they might with impunity do in the way of harassing Garrison, they decided that he might as well meet the electorate at first hand and learn its opinions on Abolitionism. To this end a rope was knotted around his waist and he was lowered from the second-floor window to the tune of thunderous howls and cheering from the friends of the Union. It is doubtful if they would have seriously injured the good man, but the clothes were torn from his back and there was loud and blood-chilling talk of lynching. A block away the afternoon calm of School Street was broken by a breathless citizen who burst into City Hall with the intelligence that they were burning Abolitionists at the stake.

Handsome and exquisite Mayor Theodore Lyman, Jr., reached for his white beaver hat on the letter press, glanced briefly in the mirror to see if his ruffled shirt was still starched, and called for whatever members of the watch might be lounging in the ward-room. He came to the head of State Street just as a fountain of torn blue broadcloth and fragments of cambric erupted above the heads of the crowd to indicate that Garrison's coat and linen were being sacrificed. By the time the peace officers had fought their way through to him the eminent reformer was reduced to the nether garments favored at the time and one surviving congress gaiter. Mayor Lyman followed through the lane opened for him, bowing to such citizens as he recognized and courteously refusing snuff until the present press of affairs should be over. It was noted by several that his silk waistcoat was cut in the new manner with four gold buttons instead of six.

Whether the mayor was more concerned for the civic peace or for the immodest exposure of Garrison is not in the record. In any event he discharged an officer to find a hackney coach on the rank outside Topliff's News Rooms and bundled the battered Abolitionist into it when it arrived. There was some difficulty in getting through the mob which by this time was seriously considering offering defiance to the mayor himself but, save for the damaged shins of several youths who attempted to reach the horses' heads and fell under the wheels of the carriage, nobody was injured. Garrison, for safe keeping, was driven to Leverett Street jail where he spent the night in his second-best suit which Mrs. Garrison sent in from his home just around the corner. After he had been released next morning the turnkey found written on the wall in the best Monte Cristo manner: "William Lloyd Garrison was put into this cell on Wednesday afternoon, October 21, 1835, to save him from the violence of a respectable and influential mob, who sought to destroy him for preaching the abominable and dangerous doctrine that 'all men are created equal' and that oppression is odious in the sight of God. Hail Columbia. Cheers for the Autocrat of Russia and the Sultan of Turkey! Reader, let this inscription remain till the last slave in this despotic land be loosed from his fetters."

The mannered mobbing of Garrison was far from being the climax of the anti-slavery movement in Boston, but it was a high point in the comedy of its early exploitation. The years following 1835 saw such personages and figures drawn into the Abolitionist ranks that almost overnight it achieved the status of a swift-moving drama of powerful social forces representing a new order in gestation. The exploitation of the reform movement remained largely in the hands of idealists and churchmen, Charles Sumner, Theodore Parker, Stephen Phillips, Harriet Beecher Stowe, Thomas Wentworth Higginson, and other nominal leaders and prophets who, in the language of another generation, would be described as "front men." But behind the oratory and humanitarian benevolence of incessant meetings in Faneuil Hall, snowstorms of pamphlets, and the ever dramatic attitudes of amateur and professional friends of the serfs, less spectacular but far more significant influences were working. It was becoming increasingly apparent to the entrepreneurs of State Street and Atlantic Avenue that new and illimitable vistas of opportunity were daily being opened by the rapid progress of a growingly industrial time. Transportation was assuming characteristics of ease and speed which were to remain unaltered for a full century. The end of the fourth decade brought promise of enormous tangible wealth from unexpected sources in the quartz lodes of California. And machinery was about to revolutionize every industry involving the handling and manufacture of cotton. Adroit planning might overnight elevate New England to the commercial leadership of the land, and Boston banks, railroads and Boston-financed mills would furnish the financial sequel to the brave days and profits of the clipper trade. Slave-labor and the prosperity of the South stood in the way of the achievement of these good ends, and there were humanitarians ready to hand to assist in the undoing of both in the name of the Great Jehovah and the Boston Female Anti-Slavery Society. It was almost too good to be true, and not the least satisfactory aspect of the scheme of things was the circumstance that it was quite unnecessary for the really influential persons of the community to associate themselves with an increasingly popular and socially dubious cause.

It is difficult to look back over a hundred years and appreciate the heat and feeling which characterized the slavery controversy in Boston in the three decades before the Civil War. The temper and unrestrained qualities of the oratorial debauches of the period are in themselves amazing as manifestations of a generation but little removed from a Puritan reticence and disdain for the ornamental and baroque.

"Across the Stage of Time," thundered Theodore Parker from the platform of the Boston Music Hall,

the nations pass in the solemn pomp of their historical procession. What kingly forms sweep by, leading the peoples of the past, the present age! Let them pass—their mingled good and ill. A great People now comes forth, the newest born of nations, the latest Hope of Mankind, the Heir of sixty centuries,—the Bridegroom of the virgin West. First come those Pilgrims, few and far between, who knelt on the sands of a wilderness. . . . Then comes the One with venerable face, who ruled alike the Senate and the Camp, and at whose feet the attendant years spread garlands and laurel wreaths calling him First in War and First in Peace and First in his Country's Heart, as it is in his. Then follow men bearing the first fruits of our toil, the wealth of sea and land, the labors of the loom, the stores of commerce and the arts. A happy People comes, some with shut Bibles in their hands, some with the nation's laws, some uttering those mighty Truths which God has writ on Man and men have copied into golden words. Then comes to close this long historic pomp —the panorama of the world—the Negro Slave, bought, bonded, beat.

It was, in the best sense of the words, a holy show.

Chapter XII

RECEPTION COMMITTEE

THE nineteenth century was seemingly an era of almost continual pilgrimage to the Athens of America. The patronizing Charles Dickens was moved to risk the North Atlantic and the subsequent and even more fearsome perils of New England train brigades and steam-packets to experience its august charm. Matthew Arnold, upon being served his first fish-ball at the home of James T. Fields, leaned forward, his whiskers bristling with fright, to exclaim to his wife, "Frances, Frances, there's something dead inside m' bun!" Prince Henry of Prussia and the Grand Duke Alexis brought the cachet of smartness implicit in Burke's Peerage to the austere but far from hostile democracy of its faubourgs. Boston Museum and the Parker House were as integral a part of the American grand tour as the Astor Library in New York or Mrs. Potter Palmer and the stockyards in Chicago a few years later.

And the two greatest occasions for civic hurrah during

Boston and the Boston Legend

an interlude when so many keys to the city were being given away were the welcomes extended to the Marquis of Lafayette and Edward, Prince of Wales. Lafayette returned to Boston, an old man, in 1824 and history records few parallel debauches of sentiment and sentimentality. There had never before been so many people in town as flocked from all over New England to welcome with cheers, tears and salvos of oratory their ally of revolutionary times. The old gentleman was lodged in the building at the corner of Park and Beacon Streets, opposite the State House, where later George Ticknor, the publisher, made his home, and from dawn till dark and long after crowds stood outside to cheer the warrior's every appearance at a window and even his shadow falling across the shades after lamplight.

Every token of municipal and private hospitality was shown Lafayette. The school-children of the recently chartered city turned out in thousands to participate in drills and figures on the Common and to present him with the bouquets of flowers which were fragrantly inseparable from all public occasions and were then carried by men as they are by women now. Old soldiers pressed through the crowd at the State House to recall to him battle incidents at Yorktown and Brandywine. The widow of Governor Hancock, when Lafayette, perceiving her on her balcony, saluted the old lady, burst into tears at the memory of departed times recalled by the gesture and exclaimed, "I have lived long enough." Wendell Phillips, a lad at Latin school, remembered the parade in his honor as "a sight which should live in the memory forever—the best which Boston ever saw." In an age when sentimentality needed no excusing it was all a happy reunion, with tears and bunting and band music in the unabashed manner of the American holiday of tradition.

Reception Committee

The year 1860, with the Union threatened with dissolution and the arsenal at Springfield running night and day in double shifts, found all North America in a fever of excitement over the advent of Edward, then Prince of Wales, who, as Baron Renfrew, toured Canada and the principal cities of the United States to the accompaniment of such drum-whanging, cannon-firing and hurricanes of florid oratory concerning trans-Atlantic handclasping as has never been paralleled before or since. Canada welcomed him with music festivals and a deluge of patriotic rum punch. Small towns in the Middle West presented souvenirs in the form of lampshades, corned beef, hand-painted vases and a collection of live turtles. He gazed over the lawns and terraces of Mount Vernon and returned to his landau to find it filled with walking sticks cut from a multitude of Washington elms; his eyes were treated to the magnificence of the Astor Library and Cooper Union in New York, and a monster ball at the Academy of Music inaugurated social jealousies surviving to this day in Knickerbocker families. He arrived in Boston in October to view the Athens of America at first hand and participate in a communal, social and fraternal flag-raising of Homeric proportions.

Even the train which whisked him over the Berkshires from Albany behind the locomotive "Prince of Wales" was a miracle of elegance. The eyes of spectators at Pittsfield and Palmer bugged out at the magnificence of his "imperial salon wagon" with its wealth of turkey carpets, cloisonné, hand-stitched antimacassars, silk hassocks and solid silver "drinking accommodations tastefully set forth upon a marquetry table." The Prince himself was amazed at the "conveniences of the toilette which furnished running water from a mysterious source." The caravan of opulence, which included two "burthen cars" of animal, vegetable, sentimental and lithographic souvenirs, swept

Boston and the Boston Legend

into Longwood to a leitmotiv of screaming urchins, cannon-fire, discharges of aërial maroons, and the polite huzzahing of the frock-coated reception committee. Boston was beside itself with satisfaction, and outrageous pride shone on every face as Edward Everett welcomed the distinguished visitor to the community whose first citizens had, but a few years before, delighted to empty their slops on the English king's lieutenants as they went about their business in its muddy thoroughfares. The town was in a dither of ecstasy and even the New York newspapermen were impressed.

"Boston, the city of cow paths and revolutionary reminis-cences was alive with a double excitement last night," the correspondent for James Gordon Bennett's *Herald* said in his story, filed by "magnetic telegraph" that evening,

and the Prince divided the public curiosity with the great Bell and Everett demonstration. Kept wide awake by the Republican parade of the night before, Boston seemed last night as if it would never rest again. The streets were crowded and blockaded with people, and all sorts of cheers and all sorts of music made night and this early morning hideous or melodious, just as people chose to take it. The *Herald* despatch of yesterday left the Prince snugly ensconced in his hotel, and after partaking of a magnificent dinner the royal party determined to spend the evening quietly at home and go to sleep early, if the people would let them. But the people wouldn't. If there had been another Stamp Act to resent, more independence to gain, and a new Seventy-Six to be "fought and bled and died" through, there could have been no more noise and confusion, no more drum-ming and fifing, no more training, marching and Yankee Doodling, than there was last evening. The crowd which received the Prince at the hotel had hardly dispersed before it reassembled in such largely augmented numbers that it seemed as if each person had only de-parted to return with a body of new recruits. Fireworks, illumina-tions and transparencies made most of the streets as light as day.

The people, turning out in all directions, lined the streets, each corner seeming as if all the population had gathered there, and left the remaining portion of the city vacant. Boston, which, large as it is, important as it is, and venerable as it is, really looks by daylight

124

In Louisberg Square Boston

LOUISBERG SQUARE

Reception Committee

only like an extended town, seemed quite metropolitan, and would not have been recognized by its oldest inhabitant, except by its crooked streets; and to add to all the rest, pushing its way through the crowd, and seeming from its numbers a small population in itself, the Bell and Everett procession blazed along amid a glare of colored lights.

The covering of Boston's pageant of royalty by the press was extraordinarily detailed, and in describing the grand ball at the Boston Theater which climaxed the happy occasion the *Herald's* reporter alone filed more than fifteen thousands of words which were transmitted over the newly organized American Telegraph Company's wire to New York in a day when news codes were unknown and every letter was signaled by full Morse transmission. The running story was augmented by last-minute dispatches as to the Prince's changes of dance partners at half-hour intervals until two in the morning in time to make the late city edition for the breakfast tables of Murray Hill and Gramercy Park.

Nothing like the Grand Ball at the Boston Theater had ever been seen before and it is doubtful if it has so much as been approximated since, and the faithful play by play account of Mr. Bennett's star reporter deserves the attention of connoisseurs of vanished and Byzantine elegances:

The Boston Theater seemed to have doubled its size, so immense was the space which was to be crowded with "fair maidens and brave men." Even after the Academy of New York, with its magnificent *coup d'oeil* of light, flowers and beauty, the Boston ballroom did not seem second-rate or *fadé;* but, on the contrary, so unique and original were the designs by Messrs. Hoyt & Chutz, and so admirably were those designs carried out, that even the suite of the Prince were delighted, and acknowledged that, in the matter of ballroom decorations at least, the fertility of human invention is wonderful. The Boston ballroom was about the same shape as that of the Academy, and was formed in the same way, the parquette and

125

stage being floored over. The smaller size of the house, however, gave the Bostonians the advantage in a cosy, comfortable, enjoyable feeling which very great rooms always lack, and without which a great ball is simply a great nuisance. One felt at home immediately upon entering the building, and prepared to enjoy himself as naturally as if the affair were a private party.

Entering the room from the doors directly opposite the stage, the eye, dazzled by the light from a thousand burners, cannot at first take in the full beauty of the scene. As usual, an attempt was made by the decorators to transform the stage into a marquee, or imperial tent. This has been the custom from time immemorial. All decorators attempt it, and all fail. At the Japanese ball, at the Academy, everywhere, the stage must be transformed into a marquee, and refuses to be transformed into any such thing. The same attempt at transformation was made here, and with the same results. The stage would not look like a marquee, or even a pavilion; but it did appear like a large room, removed and separate from the main hall, and decorated only as scene painters and ball committees can decorate. The private boxes were hidden by groves of evergreens, from the deep shades of which peeped pure white statues, as if the wood nymphs were observing the display and were eager to join in the dance. These groves flanked the entrance to the stage, and above them were crimson curtains, rising in beautiful folds to the proscenium drapery, which was formed of an immense American flag, most gracefully arranged. The roof of the marquee was painted in arabesque work, in eight varied colors, with fantastic designs, and from this ceiling was suspended three chandeliers, of a style similar to the arabesque designs. Falling from the ceiling to the sidewalls were crimson curtains, relieved by gold bands, and sloped and lapelled in Turkish style, producing a most beautiful and novel effect. The side walls were painted in imperial purple, with ornamented squares, and relieved by panels framed in gold and painted in lighter colors and more varied designs. From each of these panels—four on either side of the marquee—depended side chandeliers, in ebony and gilt, under which, upon ornamented pedestals, were vases of natural flowers, from Ever's gardens at Brighton. Between these chandeliers were large pier glasses, gilt framed and flower wreathed, and the reduplications of three mirrors seemed to increase immeasurably the size of the room. In the corners, at the extremity of the tent, were also pier

126

Reception Committee

glasses half concealed by common curtains, and just beyond them were evergreens and flowers, forming beautiful supports to the back scene, and relieved by statues of Ceres and Hebe.

Looking from the entrance of the marquee towards its extremity, the effect was perfectly bewildering. Besides all these decorations, which the reader must frame in a picture for himself, the eye was attracted by many little details—a stripe of gilt, a happy flourish of the crayon, which cannot be described upon paper, but which aided the general effect. Then immediately opposite, half hidden by trees and flowers, among which a white fountain bubbled up its crystal waters, falling again in diamond drops beneath the brilliant lights, an immense picture of Windsor Castle frowned splendidly and completed the *tout ensemble*. Johnson had surpassed himself in this picture. From the turrets of the magnificent castle floated the royal standard. Around were trees, picturesquely arranged and grouped with the real evergreens in the foreground, while by happy fortune the artist had succeeded in catching that hazy, misty, half-clouded sky peculiar to English landscapes. All of the royal party recognized at once the fidelity of this picture and repeatedly expressed their admiration, not only for the artist's skill, but of the good taste which thus beautifully and unostentatiously suggested the presence of the Prince and connected his home with his appearance here. Seats covered with green cloth were arranged around the marquee, and the royal party were seated upon velvet sofas.

Turning toward the entrance of the marquee and looking out upon the body of the theater, the *coup d'oeil* was surprising, and each detail only heightened the pleasure of the first impression. The horseshoe shape of the theater is that most favorable for fine effects and the result was all that could be wished. From the ceiling, which was most richly frescoed and painted in gold and white, hung a large chandelier, an inverted dome of gaslights and glass, glittering and glazing indescribably. This and side brackets along the walls gave sufficient light for a dozen such halls, and brought every decoration into full view. The theater has three tiers each of which was differently adorned. Objection might be taken to the motif of the decorations—which was mainly gilt and colors—and might have found fault with the gaudiness and lack of simplicity which characterized the affair, but it is certain that everything which could be done with this style of ornament—and it is capable of magnificent

127

effects when entrusted to good hands—was accomplished in the ball-room. From the uppermost tier gilded pillars, with arches connecting them, supported the roof, and were left undecorated, except by slight draperies of red, white and blue flags. The front of this upper tier was covered with a hanging of crimson cloth, fringed with blue, and a blue border, draped in festoons and studded with gilt stars, ran along the upper edge of the balustrade. Each of these festoons was held by a bouquet of natural flowers from which depended a long blue banneret, ending in a gilt ball which hung below the balustrade and over the tier below. The second tier was hung with orange-colored cloth, fringed with blue and festooned with crimson and wreaths of flowers. At equal distances along the front were shields alternately bearing the Prince of Wales' feather and the mottoes, "Justicia," "Concordia," "Amicitia," and other Latin inscrip-tions. . . .

Eleven hundred double and two hundred and twenty five single tickets were sold for the ball, the receipts being about twenty thousand dollars.

The ballroom was crowded early, and by ten o'clock was a perfect jam, all the house except the highest tier being filled, and even the dressing rooms and lobbies crowded. Three thousand persons were present.

At a few minutes after ten the Prince arrived, and was received by Mayor Lincoln and party in the reception room. After a moment or two he was conducted into the box, and spent five minutes survey-ing the brilliant scene.

The affair opened something like that in New York, for all the committees, being anxious to speak to the Prince, and leaning for-ward to do so, crash went a large vase of flowers, scattering its contents over the Prince. There were profuse apologies, but the Prince was laughing so heartily that he could not hear or speak.

As the party entered, one of the bands—two were provided—struck up a long fantasia, which ended somehow with "God Save the Queen." The party then moved through the crowd, which opened before them, and proceeded to the rear of the marquee; but the crowd so pressed around that they could not form a set, and they proceeded to the centre room, where two sets were formed, the Prince opening the ball with Mrs. Mayor Lincoln, who was dressed in white, with wreath and trimmings of natural flowers. The first dance was a quadrille, and Capt. Gray and Mr. Warre of suite

THE SOUTH STATION

danced in it. The crowd was very great, and curiosity seemed no less great or more restrained here than elsewhere.

The third dance, a waltz, the Prince danced with Mrs. Wise, daughter of Edward Everett and a relative of Governor Wise, of Virginia.

The next, the Lancers, the Prince danced with Miss Crowning-shield, the daughter of an eminent lawyer.

Mr. Geo. Upton made himself conspicuous by trying to clear a space for the dancers, and at the conclusion of the Lancers asked the Prince to take a walk. The Prince replied that he would walk about and return to the same spot, in order to mislead the crowd. The device was not successful, however. Yankees are not to be caught by such dodges.

In the next dance, a quadrille, the Prince's partner was Miss Emery, grand niece of Lord Lindhurst.

The next, a polka, the Prince danced with Miss Bigelow, daughter of the Chief Justice.

Canadian officials abound, and many of the Prince's Canadian suite are present.

One meets many New York faces. Among them that of Brady, the photographer, who received as an especial favor and mark of esteem, a special ticket from the Prince himself, who, hearing Mr. Brady had no ticket, sent for one and presented it to him.

The dresses of the ladies are superb, but, in consequence of the crowd, do not appear to great advantage. Many ladies came only in evening dresses, not intending to dance.

The floor is partly cleared now, however, and there is plenty of room for all. This ball is the last which the Prince will receive, as stated, and is, undoubtedly, the best. It must be pronounced a decided success.

One O'clock

The Prince has just gone into supper, and the supper room is overcrowded.

This marks the passage of the Rubicon of the ball, and its success is beyond doubt.

At two o'clock, with the forms of his paper closing in the distant and gaslit reaches of Fulton Street at Nassau, it is to be presumed that Mr. Bennett's reporter sent his last "take" of copy to the magnetic telegraph office, called it a day and set out to enjoy at first hand the heady pleasures of the most august, magnificent, and certainly the most orchidaceous social event in the history of Boston.

Chapter XIII

HIGHBALL AND JOHNSON BAR

THE first train brigades to clatter jerkily out of Boston at
a desperate acceleration of fifteen miles an hour on the
network of single-track roads which spread like the spokes
of a wheel over the New England countryside during the
thirties and forties were controlled in their fearsome progress by semaphores operated by beaver-hatted dispatchers
and by that most ancient of railroad symbols; the highball.
After a hundred years the highball, a painted globe run
up a pole on halyards, still signals a clear track ahead over
the rights of way of the world, and when steam transportation came to Boston it signaled the conquest of a continent
through the associated agencies of Samuel Colt's patent
firearms and the diamond stack locomotive. The firearms
and many of the locomotives were destined to come from
New England, and the financing of most of the roads that
were to open up the American West came from the industrialists and bankers of State Street.

At the very time when Boston clipper captains were
carrying their house flags and commercial destinies to the

Boston and the Boston Legend

farthest landfalls and roadsteads of the world, shrewd mill owners and domestic traders were appraising the first steam engines and finding them omens of promise. Boston's predilection for rail investments has survived even the final catastrophe of the New Haven, and to this day the strict trust investment laws of Massachusetts are singularly favorable to rail stocks and bonds.

The first railroad in the United States is generally understood to have been a gravity-operated car system for lightering Quincy granite out of the hills for the construction of such projects as Bunker Hill monument, Boston's Horticultural Hall and New York's Astor House, but the first railroad in the accepted sense to run out over the Roxbury Flats was the Boston and Worcester which was opened for operation in 1835 and has been running ever since as part of the Boston and Albany. From the outset there were four passenger trains a day each way and one mixed train of passenger and "burthen" coaches every noontime. The distance was forty-five miles, and so heavily patronized was the road that within a decade it was doing half a million dollars' business annually.

Second in importance was the Boston and Maine which, by the middle forties, had two branches running north into New England, the Eastern and Western Divisions of today, and which, by reason of the rich farming districts it touched and the rising industrial tide in mill towns, was regarded as the most promising of the several roads with Boston backing. At first the farmers had been fiercely opposed to the laying of rails, particularly toward the west. Twenty-five cent corn was a terror to them. "The project can be none other than ruinous," declaimed the *Worcester County Gazette* in 1829 when the problem of charters was before the Great and General Court. "Everything wanted for our markets will be furnished from abroad and our

Highball and Johnson Bar

farmers must at once quit the business of agriculture. . . . Why, then, the question will naturally suggest itself, are we wishful of anything that must radically change our character, if we are at present a people thus prosperous and happy?" The turnpike companies and toll operators, naturally, sided with the farmers, but it was the mill owners who finally jammed the measure through the legislature when they found Boston was but an hour and a half distant from Lowell and Haverhill by rail as against two days through the Middlesex Canal.

It was in 1848 and over the Boston and Maine's Western Division that the first mile-a-minute run of history was achieved, and the legend of that epic event survives in the files of Boston newspapers to be rehearsed on rail anniversaries or in Sunday features whenever an aged conductor retires, full of congratulations, presentation watches and nostalgia for an era of railroading he cannot possibly remember.

The road had become the delighted possessor of a new locomotive built to its order in England. It weighed ten tons, could develop, with a good hardwood fire, power equal to a team of thirty-five horses, and was called the "Antelope." Charles Minot, General Superintendent of the line, was an astute fellow and, even in the days before high pressure promotion and press agents, aware of the uses of publicity, and he summoned to his office his veteran engine driver.

"Pemberton," he said abruptly, "can you make the Lawrence run in twenty-six minutes flat?"

"Twenty-six miles in twenty-six minutes? It's as good as taking your life in your hands," was the reply.

"You take it and I'll ride with you," said the general super, and the next day the most intrepid reporter from each local paper showed up in Haymarket Square, his will

neatly filed with his editor and a large bandanna handkerchief in his pocket with which to secure his best hat to his
head. All along the line the switches had been spiked to
prevent spreading. Every crossing was guarded by railroad
men and local constables and the populace were out along
the right of way to see what they might see. Largely, it is
reported, they were skeptical.

With a terrific amount of snorting and a shower of
sparks that sent neighboring shopkeepers hastening to their
roofs with wet mops, the Antelope got under way. There
was no securing the cylinder cocks from the engine cab in
those days, and after the train had run a few rods to
gather momentum the fireman dropped off, ran ahead,
closed them and leaped aboard again as the drivers passed
him. The reporters held onto their seats and grew pale.
Somebody produced a flask of Old Tannery Dew, and at
Somerville crossing Charlie Minot was wheeling her at a
breathless forty and Pemberton was aiding the fireman to
toss dry pine into the firebox.

At Malden the single coach was felt to be on the rails
only at infrequent intervals, and the reporters were lying
on the floor inquiring of one another and of God why they
had ever embarked on this ultimate folly. At South Reading
the Antelope came into view on the Crystal Pond stretch in
such a blaze of brass, red paint and rolling woodsmoke that
Cyrus Wakefield, the town's first citizen, was observed
jumping up and down in his congress gaiters from sheer
delighted excitement. At Reading the village drunkard took
one look at the demon that streaked across his vision and
was strictly sober for a fortnight thereafter. At Ballardvale
Minot leaned far out on the pounding gangway and smelled
hot metal, in the course of which discovery he lost his hat,
a new white beaver that had been brought him from Locke
in London by Mr. Bartlett, the bookseller in Cornhill. The

Highball and Johnson Bar

Dreyfus self-feeding oil cap had yet to be invented and when the steam chest became overheated the fireman crawled out on the running board with an oiler in his teeth and clung perilously to the cow catcher while sousing the running parts with liquid paraffin. As the Antelope sounded a piercing scream on her whistle for North Andover crossing a loose stretch of track was encountered and the strap iron rails, torn from the granite ties by the speed of the train, flew up behind in a shower of curling snakeheads. It was, too, just twenty-six minutes to Lawrence. The reporters were in no shape to write their copy until they had been treated at the nearest sample room by the populace, and most of the gilt and red lacquer was blistered off the Antelope. It was the first time mankind had ever achieved a mile a minute over a protracted run and the passengers said they never purposed to duplicate the performance. It was plainly against the will of God.

But railroading was clearly there to stay, and in 1847 there were eight railroad stations in Boston and regular schedules were maintained on the Boston and Maine, Fitchburg, Boston and Worcester, the Eastern Railroad, the Boston and Lowell, Boston and Providence, Old Colony, Boston and Dedham and Boston and Stoughton. Coaches for six and one-half cent fares transported passengers from terminals to hotels and designated inns. When Charles Dickens pursued his querulous progress of discourtesy to New York he went by rail to Worcester, by another train to Springfield, down the Connecticut River to Hartford by packet, to New Haven by rail, and thence to Manhattan aboard a Long Island Sound steamer.

The progress of steam and steel throughout New England was by no means the stormy epic of conquest which later characterized the building of the great transcontinental lines. It was a small-scale local enterprise, carefully considered and conservatively financed by gentlemen in blue tailcoats and stock collars who, like Galsworthy's Forsytes, considered anything which yielded over four per cent with arbitrary suspicion. The original roads out of Boston were homely country affairs, engaged in short hauls, but they paid their dividends every quarter and furnished the impetus for the era of the iron horse that was to follow.

Rail travel in New England, as elsewhere, during the forties was casual, informal and not entirely devoid of personal peril. Train dispatching was no very precise science and progress over the right of way was more or less at the pleasure and discretion of the train crew. Semaphores were operated from signal towers, where they might be seen a distance of a mile, if the local agent were not otherwise occupied, but the avoidance of wrecks was largely dependent upon the wakefulness of the engine driver. Trains stopped to "wood up" at frequent intervals and, as the lengths were not always correctly cut, the fireman was often visible atop his tender, bucksaw in hand, while the engineer fed the firebox and watched the throttle. Conductors and brakemen sat on the roofs of the cars in seats protected by a chaise top, and the only heat in passenger coaches was a cannon-ball stove to which the brakeman kept the key. The White Mountain Division was not popular in winter.

The progress of a Boston and Maine train in 1846 is chronicled in the diary of a contemporary:

That long array of cars, laden with stone, onions and fish, ice, slippers and bricks, interspersed with passengers, moves in slow procession on its winding way to Boston. They stop at Danvers for the onions, near the Salem pastures to collect the boulders; at Brown's Pond for the ice, at Grave's End for the fish; at the print works for the slippers; and opposite Breed's Hotel [then a well-known drinking place] in Lynn to receive the inanimate and moisten the animate clay. I will take leave of our friends at this exciting spot and take

passage in the regular train of the Eastern Rail Road which whistles
by like a rocket on the air line to Boston.

During the sixties and seventies most of the locomotives
running out of Boston were constructed at Taunton, a few
miles south of the city, where two designers, William Mason
and W. F. Fairbanks, built the finest American engines of
the period. The graceful diamond-stack eight-wheelers with
their brightly painted cabs, gilded name plates and ornamental brass work were the finest and speediest of their
time and some of them, originally sold to the Old Colony
or Eastern roads, saw half a century of service before being
scrapped or sold to South American plantations. In 1856
Mason built two engines, one of which, on her trial trip
on the Taunton Branch Railroad, ran four miles start to
stop in three and a half minutes in a time when airbrakes
were unknown and trains were hand-braked to a stop. Many
of the thousand Taunton engines turned out at these two
shops were to play dramatic rôles in opening up the empire
of the West, but the greatest achievements of Bostonians in
financing the trans-continental roads were, of course, those
of John Murray Forbes, who built the C. B. and Q. and
brought the Michigan Central to Chicago, and the scandalous but effective agency of floating the Union Pacific.

The financing of the Union Pacific was largely accomplished through the great Boston banking houses of issue
of the late sixties, and through the agency of the holding
corporation known as Crédit Mobilier it achieved a *succès
de scandale* comparable, at the time, to the other outrages
of the moment—the railway enterprises of Fiske and
Gould; Tweed's Tammany brigandage; General Schenck's
dubious speculations and the more anonymous but no less
profitable undertakings of Wall Street entrepreneurs.

In simple terms, Crédit Mobilier was a corporation

Boston and the Boston Legend

through whose agency the stockholders of the Union Pacific, an impressively large number of whom were Bostonians of Beacon Street respectability, sought to collar for themselves all the profits accruing from the construction contracts let by the road's executives. The evolution of this sagacious device, subsequent investigation disclosed, could justly be credited to Oakes Ames, then sitting for Massachusetts in the House of Representatives in Washington, who, with the enthusiastic assistance of the other majority stockholders in the venture, built and equipped the entire railroad by awarding contracts to locomotive and engineering concerns in which they themselves were heavily concerned. It was a naïve device, but sufficient in a naïve era. It netted its happy participants about 340 per cent up to the end of 1868, when the road was nearing completion, and those Boston financiers concerned with the profits were highly gratified. New cast-iron stags appeared on lawns and the top-hats of State Street saluted each other of a morning with even more than customary unctuousness.

In order to insure against interference by his colleagues in Washington, Congressman Ames had distributed among friends in high places in Pennsylvania Avenue a large amount of Crédit Mobilier stock at par. These gentlemen, too, were grateful to Union Pacific and included, as subsequently appeared, a number of the most influential men in public life: Schuyler Colfax, the outgoing vice president, Wilson, his successor, James Brooks of New York and Patterson of New Hampshire. A number of high-minded members of Congress, however, none of whom had been able to get in on Crédit Mobilier at the issue price, entertained strong ideas about the whole transaction, and a nation-wide scandal resulted from the investigation and reports of the Poland and Wilson Committees. Ames and Brooks received votes of censure from their respectful associates in the house. At the expiration of his term Oakes Ames and his brother, Oliver, who also had been closely associated with Crédit Mobilier and had sold vast quantities of picks and shovels to the road from the Ames Plow Works, retired to North Easton where they were the nabobs of the shire until good living and apoplexy closed their careers in an approved and dignified manner. The effects of the scandal were far-reaching. Pious folk everywhere, in measured language, condemned the conduct of everyone connected with Crédit Mobilier, and were firmly determined to get in on the ground floor the next time any such venture appeared on the financial horizon.

But the Union Pacific became one of the great American epics with General Jack Casement laying ten miles of track a day for his Boston backers and a side bet of $10,000, and then racing an engine forty miles an hour over the track to prove it sound. And eventually the last tie of polished California laurel was laid, the last spikes of Nevada silver and California gold were driven.

> What was it that the engines said,
> Pilots touching head to head,
> Facing on a single track
> Half the world behind each back?

They rang church bells and fired cannon salutes from coast to coast on May 10, 1869, and in State Street quite a number of clerks were given half an hour extra for lunch while their employers celebrated the event in a conservative mug of ale with Stoughton bitters at Parker's.

Perhaps the last florid gesture of Boston railroading before the business of wheeling the nightly fish express over to New York and bringing the brokers home on the Yankee Clipper became a routine was the White Train of the nineties which made the New York run in six hours flat.

Boston and the Boston Legend

The magnificence of this limited, which rolled over the old air line through Connecticut every afternoon at three o'clock, fairly staggered travelers of the puff-sleeve and livery-stable era. "The parlor cars are furnished with velvet carpets," reported an awed contemporary, "silk draperies and white silk curtains; the chairs are upholstered in old gold plush, and large glass mirrors set off the car handsomely. Three of them have a state-room and twenty-six seats in the main saloon and the other four have thirty seats each. The royal buffet smokers which will be run in addition to the ordinary smoking cars are decorated in the same manner as the parlor cars and contain twenty-four handsomely upholstered chairs for parlor car passengers. The Pullman Palace Car Company has designed a special dining-car for the train." When the semaphore arm dropped at the South Station and the engineer of the White Train, attired in a white coat and snowy cap surmounted with his goggles of office, edged open his throttle, slowed for his air test, and eased the Johnson bar back to a fifty degree angle until, at Walpole, his cross heads were but a gleaming blur, he represented the *fin de siècle* of steam and steel out of Boston.

Another Boston railway which is, like Thompson's Spa and going to funerals, a characteristic institution is the narrow gauge line known as the Boston and Revere Beach road. Like the celebrated miniature line which once connected Nantucket town and 'Sconset, it is one of the few less than standard width roads still operating in the country, and its diminutive brigades and coaches crammed with commuters or holiday-makers, as the season and time decree, can be seen streaking daily from its Lynn terminal to the greater metropolis.

Despite the circumstance that the sensational debauching of the New Haven Railroad's finances brought grief and

140

consternation to half the first families of Boston, the road has always remained in the status of a household institution to be tolerated, cherished and even petted. The loss of a topcoat aboard the Merchant's Limited by the writer's father approached the proportions of a *cause célèbre* for years, and communications between the aggrieved passenger and the company's officers were maintained through five presidencies of the line. To this day Fred Wright, the ranking Pullman porter on the run, and senior conductors in blue tailcoats argue possible hypotheses to explain the disappearance of this epic surtout, and annual reports on the investigation of the mystery have been regularly turned in by New London station masters. Most Boston families maintain some similar tie of affection with the New Haven. That the line recently inaugurated one of the world's fastest trains in the form of a streamline Diesel clipper which slams its way across the countryside at a hundred and ten miles an hour cannot induce Bostonians to regard the road as anything but a delightful and perhaps vaguely irresponsible household tradition.

Chapter XIV

"BOX 52, LET HER ROLL!"

WHEN, on the evening of November 9, 1872, the first district alarm was pulled at Box 52 and Dan Marden, foreman of Steamer No. 7 shouted the traditional "Let her roll," the Boston fire department was regarded as a highly modernized force. In 1854, accompanied by blasphemous comments of the firemen themselves, the telegraphic alarm system of Dr. William F. Channing had been introduced, and in 1860 the old hand pumper had been banished from metropolitan precincts. Departmental diehards viewed both these changes with the customary alarm and prophesied that no good would come of abandoning the traditional roof to roof bawling of "Fire" and the highly esteemed gesture of cutting out rival hand pumpers at the hydrant and turning on them the first stream, quite regardless of whatever conflagration might be under way about their ears.

"Box 52, Let Her Roll!"

There were still hand pumpers in the outlying districts and a good many of these were to see service in the ensuing twenty-four hours, but in the city itself horse-drawn steamers were the delight of urchins and grown folk as well. Signals were dispatched by departmental telegraph only a little less efficient than that of today, and the City Hall bell told the location of the blaze so that the citizenry might enjoy the spectacle before the roof fell in. Firegoing then as now was esteemed a holiday occasion and dignified gentlemen in top-hats were heard to remark, "Ah, the wing is nicely alight now" when it was apparent that overwhelming catastrophe was inevitable to someone else.

On this Saturday night, Bostonians who recall this most epic of conflagrations will tell you, there was a singular calm on the city. As a matter of fact, the town still "kept Saturday evening" as a prelude to Sunday and there was less going and coming in the streets, fewer hacks on the cab ranks, more infrequent horse-cars than usual. To Foreman Marden of the T. C. Amory it looked like a dull night and he remarked as much to Charlie Riley, the engine-man, who was contemplatively cutting off a chew of Old Plug with his pocket knife. As a matter of fact, everyone in the house looked forward to a fireless weekend if for no other reason than that all the horses were ailing from the tremendous epidemic of epizoötic, and for a week all calls had been answered in hand towed engines.

At 7:24 exactly the striker in the engine room exploded into action, the call board indicated Box 52, and on the roof of City Hall the bells carried the intelligence to the city that at the corner of Summer and Kingston Streets somebody had pulled the box in front of the establishment of Messrs. Tibbitts, Baldwin and Davis, wholesale dealers in dry goods.

As a matter of fact, the four-story building with an ornate

143

granite front was at that moment ablaze from cellar to ornamental and florid zinc cornice. It was one vast bonfire of hot black flames that roared out its windows and into the quiet streets, melting off the metal shutters so that they rained down to the sidewalk in a disagreeable Niagara and bursting up through the ventilators in the roof fit to be seen for blocks. The building had boasted an elevator serviced by a steam engine in the basement and it was generally supposed that it was in these subterranean offices the fire had got a brisk start before it blew out the windows over the startled head of a passing watchman.

Steamer No. 7, the T. C. Amory, rolled around the corner and up to the hydrant just a hundred and twenty seconds after the alarm, drawn by a hastily recruited team of boys, bar loafers and regular firemen. Its hose cart and ladder were there just before it, and by the time the first connection was made sparks were shooting out of its stack and its pistons were gleaming and flashing red in the firelight. Engineman Riley, probably still in possession of his Old Plug, leaned over and tied down the whistle cord. He was going to need more coal before this evening was out and he might as well start whistling for it right at the beginning.

Hard on the heels of No. 7, the Barnicoat and Foreman Joseph Pierce came around the corner, laying hose as they rolled. Pierce took one look at a flaming cascade of hoop skirts which was being blown out the windows of Alexander K. Young and Co., on the top floor, and advised Marden to pull another alarm. Between then and eight o'clock five alarms came through from Box 52. Foreman Marden was just reaching for the hook to pull a sixth when the cornice, four floors overhead, came loose. It slammed down to the sidewalk in an extravagant deluge of crumbling stone and white-hot sheet zinc, taking with it a

E H Suydam
Post Office Square

POST OFFICE SQUARE

few remaining steel shutters and, more important, the telegraph wires. The general alarm had to be sounded through Box 123 down the street and Foreman Marden's white helmet was badly scorched.

The Chief of the Fire Department, J. C. Damrell, was on the scene by this time, his Horace Greeley whiskers bristling with professional pride and pleasure and foreseeing, with a deal of accuracy, a great quantity of smoke to be eaten in the next few hours. The premises adjacent to the source of the fire were half consumed and geysers of sparks and embers, caught up in the terrific fire draft, were being impartially distributed throughout the neighborhood. Engine companies arrived every minute. Hose was being laid from six blocks away with pumpers stationed at intervals to keep up the pressure, but even so the water supply was totally inadequate to the occasion. It was so hot in Summer Street that hosemen and nozzlemen lay in the flooding gutters and directed their streams from behind fire shields and impromptu barricades of wet packing cases.

By nine o'clock that evening Boston firefighters knew that the pressure and water supply at their command were inadequate for conflagrations in five- and six-story structures and that Mansard roofs had many of the qualities of Greek fire. Fire in the wooden lofts on top of stone buildings was absolutely out of their reach, the roof gun and water tower not having come into being yet, and while they might wash out even impressive blazes on lower floors the city was becoming bravely alight from roof to roof. Then, too, it was the first great fire in a comparatively modern city and the discovery was made that granite could chip and flake and disintegrate surprisingly under sufficient pressure and that supposedly impregnable iron pillars could melt through and let the whole façade of a structure down into the street like the crack of doom. Window-sills and

Boston and the Boston Legend

ledges dissolved in glowing fragments and fire escapes came down in a nasty tangle that ultimately melted and flowed into the gutters.

Roaring into Otis Street, a narrow East and West causeway in the midst of the retail district, the blaze really got out of hand. The short thoroughfare ending in Winthrop Square was an ocean of fire from end to end. "Beebe's Block," an imposing six-story structure with tall colonnades and the inevitable Mansard roof, devoted to retailing dry goods, became a fountain of fire that splashed and rippled over half a precinct when its roof went and the bulging walls cracked out with explosive gouts of deep red flame. Gas detonations and the fire draft filled the air with blazing kid gloves and bolts of muslin, stationery, hats, caps and even hides, and the destruction of a great lithographing plant distributed half a million gaudy chromos to the winds.

By the time the fire had worked northwards to Milk Street, perversely enough going directly against the wind, Boston was telegraphing for aid to a score of neighboring cities. Sixty miles away in New Hampshire the blaze was seen and appeared so close that farmers started over their fields in its general direction under the impression it could hardly be more than a mile distant. At Wakefield, twelve miles northward, the local call firemen were gathering in front of Doc Richardson's drug store preparatory to starting over the road pulling their hand pumper to the scene of the fire. The writer's father overtook them in his horse rig at a dead gallop in Greenwood, but his leather house in Pearl Street had gone before he could get to town. In Newport, Rhode Island, they were starting apparatus northward and at Providence two gondola cars of firemen and engines were waiting to be coupled on the early morning train from New York. Boston was going up in smoke and in far distant cities clergymen polishing their next morning's

"Box 52, Let Her Roll!"

sermons were preparing timely references to the major afflictions of history.

In the middle of a curve of Franklin Street stood the municipal flagpole, a hundred feet high and surmounted by a gold ball. The crowds, when they saw its length in flame, groaned and wept as though it were an omen. In Washington Street the premises of the *Boston Evening Transcript* were spouting fire, and melted lead from the composing room was cascading down the stairs into the counting rooms. Next door in Currier and Trott's building, occupied by the *Saturday Evening Gazette,* men from the insurance and protective associations were tamping charges of dualin into place in the hope that by dynamiting the structure the Old South Meeting House might be saved. As a matter of fact it was. At the other end of town, along the water-front, Prentices Wharf and Russia Wharf were settling on their piles into the harbor, their great pier sheds reduced to beds of coals and their fronts having fallen into Broad Street. The shoe and leather capital of the world along High and Pearl and Congress Streets was burning sullenly and under a dun and oppressive cloud of smoke.

It was inevitable, even in a day before the telephone, that all Boston should be aware of the conflagration. As a matter of actual record the fire did not "destroy" the city. It consumed an enormous fan-shaped wedge running from the water-front to Washington Street and from South of Summer almost to State Street. The extent of the calamity resulted from the condensation of wealth and resources in the business district afflicted rather than in the geographical latitude of the flames. The better residential districts of the city, of the Back Bay and Beacon Hill, were never seriously menaced and, aside from the clamor of engines in the streets and the excited voices of pedestrians, might never have been aware of the conflagration. Young Robert

Boston and the Boston Legend

Grant, later to become Boston's foremost magistrate and a novelist of note—for he wrote *The Chippendales*—was emerging from a private concert on Beacon Hill late in the evening and walked down to Washington Street to observe the spectacle. The fire lines stopped his progress a little north of the Old South Meeting House and when his evening stick chanced to slip through the grating of a drain, he remarked to himself that he should come by the next morning and retrieve it. Next day the spot was a wilderness of ruins, for, like many people, he did not imagine he was witnessing the inception of a holocaust of a major order.

But before midnight the entire populace, reinforced by swarms from Charlestown, Brookline, the South End and the suburbs, was on the scene. Merchants in evening dress filled carpet bags and waste baskets with valuable documents they would not trust to their vaults. A host of teamsters reaped fortunes for the hire of their vehicles to doomed warehouses. There was some looting and a vast deal of drinking.

The whole city, in fact, was filled with jittering inebriates. In Chicago, the year before, the saloons had kept open till their roofs were ablaze and did a land office business, and the same manifestation was widely observed in Boston. There were souses everywhere. They tripped over hose lines and hurrahed and howled when roofs fell in. They fell into manholes and had to be pumped out by the impatient and overworked police. They escaped death under disintegrating walls by the proverbial grace of God and broke their heads falling out of windows while trying to see if their own houses were on fire yet. Something in the nature of the calamity suggested drinking to everyone, and firemen, silhouetted against the flames, were observed to be holding a hose in one hand and a black bottle in the other. Youths, smelling like the Medford distillery, whirled and revolved

"Box 52, Let Her Roll!"

and fell down with screams of laughter in the gutters for all the world as though it were Fourth of July. It all ended with black looks from the ministers who were out, and an order, from the chief of police, closing the saloons toward morning. After that the catastrophe was more decorous.

Sunday morning dawned on a tremendous yellow pillar of smoke which rolled, like a symbol of doom, slowly over the harbor and the ocean. The fire was moving northward by day with the same appalling and irresistible force that it had spread during the night through the retail and shoe and leather districts of the middle city. The heroic efforts of firefighters, civilians, protective watchmen and volunteers of all sorts had diverted the flames in their northward progress along Washington Street just in time to save the Old South Meeting House. A curtain of water from a score of pressure hoses and the presence of a swarm of men with buckets and blankets on the roof and upon the steeple is shown in the lithographs depicting the spectacular rescue of the structure. The fire, having burned out the *Transcript* offices, swept through Hawley and Devonshire and across Milk in its progress even after all the fire-fighting forces of Boston and its neighbors were massed against its front.

It was really the old Post Office and United States Treasury building which fronted on Milk Street that stopped the conflagration toward evening Sunday. Engulfing Lindall Street, a narrow mall in the rear of the treasury, in a billowing sea of flame the fire was met and held in the spacious, rococo corridors and rotunda of the federal offices. The mail had been hastily removed to Faneuil Hall, but the flames penetrated the structure, seared its ornate woodwork and furniture, melted the dome of colored crystal, fired the window sashes and cracked the granite of its exterior in a hundred places. But the firemen on the State Street side washed it out with streams from a dozen steam

149

pumpers roaring at top speed and ranged along Merchant's Row and Doane Street. Barricaded behind overturned desks and the counters of its great hall with the black hose snaking out behind them into the din and yellow confusion outside they met and held the fire twenty-four hours after the first alarm.

At the time the entire police force of metropolitan Boston was five hundred and twenty-four men, and to the civil authorities it became apparent as Sunday drew to a smoky and hysterical close that, exhausted as they were, these would not be sufficient to maintain order throughout the city. At the request of Mayor William Gaston, six battalions of the state militia were mobilized and, although martial law was never declared so that these had no actual authority, the crowds naturally imagined they had and their presence was respected accordingly. At the same time it was discovered that the gas in the city's mains was an additional fire and explosion hazard and the cocks were turned off, so that what illumination Boston had that night was abated and far below normal. Editions of the next day's papers were prepared and the forms locked in composing rooms illuminated by candlelight. In private homes kerosene lamps reappeared after years of disuse, and in some cases it was reported that whale-oil lamps, dating from half a century earlier, before the first gas mains were laid, were put back into useful service.

The spirit of the city, in many instances, assumed overtones of lightheartedness and even of the carnival. Merchants who had been wiped out and over the ruins of whose warehouses the streams were still being played by exhausted firemen declared that old Boston had known worse things than this. Why, look how even Chicago was recovering from a similar destruction!

At the time of the great fire Boston was still a relatively

"Box 52, Let Her Roll!"

small community of 250,000, so that the loss of sixty-five acres of urban real estate and possessions, machinery, stocks in trade and manufactured goods of a value of $75,000,000 was an almost staggering catastrophe. Large sums of currency and negotiable paper, too, were destroyed, against which no insurance could be issued. Of this sum, $52,300,-000 more or less, was covered by solvent insurance companies, a large portion of the balance being secured by policies with Massachusetts underwriters bankrupted by their enormous liabilities. The toll of the fire included fourteen lives, seven of which were those of firemen, the other half civilians.

Perhaps the greatest single architectural loss was that of Trinity Church, the plans for whose new structure, later to be erected in Copley Square were with its stained glass windows by William Morris and Burne-Jones, happily, at the time being drawn. Built in 1829 of granite with a square heavy tower, it was at once a landmark and scene of the rise in favor and fame of the young Phillips Brooks who had come to Boston from Philadelphia in 1869.

Brooks, quite naturally, was warmly attached to the stern old church as is evidenced by one of his letters written shortly after the fire.

The desolation of the fire is bewildering [he wrote]. Old Trinity seemed safe all night, but toward morning the fire swept into her and there was no chance. She went at four in the morning. I saw her well afire, inside and out, carried off some books and robes, and left her. She went majestically and her great tower stands now, as solid as ever, a most picturesque and stately ruin. She died in dignity. I did not know how much I liked the gloomy old thing until I saw her windows bursting and the flame running along her high old pews.

In Mr. Blackstone's time the land running eastward from Shawmut to the harbor-front had stretched away in low rolling meadows which, as the city spread out from Beacon Hill and the North End had gradually become first a partly residential district and, just before the fire, the most important mercantile and warehouse region of the growing city. From Tremont Street to the water-front had been an unplanned maze of causeways and main arteries, bisected at improbable angles by narrow thoroughfares and cross streets, but when the fire was over an observer could stand in Washington Street and look south and east to the salt water over an unbroken perspective of ruins and leveled masonry. In general outline the course of the destruction had been fanshape, the narrow end at Russia and Prentice's Wharves, the full expanded width along Washington Street, only a block removed from the open reaches of the Common itself. The desolation was so complete that it was impossible to find the routes of the streets themselves in some sections. The southernmost limits of the fire's progress were just a little to the north of the present location of the New Haven Railroad's South Station.

It is difficult to imagine the excitement the intelligence of the holocaust created throughout the country. The first dispatches of the then growing conflagration, sent out shortly after midnight Sunday morning, were carried by the Sunday editions everywhere, usually in the form of short, stop press notices. New York's Sabbath was devoted to no other topic either in private or public. At clubs and hotels groups of business men met to discuss the latest bulletins with which the Western Union Telegraph Company kept them supplied. Trains arriving at Forty-second Street were met by anxious groups of reporters and the photographers of the time—pen-and-ink sketchers, who executed fire pictures for their papers from the accounts of eye witnesses. In scores of churches preachers derived almost as many morals from the catastrophe, the most practical of which in Man-

"Box 52, Let Her Roll!"

hattan appears to have been that drawn by Dr. Bellows at the Church of All Souls where he delivered a powerful address on the subject "Parsimony in Building," a theme generally understood to be aimed in the particular direction of the culpable Mansard roof.

The New York newspapers, with a display of initiative and energy which could scarcely be surpassed by the most imaginative managing editor of today, carried the most complete and graphic accounts of the fire on Monday morning. The *New York Tribune,* from reporters and correspondents on the fighting lines of Summer and State Streets, printed thousands of words of dispatches, including an hour by hour account of the progress of the blaze, a complete list of the destroyed properties, maps of the Boston business district, the assets and Boston liabilities of scores of insurance companies, stories on the local angle of the calamity and other features which many might imagine the devisings only of recent high-pressure reporting. The entire front page of the *Tribune,* an inside page of news and the full editorial page were devoted to the great fire of Boston, and for a week, in gradually diminishing proportions, it was the leading news of each successive day.

On Tuesday morning the *Tribune* concluded a lengthy dispatch with the following paragraphs describing the decline of the fire and the subsequent invasion of the town by a vast host of sightseers and other curious visitors:

When Chicago was burned the railroads carried thousands of people out of the city free of cost, for everybody wanted to get away; but at Boston nobody goes away and everybody tries to come in. Even ladies venture into the midst of the furnace. They have been clambering all day over the ruins of their husbands' and fathers' warehouses and listening with a sort of pride to their escorts describing the magnitude of their losses. Tonight some of the bolder

Boston and the Boston Legend

or more romantic of the gentler sex, who have won the favor of the Commanding General, and what is perhaps more difficult, persuaded the guard to respect the General's pass, are groping among the flames for the sake of the sensation. There is danger in the adventure for there are tottering walls to avoid and vaults loosely covered with rubbish, and flying sparks and beds of hot coals over which the white powder of crumbled granite and freestone has spread a treacherous sort of crust.

A horrible slime is getting deep in many of the streets where the coal from steam fire engines, the ashes, the stone dust and the charred refuse from the building are mixed with the streams of water bursting from the hose. Still, taking all things into consideration, I doubt whether a great fire has ever before been conducted with such order and so little discomfort.

On the same day advertisements appeared in papers throughout the country to the effect that a full and graphically detailed illustrated story of the great fire of Boston would appear Wednesday in Frank Leslie's weekly newspaper, while before the month was out at least one chronicle of the event appeared in book form. Very likely by Monday evening "Carleton," the anonymous author of this precipitous broadside, was puttering about the ruins of Shreve, Crump and Low's "magnificent palace of bijouteries," soiling the cuffs of his "stylish gents pants from Collin's celebrated outfitters," and making an occasional excursion in the direction of Parker's in School Street to wash the dust from his throat with a glass of something stronger than Stoughton's bitters. The field of belles lettres is somewhat the more ornate for his subsequent essay.

The year before, when the Chicago fire had set an all-time record for American conflagrations, in point at least of magnitude, the merchants and townspeople of Boston had rallied to offer Chicago credits, manufactured articles and aid of every sort in her emergency. The first wire from the East was signed by Mayor Gaston and read, "What do you need?" The same day Kidder, Peabody had offered the Chicago relief committee $100,000 credit to aid the destitute, while carloads of blankets, lanterns, crockery and thousands of crates of household necessities of every sort had poured into the Western railway terminals before the paving stones of gutted Wabash Avenue were cool.

Now it was Chicago's turn, and with almost hysterically fraternal sentiments, as "May Heaven sustain your noble people," and "God bless Boston," the sum of $100,000 was offered for immediate delivery for public needs, and the telegraph wires were fairly clogged with succeeding offers from this and scores of other American communities. New York was foremost in the common attention, Brooklyn appropriated $100,000 overnight, Pittsburgh, Cincinnati, Milwaukee and Washington were close behind. Boston was deluged with aid, staggered by the generosity and kind sentiments of the rest of the country.

Actually, the number of persons deprived of homes and livings was vastly smaller than in the Chicago fire, and Boston, long an established community with machinery for relief of its own, was able to provide temporary support and, shortly thereafter, permanent employment for those who had been thrown out of work.

It was not until later in the week that the work of digging out the ruins was practicable and in many instances vaults and safes retained sufficient heat to prevent their being attacked until six or seven days after the conflagration. Safe-making in those days was not the science of today and hundreds of thousands of dollars worth of banknotes, drafts, bonds and other negotiable securities were found, when the innermost compartments were opened, to have been reduced to ashes. The vaults of the writer's father in Pearl Street contained nothing of value beyond a coagulate mass representing what, at the close of business Saturday,

Boston and the Boston Legend

had been a few hundreds of dollars in gold coin which had not been deposited at the bank. The valuables in the Everett Bank, Bank of North America and the Revere Bank were found intact, but at the Freeman's National Bank in Summer Street, near the scene of the beginning of the fire, more than $1,300,000 worth of paper, secured in an outer vault, was destroyed. When the flames had reached School Street on Monday, $11,000,000 had been removed from the vaults of the Five Cent Savings Bank and taken to the Charles Street home of its president, Paul Adams. Distrustful of the efficacy of the squad of plain clothes police assigned to its protection, Mr. Adams, according to tradition, sat out the next day and night in his front hall, attired in the top-hat and frock coat of his office, and with a double barreled gun charged with No. 2 chilled shot pointed in the general direction of that portion of the front door indicated by the bolts securing the brass eagle-knocker outside. A bank president's responsibility in that time might be a very immediate one.

Among other amazing phenomena revealed by subsequent check-ups was that of the air current created by the conflagration which carried brands from the scene of the fire for immense distances. Scraps of account books and the binding of a merchant's ledger were picked up in East Weymouth, far to the south of Boston, on Sunday morning, and a fifty dollar bill, badly scorched, was found in South Abington, twenty-one miles away.

By the end of the week the devastated section of the city showed signs of recovered order, and although smoke still curled from numerous cellars and the protective agents were still engaged in tearing down tottering towers and chimneys, little shops, barber's saloons, bars and chophouses were springing into being under canvas or in hastily erected sheds and pine-board shelters. "Closed during the

"Box 52, Let Her Roll!"

hot spell," read a sign hung over a gutted doorway. "We have removed from this location," announced another plastered across the sole remaining wall of a tailor's establishment. "Evicted but not dejected," said a third, and a shoe-store proprietor whose stock had been looted by the crowd as the flames bore down on it, advertised that if anyone had drawn the wrong size footwear they might come and exchange it for a pair from his new supply. One eating establishment, reopening under canvas on the site of its former home, actually cooked its first few dinners on the glowing embers in what had once been its cellar.

Private enterprise was equal to the task of rebuilding Boston. The insurance companies of Massachusetts, nearly every one of which was bankrupted by the extent of the calamity, were given permission to reorganize. New and, happily, less ornate structures rose within a few months on the site of the destruction. The guilty Mansard roof was banished in perpetuity and the florid cornices of the sort that had come so near to obliterating Foreman Marden were less in vogue. More capacious water mains and frequent and improved hydrants promised a more suitable supply of water in the event of future emergencies. In two years all sign of the conflagration had disappeared and in a slightly longer period the ministers of the town and its leading after-dinner speakers had even wearied of the once compelling phrase "springing Pheonix-like from the ashes." The great fire was a thing of the past.

Chapter XV

THE COMMON

HEART and hallmark of Boston, shady, serene and untouched by the mutations of the three centuries that have passed since a portion of Mr. Blackstone's orchard was set aside with adjacent pastures for its creation, Boston Common is what generations of visitors have asked for first and remembered longest.

The fifty acres of the Common is Boston's last and firmest tie with the townships of New England, where there is inevitably a common or a green, the site of bandstand, soldier's monument, ornamental waters and park benches, or as at New Haven, the ancient bill-post where the decrees of town fathers and sheriffs' writs have been nailed from time immemorial. It is a symbol of the simple rural antecedents of a metropolis and a reminder of times when the privileges of citizenship were less confined in a more ingenuous and probably happier community. And it is, in a way, representative of the still largely unimpeached character and integrity of Boston, because in almost any other American city a commercialized time spirit and the fatuous devisings of expansionists would have made short work of so spacious and potentially profitable a domain. But since 1640 when the law provided that "there shall be no land granted for house-plott or garden," no street has violated its walks and lawns, nor has any gainful enterprise, save that of paper boys and hokey-pokey wagon merchants, found foothold within its reaches. Frail ladies of the evening are accustomed to smile provocatively at the sailors who lounge about the Park Street subway entrances, but this, in the absence of precise statistics, scarcely ranks as an established commerce, and the Common today is essentially what it was in the time of Governor Winthrop.

Four sides of its pentagon are walled by the façades of tall buildings showing their white Vermont granite cornices and flashing electric signs above the tree-tops by day and night. The gilded dome and mellow brick of the State House overlook it from what was once John Hancock's pasture atop Beacon Hill. The clubs and publishing houses of Mr. Bulfinch's Park Street, and the retail stores of Tremont and Boylston Streets wall it in on the East and South, but to the West there are the open reaches of the Public Garden, and beyond lie the three thousand acres of the made land of the Back Bay. Strangers to Boston wonder about the name of the town's first residential district, but when the first railroads ran over the Roxbury Flats in the thirties the region was actually a desolate fens and marshland which has since been filled in. To this day its houses sometimes sag and settle from time to time on the pilings driven deep in the ooze from which dredgers have sometimes recovered ship's keels and fish nets lost by dwellers on these shores long ago and before the dawn of recorded times.

Actually the Common as a public property dates from the year 1634 when the town, by universal assessment, purchased his orchards from Mr. Blackstone for thirty pounds and laid out a municipal training field there for the military, and ever since then it has been more closely bound up in the general life of the community than any other single Boston institution. In some way it has affected almost every period of the city's life. The British maneuvered there, and the Ancient and Honorable Artillery company holds its drum-head elections there annually to this day. It has seen riot of public jubilation, the swaggering of Colonial dandies, at least one fatal duel, and still lends a refuge, much as does Hyde Park in London, to the crackpots and the furious who preach a flat earth or the destruction of all things of a Sunday afternoon. During the Great Fire millions of dollars' worth of goods were stacked there, and at the time of the Sacco-Vanzetti controversy Edna St. Vincent Millay, who a moment or two before had been very bold against "the interests," fled down its paths from a grinning policeman to the hoots and catcalls of small urchins paddling at the Frog Pond. The Common has seen a lot.

The paths of the Common, according to universal credence, were laid out by the wandering of the cows which were pastured there until comparatively recently. They are shaded by handsome trees, some of them rare and costly, which the city provides. There are, too, tennis courts, football fields and diamonds, the tombs of the Central Burying Ground where lie the ashes of Cook Julien of the Restorator, the municipal bandstand and the kiosks of weather bureau and subway, and promenading down its sloping walks, on summer evenings when the church bells are ring-

E.H.Suydam
Old Park Church
Boston

BRIMSTONE CORNER, PARK STREET CHURCH

ing for late meeting, one can imagine the ghosts of towns-men in cocked hats who knew these same rounds when the king's men were in Boston, when officers in the scarlet mess jackets of a score of famous regiments were drinking old Boal at the house of the royal governor and roaring out "Down Among the Dead Men" fit to be heard across Roxbury Flats.

The story still persists, too, of how John Hancock on a later occasion, when he was giving a dinner for the Marquis of Lafayette who had helped send the king's men packing, had run out of milk for punch and how he ordered his servants, in the name of the city, to milk every cow on the Common, regardless of ownership in order to protect the town's reputation for hospitality. There is no record that any citizen ever questioned his action, and the tradition of grazing cattle on the Common is still preserved by a restriction on one of the house-lots on nearby Mt. Vernon Street requiring the owner to preserve a passageway from his land to the Common adequate to admit a cow.

The only fatal duel ever to have been fought in Massachusetts, according to the archives, took place on the Common in 1728. Whether or not the record is to be credited in chronicling only this unique death from such an encounter in a time when the practice was extremely widespread, especially in Tidewater Virginia and the Deep South, may be debated. Surely many other duels must have been fought in Massachusetts, if not among the Colonists, almost certainly among the king's officers quartered there at various times. That none of them were fatal in an age when surgery was still largely the business of the local barber would seem a matter for remark.

The difference of opinion between Benjamin Woodbridge and Henry Phillips arose in the tap-room of the Royal Exchange. Its subject was never known, but even in an age innocent of gossip paragraphers to solve all riddles in the morning editions, the word spread that it was an affair of gallantry, and both gentlemen, in pursuance of the conventions in such matters, retired from the Royal Exchange and left the drawing up of a cartel to others who had agreed to be their seconds.

The meeting was at dawn the next day at a secluded spot believed to have been near the Powder House. The seconds in attendance and the surgeon examined the military sabers which had been selected as weapons for similarity of length and weight. The principals removed their cloaks, hats and boots, standing in their stocking feet for more secure purchase on the damp grass, saluted, bowed and engaged their blades. A few minutes later Woodbridge slipped to one knee in an attempt to come under his opponent's lightning parade, thrusting forward and blindly up. The sword passed under Phillips' arm, and Phillips ran him through the heart as he crouched unsteadily before him.

The man-o'-war *Sheerness* was sailing for the Carolinas that morning on the tide, and before a stroller on the Common had come across Woodbridge's body Phillips was aboard her, and Oliver's Dock and Wind Mill Point were falling rapidly astern. For although there was no law in Massachusetts which forbade dueling, there is no doubt that the Puritan community would have regarded the encounter as murder for all the punctilio with which it may have been carried out. There was a vast pother over the affair and the coffee-houses and drawing-rooms of the town talked of little else for days. Phillips, according to legend, never returned, but in the Granary Burying Ground there is today a headstone which tells that Benjamin Woodbridge, son of Henry Woodbridge, Esq., died July 3, 1728, in his twentieth year. He was Boston's only recorded victim of the code duello.

The Common

Passing regulations for the government of the Common has been a favorite pastime with the town and city fathers as long as they have had statute books. At one time in the seventeenth century, when sanitation was not all it is now, an order was framed "that noe person shall throw forth or lay any intralls of beasts or fowles, or garbidg, or carion, or dead Dogs or Catts, or any other dead beast or stinkeing thing, in any way, on the Common, but ar injoynd to bury all such things that soe they may prevent all annoyanc unto any." Things were better for a time and "dead Dogs or Catts" were evidently put away with more care, but five years later the citizens were apparently throwing intralls and stinkeing things out with little regard for their neighbors and stern measures had once more to be adopted. "Whereas the Common is att times much anoyed by casting stones out of the bordering lotts and other things that are offensive, itt is therefore ordered, that if any person shall hereafter anoy the Common by spreading stones or other trash upon it, or lay any carrion upon it, every person so offending shall be fined twenty shillings." The volumes of statutes ruling Boston Common would fill a fair-size library.

Until the middle of last century the great sight of the Common was the Old Elm. Nothing in Boston so excited the imagination of the burgesses or aroused such wonder in pious visitors, for it was established both by the town records and in the estimates of scientists that the tree had stood there long before the coming of the first white man to Massachusetts Bay, and in 1722 it was full grown to magnificent and impressive proportions. It survived the turbulent times of the Revolution, although nearly destroyed by a great sleet storm in 1832, and in the fifties was so venerated a relic that Mayor J. V. C. Smith ordered its site protected by a heavy iron fence. Legend has it that William Robinson and Marmaduke Stevenson, convicted Quakers, and that

163

Boston and the Boston Legend

Margaret Jones and Anne Hibbins, witchcraft victims, were hanged from its branches, but historic evidence is lacking to support this. From time immemorial all hangings, a form of public festival much appreciated by all present except the victim, were staged on the Common, but in 1826 the custom was discontinued and there was a deal of muttering about depriving the citizens of their innocent amusements.

The shady Mall along Beacon Street side of the Common, where today blue-veiled nursemaids stroll with their charges en route from The Hill to the swan boats of the Public Garden was laid out more or less by accident. During the second war with England there was widespread fear of an attack on the city by the British, and a defense fund was raised by public subscription. When the raiders failed to materialize the problem arose of what to do with the cash, and a vote gave its use to the construction of this celebrated promenade.

During the nineteenth century it was the custom of the first citizens of Boston whose homes were near the Common, either on Beacon Hill or in Summer Street and Temple Place, to take a morning constitutional along the Mall. Daniel Webster, Edward Everett and Rufus Choate were accustomed to the salutes of passers-by, and it was once while covering the same steps he had known while pasturing his mother's cow as a youth that Ralph Waldo Emerson came across Walt Whitman, shambling along the gravel with the script of *Leaves of Grass* in his pocket. They stretched out on a park bench together and Mr. Emerson, whose sense of propriety was outraged beyond measure by some of the Magnificent Idler's themes, attempted to dissuade him from including them in the volume. Shiftless Walt, however, knew more of life than the Sage of Concord ever would and would not be saved, and they parted,

The Common

Emerson fully believing that the fellow was possessed of demons.

As late as the middle of the century smoking was forbidden on the public thoroughfares of the city and Smokers Circle on the Common was set aside for the accommodation of addicts of the weed. Good citizens on the way to Park Street Church or Old South Meeting House, and especially bonneted and black-mitted spinsters, gave the location a wide berth upwind and mentally noted as brimstone candidates the top-hatted gentry whose cheroots suggested to the less specifically informed all the vices of Sodom, or at least Gomorrah.

For many years when winters were more severe than they are today and even now when there has been a sufficient snowfall, the hillslope, which dominates the West side of the Common, rolling away toward the stretch of Charles Street that separates it from the Public Garden, is the favorite coasting spot of town. Nor was coasting in those ingenuous times a sport for urchins only, and contemporary prints show gentlemen, bearded as heavily as the writer's Uncle Cyrus, and sporting plug hats, manning enormous double-runner sleds ten at a time, and being pitched off at the curves in postures of surprising inelegance. Sled-racing clubs vied with one another, craftily sanding the runs selected by their opponents and shouting "Lullah," a sort of local and early equivalent of "fore" or "coming through," as they swooped down, turning themselves over into snowbanks just in time to avoid dashing their brains out against Charles Street fence.

Among the favorite racing sleds of the time were Dr. Frank Wells' Comet; the Eagle of James Lovett; Multum in Parvo of Francis Peabody and Horatio G. Curtis's Tuscaloosa. Almost invariably an afternoon of racing ended in a magnificent battle between South End and West End adherents. Screaming and slugging they joined in bloody battle, and a riot of nose-pasting and ear-chewing and face-grinding ensued until the police, summoned from Joy Street Station, came on the run, when both sides joined against the common enemy. Everyone went home to tea spitting teeth and rejoicing in a day well spent.

The portion of the Common today given over to loafing sailors and old ladies feeding the pigeons, bounded by Park and Tremont Street, is known as Brimstone Corner by reason of the white-hot sermons preached by Dwight and Beecher in Park Street Church across the way. It was a pastoral spot in the nineteenth century with the horse-cars turning leisurely up Park Street toward the State House and tall trees where now the subway kiosks stand in a wilderness of granolithic pavement. During the Boston police strike it was the whim of a mob to institute an enormous crap game there in defiance of all law and order, a hoodlum gesture which was interrupted by the arrival of a company of militia who promptly shot the ringleader, bayoneted a couple of others, and threw the rest into jail as a reminder that there was still law of a sort in the town.

The Public Garden (to make it plural is to stamp one as uninitiated in the ways of Boston) is, in reality, a handsome floral subdivision of the Common itself. After the Revolution it was vaguely known as "the marsh at the bottom of the Common," and was occupied only by five enormous rope walks which supplied cordage for the then ever crescent maritime trade of the water-front. The opening of the rope walks, however, must have been colorful to the point of rowdy, as there were free refreshments, a surge of the most florid oratory by local spell-binders, and such an occasion was never considered a success until a bemused citizen had

The Common

fallen head first into a barrel of Medford rum punch and been rescued amid vast popular acclaim.

Before ever it was the Public Garden the made land was the subject of numerous attempts to subdivide it for commercial purposes, the building along the West end of the Common of Charles Street having vastly enhanced its real estate value, but just before the outbreak of the Civil War the Massachusetts legislature secured the property forever as a public park.

At first it was surrounded by the high iron fence which to this day protects its lawns, and circuses were quartered there. No urchin was an accredited member of his neighborhood gang until he could vault this the moment a policeman's helmeted head was turned. Later its fine gardens were laid out, the ornamental waters introduced, and when Martin Brimmer was Mayor, Robert Paget designed the swan boats which now ply its surfaces to the delight of embarked juveniles and spectators from the bridge. In winter there is skating on its gelid surface, and at the entrance facing the reaches of Commonwealth Avenue with all its implications of Bostonian propriety and conservatism, there are heavy bronze gates duplicating those at City Hall, symbolizing the freedom of the ancient town.

Chapter XVI

AT THE SIGN OF THE CORNFIELDS

ALL the world knows that Frederick's Duck at the sign of the Silver Tower in the Quai de la Tournelle is the oldest restaurant in Paris and that it has been serving its celebrated *caneton à la presse* to the world's gourmets for the past three and a half centuries. At Frederick's they give patrons the number of their duck on a postcard as a souvenir and by now the number must be running on into the astronomical. But if they were to give the series numbers of Cotuits, served chill and brine-weeping, over the worn mahogany bar at the Union Oyster House at the corner of Marshall and Union Streets the figures would probably approach infinity as a limit. For the Union Oyster Bar has been serving shell fish for well over a century in its own right, and in the matter of comparatives is as authentic an antiquity in the market district of Boston as the Tour D'Argent on the Left Bank of the Seine.

At the Sign of the Cornfields

Union Street was laid out in the year 1636 and was variously known to the goodmen of the early township as the "street that goes to the pond," "Union Street" and, happiest of all, "Fore Street leading to Starr Tavern." North of Hanover Street it was still a festive avenue, since that part of it came to be known as Green Dragon Lane Tavern. In 1714 one William Patten, a native of Charlestown, "petitions to sell strong drink as the inholder at the Green Dragon in the room of Richard Pullen who hath quitted his license there."

But the structure that is the Union Oyster House was built so long ago that there are no municipal records to tell posterity when its massive sills were set or who joined its hand-hewn rafters. All that is known is that as an oyster bar it has been doing continuous business since 1826 and that for more than a century previous to this the building had been a local landmark.

Previous to the date when it became a fish-house, it was the place of business of Thomas Capen, importer of silks and fancy dress goods, and was picturesquely known as "At the Sign of the Cornfields." Thomas Stoddard bought the Capen House, as it came to be known, in 1742, and this is the first record we have of its existence. It was inherited by his daughter Patience and her husband, Hopestill Capen, and thence passed to Thomas Capen, the Cornfields draper. In the fall of 1769 Benjamin Thompson of Woburn, afterwards Count Rumford, was apprenticed to the elder Capen. He was exiled during the Revolution as a Loyalist, but afterward returned to be one of the most generous benefactors of Harvard College. Here at the same time Thomas Parkman, one of Boston's most distinguished merchants, learned his trade, and in the upper stories of the building Isaiah Thomas published, under the motto "Open to All Parties But Influenced by None," *The Massachusetts Spy* until the hostilities of 1776 forced its removal to Worcester.

During the war with England the house was the headquarters of Ebenezer Hancock, paymaster of the Continental army, and there is no reason to doubt that Washington himself was familiar with its even then ancient premises, but it was not until the spacious days of last century were well under way and Boston was the banking and mercantile center of the United States that Atwood and Bacon installed the semicircular bar, the narrow private compartments and an open coal range in the kitchen and hung out their sign as the most famous of Boston fish ordinaries.

From that day to this the Union Oyster House has been a cathedral, or more properly speaking, a chapel of seafood, its high altar the oyster bar, its acolytes and priests the white-coated experts who deftly render available and edible its Cotuits and Little Necks, its worshipers the patrons whose mouths water and whose nostrils quiver at the salt odor of lobster broiling on a coal fire in its kitchens. Its open fire has been replaced with grills, the mahogany surface of its bar has been refinished a dozen times, the menu occasionally amended, seasonally, of course, with an eye to the months of R, but otherwise the place is much as it was when the first proprietors served their first oyster stew —which has been a house favorite ever since.

In the last century the great of Boston were familiar sights in Union Street and behind the small-paned windows of the bar. They ranged their beaver hats, black in winter, white in summer, on its hat racks. Their coat tails hung down from the high bar stools, and they polished off oysters and clams, crabs and lobsters, quahogs, shrimp and mussels by the million, consuming schooner loads of fish every week and on banner days as many as thirty-five barrels of Cape Cod's finest and most succulent Cotuits. Daniel Webster

At the Sign of the Cornfields

was a constant customer. He drank a tall tumbler of brandy and water with each half dozen oysters and seldom had less than six plates. Then, too, came the merchants of the city: John Shepard, Eben Jordan, Theodore Whitney, who inaugurated the January clearance sale and introduced the first house-maids' uniforms, Charles Hovey, who opened Boston's first department store, Richard White, David Conrad and Richard H. Stearns. At one time Louis Philippe, afterward King of France, lived in exile on the upper floor of the building and earned a living by teaching the French language to Boston fashionables of the time.

When first it was opened the Capen House was almost on the water-front and from the backyard one could shout to the wharf where its fishing boats docked if you wanted to expedite a few dozen lobsters for an extra brisk luncheon trade. Now it is four or five city blocks from Atlantic Avenue and the water-front has been pushed back to the edge of the made land on which stand the great number of Boston's downtown markets.

Chowder and lobster stew are the house specialties and here is how they recommend that one build a clam chowder in the Boston manner: Cut up several pieces of salt pork and fry them in a kettle slowly; slice onions and fry in the same kettle. Add a quart of potatoes and a pint of clams to the kettle; cover with water and let them boil until done; add a pint of milk or, if you wish, cream, bring to a boil and serve. Of such fare it must have been that Ishmael of *Moby Dick* partook at the celebrated Try Pots Inn, Mrs. Hosea Hussey, proprietor, at Nantucket. At the Union Oyster Bar, however, one will no longer see "Dad," the venerable gaffer who for sixty-five years opened shell-fish there. He died a few winters since.

When patrons leave, if by chance they have parked their

automobile around the corner, and escape through the little adjacent alley, they will pass the establishment of Gerry the Chimney Man and Wheeler's Shoeing Forge. Boston still patronizes those two trades.

Chapter XVII

PALACE IN THE FENS

DURING the eighty odd years of her life Mrs. Isabella Stewart Gardner must have heard so much and seen so much and known so many things that gave her pleasure that she died, a little more than a decade ago, a very full woman, in the Baconian sense. The posturing Henry James once remarked that she had enjoyed "a preposterously pleasant career," but that merely suggested the enquiring vitality with which she met the challenge of a world opulent in forces and personalities and possessions that were to delight her as they must bring pleasure to any fine and gusty appetite for sensation, emotion, and sheer tactile satisfaction and beauty. And, although she was no Bostonian by birth, she became to two whole generations an archetypal representative of the qualities of intellect and independence esteemed essentially Bostonian. Today she is part of the

173

saga of the town and the authenticity of the Gardner legend is established by a tangible memorial that is one of its fine and enduring sights.

The peculiar thing about the career of Mrs. Gardner as a universal ambassador of Boston when abroad and a representative of the world when at home was that no other community in America was quite so admirably adapted to the exhibition of her abundant and by no means unconscious genius. The Chicago that gloried in the regal manifestations of the supremacy of Mrs. Potter Palmer would not have understood or appreciated her far from respectful obeisances in the direction of formal society, and the Gotham which owed an almost feudal allegiance to the cause of either the solid Mrs. Astor or the ambitious Mrs. Fish would have been terrified by her informed intelligence.

Isabella Stewart was born in New York in 1839, "plain of face and beautiful of person," and, in the manner of the times, was educated for the most part abroad. The year of the outbreak of the Civil War she came to Boston as the bride of John L. Gardner, an amiable New Englander of suitable ancestry, who will, however, be principally known to fame as Mrs. Gardner's husband. With her rise to fame it became the custom of Bostonians, particularly those who had not the privilege of her acquaintance, to refer to her as "Mrs. Jack." To intimates she was "Mrs. Jack" until the death, at the close of the century, of her husband, but after that she was scrupulously spoken of as Mrs. Gardner and she tolerated no liberties with the given name of her dead husband.

With Mrs. Gardner came to Beacon Street a cosmopolitan and highly articulate personality which, for more than sixty years, was to be at once the delight and terror, the pride and anguish of a community which was alternately to applaud her as an ornament in its midst and hold up its black-mitted hands in scandalized disapprobation of her more extravagant gestures. She had money of her own in ample supply and when her husband, with Chesterfieldian consideration, quitted this mortal scene leaving her a very considerable sum in addition, she was already established as a patron of the arts, especially music and painting, a fascinating and outrageous member of local society, and a figure upon whose extra-mural activities city editors checked with nice and regular precision.

For from the outset Mrs. Gardner was news, and in a society where entertaining Major Higginson at tea and sleigh-riding on the Brighton Road on Sunday afternoon were the ultimate public activities endorsed by decorum, she soon became far from anonymous. Small, birdlike and fragile, she was, however, exquisitely proportioned and she attracted men and dominated them in a manner at once flattering and possessive. The vivacity of her manners and her abundant feminine graces gave her admirers a generous return on their investment of attention. Never averse to association with men younger than herself and who, incidentally, aroused her far more by their importance or essential personality than by the mere charms of their persons, she was one of the first to patronize and exploit John Singer Sargent. He painted her for the first time when he was but thirty in the now famous pose with a black shawl drawn tightly across her hips to accentuate her figure, and the result, for some reason quite incomprehensible even in the light of the reticences of the time, aroused so much talk in the precincts of the Somerset Club and other exalted circles where the reports of Bull Run had not yet been confirmed that she had it put away out of the sight of all eyes until after her death.

Heartened, however, by the easy fame attracted by this

expedient, she set out upon a series of gestures the dinner-table reports of which were to cause butlers to blanch the length and breadth of Commonwealth Avenue and cause grave editorial concern in the offices of the *Transcript*.

Jim Corbett, the gentleman of the cauliflower industry, toured the country in a vaudeville sketch, and though the public which received him in the Athens of America was largely recruited from the touts of Hanover Street and the clients of the Old Howard Theater, Mrs. Gardner was among the assembled chivalry to see and to applaud.

A fashionable coaching party which was organized one fine spring day for a tour of the North Shore, through a mistaken rendezvous, failed to pick up Mrs. Gardner before essaying the delights of Magnolia and Pride's Crossing. But as the horses were reined for the grade stop at Beverly Farms there was a valiant tooting of locomotive whistles and grinding of brakes and the errant guest leapt from the cab of a panting Boston and Maine locomotive into the midst of her friends. She had chartered it post-haste and had persuaded the terrified engineer to let her take the throttle and wheel them over the fish plates of the Eastern Division eighty miles and more an hour. He told reporters she handled the Johnson bar "like a veteran hoghead."

Sandow the strong man came to Boston, and, while timid society matrons flutteringly felt his biceps, she gave them a dig with her fingers that made the great ape let out a grunt of astonishment.

The Copley Society's annual festival was about to be staged when, in an inadvertent moment, Mrs. Gardner fell and broke a leg. She had to be almost forcibly dissuaded from being carried to the stage and dispossessing the woman assigned to the part of a reclining Cleopatra in a tableau vivant. As it was she occupied her box the next night at the opening of the opera season and heard Mascagni with her

IN UNION STREET

Palace in the Fens

back turned and her leg in its cast stretching into the dressing-room.

She drank beer at Pop Concerts at Symphony and announced to interviewers that she adored it in an age when ladies usually took their Sherry behind drawn curtains. She got the De Reszke brothers to sing at her home for tea when nobody else in town could even meet them. In an excess of Episcopal enthusiasm she scrubbed the steps of the Church of the Advent during Lent. She hired the Chinese Theater in Harrison Avenue and took a top-hatted and ermined audience down for an evening of Celestial drama. She rented a lion to walk down Tremont Street with her on a leash before operetta singers first thought of this now ancient device for luring the photographers. She appeared at the town's most formal ball of the season with a negro page, in the manner of the court of Louis XIV, bearing her train through ranks of scandalized and delighted Higginsons, Coolidges and Saltonstalls. In a town modest in the use and display of lackeyed elegance she drove out with not two footmen on the box of her landau, but three. She wore a string of fabulous matched pearls around her waist instead of her neck and had two diamonds as big as paper weights mounted on antennæ and worn in her hair so they waved ahead of her like the feelers of an insect. And if anyone raised an eyebrow at anything she said or did she merely remarked finally, *"C'est mon plaisir,"* and let it go at that.

As a patron of music she was at home in a field she knew and understood. She is reported to have paid Paderewski the sum of $3,000 to play for her at tea once at Fenway Palace when only herself and one little old lady were present to hear, but this may well be apocryphal. In any event she delighted in arranging concerts and engaging the first musicians of the world, many of them before they became celebrated, to play for the pleasure of her friends. As a

Boston and the Boston Legend

confirmed attendant at Friday afternoon Symphony Concerts she always occupied seats on the extreme right, favor-
ing the violins, in the front row of the balcony and when the
organization moved from the old Boston Music Hall she
reserved for her use the corresponding seats in the Huntington Avenue auditorium.

All this extravagance of gesture, this exotic bohemianism
was, however, merely the build-up for the supreme performance of her career: the evolution of Fenway Palace as her
salon and as a perpetual souvenir of her genius.

For years before the concrete idea of an Italian palazzo
set in the marshes of the Fenway had become a concrete
reality or even a germ in her mind she had "collected," as
the phrase had it. But her collections, connoisseurs then and
later agreed, were not the random purchases of a wealthy
amateur casually furnishing an urban residence with the
miscellanies of the magazines of France and Italy. She assembled statuary and brocades, miniatures and rare panel-
ing, tapestries and portraits long in the families of Italian
princes, columns from a Doge's palace, paintings from the
brushes of the classic masters of the dead centuries. She
bought in an orderly manner with a feeling for the esthetic
and possible inter-related values of what she acquired, so
that when she came to assemble them all in one collection
there was harmony and significance in their arrangement.

Some notion of the holy rage in which Mrs. Gardner
undertook the business of collecting may be gathered from
one episode, recorded by John Hunter Sedgwick, in the
Transcript.

In May, Berenson [her factor and confidante] asked her if she
would like to buy Titian's "Rape of Europa," painted for Philip II
of Spain and reported to have been called by Rubens, when he made
the copy of it that now hangs in the Prado, the greatest picture in the

Palace in the Fens

world. The picture was given to Charles I when he went to Madrid to negotiate for the hand of Philip III's daughter, but, as negotiations failed and Charles left in a hurry, the picture remained behind, carefully packed. In the eighteenth century it was the chief ornament of the Orleans collection, and finally it came into the possession of Lord Darnley and was hung at Cobham. The price asked was high, several times as high as any Mrs. Gardner had yet paid for any work of art, and Berenson might have hesitated to propose the purchase if he had not known that she was prepared to pay even more for Gainsborough's "Blue Boy" which he had tried in vain to get for her. But she had seen the "Blue Boy" and she had never seen the "Europa." Moreover, Berenson expected the "Blue Boy" to exhaust her funds and had offered the picture, tentatively, to another Boston collector, and Mrs. Gardner had forbidden him to bring her into any competition with her neighbors. Nevertheless, as he wrote, "it would be poetic justice that the picture originally intended for a Stuart should rest at last in the hand of a Stewart." In order that her decision might actually reach him before the other person's, he begged for a cable reply, and he got it. It was said that Dr. Wilhelm Bode of the Berlin Museum fully intended to buy the picture, but to pay the asking price was contrary to all precedent. He expected a leisurely haggle over it, and when he found that an American, and worse still a woman, had recklessly cabled that she would take the picture without argument, he was furious. Berenson wrote: "Why can't I be with you when Europa is unpacked? America is a land of wonders but this sort of miracle it has not yet witnessed"; and later, "I hope that you have received her and had your first honeymoon with her. What a beauty! Titian at his greatest, Rubens at his strongest, you have both matchless artists' dominant notes singularly combined in this one picture. How I wish I might see you in your first raptures over her!"

At length, 1900 to be exact, the cornerstone of the structure that was to be the Isabella Stewart Gardner Museum in the Fenway, and was to be generally known as Fenway Court, was laid with due ceremony. The architect had favored erecting it about a frame of steel girders as is customary in modern construction, but Mrs. Gardner had

informed him that the contrary would be the case. It would
hold itself up like an Italian palazzo or there would be another architect retained.

As the first walls were raised on the windswept marshes
of the Fenway conjecture was feverish as to whatever
Mrs. Gardner could be doing now. A cordon of guards kept
public and reporters alike at a respectful distance, but she
herself could be seen mounting scaffoldings, climbing lad-
ders and squinting down courses of newly laid brick in a
manner to terrify the workmen out of their masonic wits.
It became audibly apparent to observers, too, that she was
accompanied upon these safaris by a sort of personal trum-
peter who blew, from time to time, not altogether melodious blasts on a *cornet-au-piston*. Comparison of notes by
reporters and interested spectators revealed that these were
calls for master workmen; one toot for a steam-fitter, two
for a stone mason, three for a roofer, and so on. One day
there was a terrific blowing on the *cornet-au-piston* and a
veritable panic ensued among the workmen. Finally the
master plasterer, hat in hand, shuffled forward and was
given a lesson in his calling. That was no way to tint a wall!
Where were his wits that he should use a paint brush?
Where was a sponge; she'd show him. And the great lady,
liberally bedaubing herself with coral pink pastel, achieved
just the effect she wanted with a common bath sponge.

At length the day of the opening arrived and Boston society, half protestant, half ablaze with curiosity, prepared
for what it realized must amount to an ultimate acknowledgment of Mrs. Gardner's supremacy. Hitherto her grand
manner of living, brilliant entertainments and habits of
fashion had made her seem to the public like a leader of
society, but there was an old guard that had held out val-
iantly until 1903, when Runnymede was reversed and the
barons were brought to a very sensible acknowledgment of

FENWAY COURT

Palace in the Fens

her overlordship. As one writer remarked, she had a very Renaissance evening of it. "Up one side of the horseshoe stairway society climbed to Canossa, and down the other side it descended like the army of the King of Brentford," while its hostess received, triumphant, begemmed, generally admired, and a deal better understood than Ruben's "Earl of Arundel" or the Cellini bust of Bindo Altaviti which were prominently displayed.

From that day until her death twenty years later Mrs. Gardner was an accepted Boston fixture. Fenway Court as a museum was controlled by a corporation formed for that purpose by its founder, who lived in her own apartments on the top floor where she received intimates, heard the world's foremost musicians and passed long hours with no more pretentious company than that of her old dog, Roly.

Fenway Court is entirely different from any other museum in the world. It is in every sense a palace, designed, built and furnished to be a harmonious setting for the collection Mrs. Gardner formed. During her lifetime she was usually to be found about the premises on the days when they were opened to a limited public. A trusted Italian who had known the place from its earliest times showed them about, pointing out the "Europa," the Veronese room whose ceiling was taken from a sixteenth century Venetian palace, the "Pietà," Mantegna's Madonna and Child from the collection of the Duke of Mantua, the Cellini bust, the Giorgione, the Holbeins, Rembrandts, Tintorettos, and the later Whistlers, Degas, Sargents and Zorns.

Nothing might be touched, for everything was fragile, planned, and in its place, but one day a connoisseur picked up to examine it an ancient bell which pealed through the mansion. The guardian of treasures sprang forward. "Mrs. Gardner's ill," he said. "She's in bed, she cannot walk, but she sees, she hears through the walls. She will come if that rings again."

When she was eighty-five Mrs. Gardner died, but even this finally mortal act was planned as a fitting curtain to a life so brilliantly compelling, so full of savor and gusto. Her remains were borne into her private Spanish chapel and a pall of black velvet spread over them. At her feet was hung a black crucifix and, day and night, at either dead hand, there burned tall tapers which never wavered in the still air of the chamber. On two prie-dieus black-cowled nuns knelt in constant prayer for three days and three nights, and thus, with incense and litanies about her, there passed the most spectacular Bostonian.

In her lifetime so fascinating a personality had she been that a favorite Boston anecdote concerns a lady from the Middle West whose two wishes on coming east for the first time were to see the Atlantic Ocean and Mrs. Gardner. In later years the legend of Mrs. Gardner is almost as powerful and thousands of pilgrims yearly seek her out in the three portraits of her by Sargent which are located in widely separated rooms in Fenway Court. The first is the famous full-length picture with the strands of pearls about her waist, the portrait of much gossip which during her lifetime was locked away in her secret Gothic room. "Once contemplated," says a recent writer, "it remains in the imagination as a question that contains its own answer."

The second is a mere sketch with the face left blank, but so great is the artist's feeling for the personality he records that observers must look a second time to be certain that the face is not indeed there.

The third, painted the year of her death, shows her propped against pillows, swathed in flowing silks and her head, too, folded in a complete frame of soft veils. There

is greater tranquillity than is suggested by the other two,
and greater repose, but neither boredom nor fatigue with
life, and in this, Sargent showed her as she was always, for
she never knew either.

Chapter XVIII

NEWSPAPER ROW

THE houses of the proper people in Boston are white stone
with iron grills at the doorway, or they may be red brick
or brownstone with forsythia or lilac bushes on the lawn.
They are located on the "right" side of Commonwealth
Avenue, or the river side of Beacon Street, or in Louisburg
Square, or perhaps in Arlington Street, overlooking the
Public Garden, through which the head of the family is
likely to walk to his office in the morning, carrying a green
cloth bag of books and papers, in spite of the fact that an
expensive motor stands at the door. They are private residences, all of them, not apartment hotels or coöperative
enterprises with footmen and carriage starters, and some
of them have odd old panes of purple glass in their windows
and hitching posts outside, or conservatories openly displayed for the pleasure of passers-by.

The entry to such a house is through a white Colonial
doorway with a handsome fanlight overhead and there is

likely to be a porcelain umbrella stand or a potted plant, and a trim Irish maid or English servant in severe livery will answer if you ring. But at the houses of the proper people one common characteristic may be found every week-day afternoon at five o'clock, just as tea is being served inside, a qualitative hallmark as clearcut in its implications as coat armor or membership in the Somerset Club.

It is the last edition of the *Boston Evening Transcript*.

For something over a hundred years the *Transcript* has been placed, not carelessly flung, with a certain deferential care upon the door-steps of the people of Beacon Street and Commonwealth Avenue, or, as it was when the *Transcript* was young, Summer and Washington Streets. In winter it has been delivered as the snow blew dizzily down around the gas-lamps in the streets while roundsmen in tall helmets swung their arms briskly to keep out the chill, and in summer it has followed its subscribers to Cape Cod or the North Shore or the White Mountains, beloved of Bostonians and filled with long country hotels with rocking-chairs on the porches and geological curiosities in the form of notches and profiles.

The *Transcript* in its century of superior but by no means cloistered existence has come to be an integral part of the Boston scene, much like the Lowell family and the reputation of a fondness for cod and the young men of Harvard who dance at balls at the Somerset. But more than any of these it is a vital and representative tradition, with an altogether amazing ability for adaptation to a modern order of things. Only in the saga is the *Transcript* the foe of the new inheritors of City Hall and the unquestioning supporter of the old heirs to the State House, with its Indian crest and seal and superscription of authority and prestige. Changing times have found in the *Transcript* a more elastic tolerance than those who have heard only of its genealogical department are likely to believe. Only in its concrete and physical manifestations does the *Transcript* cleave to an earlier order.

At Milk Street and Washington, with the Old South Church beside it and Dunne, the tailor to the proper Boston people, downstairs, a chastely caste-conscious brass plate on the stairs announces "editors two flights, reporters three flights." The city-room, which is built on three distinct levels, might be the reading-room of the Athenaeum in Beacon Street. Dignified people wearing all their clothes speak to each other with courtesy and an awareness of grammar. They are the reporters and copyreaders. Young persons who neither shoot craps on the desk tops nor gather in the washrooms for long discussions of the relative merits of the Yankees and the A's transport sheaves of paper from desk to desk. These are the copy boys. The copy paper, in the old tradition, is square and yellow and of a superior texture which will not disintegrate during its progress through a writing machine. The news writers seat themselves at their desks with that assurance attributed by Lytton Strachey to Queen Victoria, confident that they will not sit on (a) their own hats, (b) an overturned pot of mucilage or (c) a copy spindle. When the paper has gone to bed for the afternoon the staff departs for home in a reasonable state of sobriety instead of barging off to the nearest saloon to become falling-down drunk before dinner-time.

The city editor is, it would seem, almost as much an admissions committee as a director of news-gathering activities. One young man recently graduated from the academic groves of Harvard who applied for the privilege of serving in a minor capacity reported that he was not consulted as to his journalistic attainments, but that there was considerable adroit questioning as to the clubs he had made along Mount Auburn Street. And certain it is that members of the Porcellian Club and Institute of 1770 are not strangers to the staff.

A short time ago when the *Transcript* gracefully achieved its one hundredth birthday and at the same time became the only daily in the land to have been owned by the same family for more than a century, a number of anecdotes were rehearsed about the venerable paper and its staff. None so charmingly and yet adequately indicates the esteem in which it is held among the burgesses by the Charles as that of the entirely correct butler who announced to his master the arrival of the representatives of the press in the terms: "Two reporters from the newspapers, sir, and a gentleman from the *Transcript*."

The most distinguished member of the *Transcript's* editorial staff during the current generation was the late H. T. Parker, known throughout the world of music and the drama by his familiar initials H.T.P. He is dead now, but the tradition of his gusty personality, his acid impatience with mediocrity and his pyrotechnic bulldog pipe which showered Boston for more than thirty years with flaming embers are part of a still vital saga in Washington Street's Newspaper Row. So penetrating and classical in their execution were Mr. Parker's reviews that it became a local legend that they were originally written in Latin and then translated for the instruction of the *Transcript's* readers. In point of actual fact, two typographers were retained in the composing room to decipher his holograph which, for legibility, compared favorably with that of Horace Greeley, since he never learned to use a typewriter and rebelliously refused the services of a secretary.

Attired in the opera cloak and chapeau claque of accepted usage, H.T.P. was an institution on first nights and at Symphony. A passionate amateur of hocks, he made an annual pilgrimage to the Rhineland, and wrote column-long

dispatches for the editorial page on the merits of Bern-
casteler Doktor Spätlese and Johannisberger Erntebringer
which, during the arid years, drove readers into frenzies.
His place at Friday afternoon Symphony was in the first
row of the balcony and he was accustomed to indicate his
disapproval of a rendition in the Continental manner by
thumping the floor vigorously with his heavy walking stick.
Upon one occasion he was reported to have pounded the
adjacent foot of Mrs. Jack Gardner and Symphony at-
tendants still pale at the ensuing exchange of cultivated
expletive. Even in a community where individualism still
flourishes unabated and unafraid, H.T.P. was a notable to
be pointed out as he steered his course down the center mall
of Commonwealth Avenue, walking, like Agag, delicately,
but, like David, armed with a wealth of shockingly lethal
epigram. He was, in amazingly even proportions, an eager
and skilful reporter, a sensitive critic, and a Bostonian and
individualist.

Only one woman stands out in the history of the *Transcript*. Miss Cornelia M. Walter, sister of the first editor,
was for five years, and in an age when feminism was all
but unknown, his competent successor in office. Her salary
was $500 a year. In 1852 the paper boasted two reporters
who received jointly the sum of $11 a week. Years later
the treasurer considered $20 a liberal allowance for news
writers.

Thus is the *Transcript* of the 1930's a curious admixture
of the old and the new. Her antiquated presses, named after
members of the Mandell family like the locomotives and
fire engines of the last century, clatter through the day's editions with a minimum of assurance that they will not fall,
like the one-horse shay, into utter ruin; while the closing
stock final is delivered to distant New England points at
150 miles an hour in tri-motor planes. And a mandate from

NEWSPAPER ROW

Newspaper Row

the past, a tradition of dominance and wealth and prestige dating from the proud clippers in the China trade, is reconciled with a more recent dynasty of Gaelic genius and origin in Boston's politics.

Other Boston gazettes, while more essentially newspapers, have never enjoyed the esteem at home or the fame abroad of the *Transcript,* nor has any, save possibly the old *Advertiser* of many years since, been so representative of the ideas and manner of living of proper Bostonians.

During the middle and latter years of the nineteenth century the Boston *Daily Advertiser* enjoyed all the bright prestige at home, if not the foreign acclaim of the *Transcript.* Edward P. Mitchell, later destined to become editor-in-chief of the New York *Sun* after the death of Dana, served his apprenticeship on the *Daily Advertiser's* staff early in the seventies and his description of that institution from his *Memoirs of an Editor* recreates a vanished day in journalism.

The *Daily Advertiser* of that day [he says] was a vast blanket sheet with a page more than double the size now standard. Its columns seemed interminable when there was one to fill. They were crammed, however, with good writing in every department. We used to believe that the regulations governing the use of English in the *Daily Advertiser* had been drawn up originally by the faculty of Harvard University in solemn conclave, and that the professors met from time to time to devise new refinements of speech and to investigate the fidelity of our observance. I remember, for example, that the word "reliable" was absolutely forbidden; the theory of the Harvard conference being, as we understood, that you cannot "rely" anybody or anything, but must rely on him or it; so that the only permissible locution would be "relionable." The prescribed synonym was "trustworthy." So strong was the influence of codified *verbotens* that I have written "trustworthy" rather than "reliable" all my life; even on the *Sun,* where the offensive "reliable" was overlooked or ignored and the odium of phraseology concentrated upon such expressions as "in this connection" or "in our midst."

Boston and the Boston Legend

The fastidious sense of responsibility toward the language permeated to every part of the *Advertiser's* establishment, extending even to the mechanical departments. Even John Mason, the lanky and cynical foreman of the press-room, used to snatch up the first copy of the first edition as it issued from the machinery and scan it with critical eye for faults in English. One midnight he came tearing upstairs with the paper in hand and pointed indignantly at a headline which announced that the veterans of this or that organization would "reune next Tuesday." "When in holy Halifax," he shouted, "did they first 'une'"?

Not only of the culture of Harvard but also of Boston's commercial greatness, Boston's political conservatism, and Boston's social propriety, was the old *Advertiser* considered to be the leading newspaper exponent. The magnates of State and Devonshire Streets and the chosen of Beacon Hill and the Back Bay were visitors to the room of the chief editor, Mr. D. A. Goddard. He was a scholarly person, tall and stooping, with a very gentle look in his eyes, but so remote was he from the sphere of the youngsters that we seldom saw him except as he passed in and out. I used to imagine that as a powerful journalist with marked habits of seclusion but far-reaching connections with the outside great he was very much like Delane; possibly the idea resulted merely from an unconscious association of his given name Delano with the name of the illustrious editor of the London *Times*. I was not in a position to know which editorial articles were his and which were written by his assistants, Edward Stanwood and Walter Allen and Henry A. Clapp, a lawyer who was also the dramatic editor and one of the best critics of the stage I have ever known anywhere.

Edward Everett Hale was to me by far the most interesting of the friends of the *Advertiser* frequently to be seen in its office.

For many years thereafter the *Daily Advertiser* continued its existence, its latter career that of the Sunday edition of the Hearst *American,* its name unchanged to preserve membership in the Associated Press.

Another famous Boston newspaper institution was the *Post's* cane. As the leading Roman Catholic organ of the community, the *Post* enjoyed a handsome circulation and one by no means diminished by its celebrated cane legend. The idea came from the genius of Edwin Grozier, for many years its editor-in-chief. Coming one day into possession of a considerable number of cheap walking sticks in some unexplained way, Mr. Grozier caused them to be distributed with the compliments of the paper to the oldest gaffer in every community of any size throughout the state where the *Post* had rural circulation. Upon his demise the cane was to pass to the new inheritor of the title as a proud symbol of his own longevity and the approval of the editors of the paper. The idea was a huge success, even though in a day of high-pressure promotion it may seem a naïve one, and throughout New England, eventually, the bearer of the *Post* cane was a distinguished codger and much admired at the cross-roads.

The *Boston Globe* is popularly reputed to have attained its position as a highly prosperous journal even in hard times by the bourgeois gesture of printing the name or picture of every resident of greater Boston once every year. People who admired seeing themselves in type or half tone naturally admired the singular good judgment of the *Globe* in selecting them for inky honor, and coffers in the vaults of the Taylor family, its proprietors, became correspondingly heavy.

The *Globe* for years occupied Washington Street premises so sensationally antiquated that reporters in the upper floors agreed among themselves that, in the event of fire, any attempt at escape would be the essence of futility and that they would quietly and unprotestingly yield themselves to the holocaust. Brother news writers from the handsome and modern *Herald* offices were accustomed to goggle unbelievingly at the open fireplaces in the offices of *Globe* reporters and at the cellarful of presses which rambled off in uncharted caverns under neighboring loft buildings and nearby streets. But the *Globe* has proved itself a consistently profitable property for many decades and the pride of the Taylor family, as represented by William and Charles, sons of the founding general.

Its star reporter, for more years than he cared to think about, was Frank Sibley, whose black hat and Windsor tie were familiar hallmarks along Newspaper Row. Mr. Sibley won his first fame covering the Cuban campaigns of the Spanish War for the *Journal* and the legend persists in Boston city-rooms that he actually and by physical propulsion urged Theodore Roosevelt up San Juan Hill. "Come, come, Colonel," he is supposed to have cried as he dragged the reluctant future president ahead through the Mauser fire, "I've got to file in half an hour and I haven't got a lead for my story yet."

Only one daily which makes a gesture in the direction of conservatism of format and maintains pretensions of complete news coverage, the *Boston Herald,* finds its way to the responsible breakfast tables of Chestnut Hill and Pinkney Street. In its ninety years of existence the *Herald* has not always enjoyed the affluence which it achieved under the direction of Managing Editor Robert B. Choate, but it has almost invariably been allied to the more responsible causes of the times. As its editor, Robert Lincoln O'Brien was a powerful, if latent figure, in Boston's affairs throughout the twenties of the nineteenth century, and its music reporter for many years, Philip Hale, ranked as one of the foremost in his highly specialized calling. His program notes for Symphony and his reports on the music events of Boston and a wider world were awaited with a breathlessness not divorced from terror, for, like H.T.P. of the *Transcript,* he was not easy to please.

The calling of the press in Boston, since the turn of the century, has not been regarded by professional newspapermen as an alluring one and by the irreverent it has, in fact, been spoken of as the "poor farm" of American journalism, largely because, aside from the *Transcript* staff, there has been little demand for the best professional technique. Wages have been low and reporters, by and large, a far cry from their gilded and envied confrères in such "good" newspaper towns as Chicago, New York or San Francisco. Boston city-rooms have produced a variety of persons bound for wider achievements in the world, ranging from Katharine Brush to Henry Cabot Lodge, Jr., and from Professor Copeland of Harvard to Bruce Atkinson, Melrose born and scholarly senior drama reviewer of the *New York Times*. John Mason Brown, Walter Prichard Eaton and the distinguished Edward P. Mitchell, all served apprenticeship in Boston news offices, but few have remained to maturity on the scene of their earliest triumphs.

Chapter XIX

VALOR AND THE HUMANITIES

For three centuries Harvard College and later Harvard University has been famous, at various times and in varying degrees, as a peculiar synthesis of theology, liberalism, civic tumult, esthetic indifference, urban society, transcendentalism and Medford rum. As America's foremost grove of the academe it has commanded universal respect among scholars and pedagogues. Its history has been liberally illustrated with intramural riot and extramural blasphemy and bad manners. It has supplied generations of eligible youths for the debutante balls of Commonwealth Avenue and it has been a stronghold of Abolitionism and strong drink. Its early years saw Harvard students and theologues alike suffering pitiful privations which they met with a moving fortitude and a vast latinity, while in later times it has been one of the most wealthy vested corporations of the world.

194

Valor and the Humanities

Almost any phase of Harvard's being offers classic examples of paradox.

Harvard is confirmed in the assurance which derives from long and secure establishment and is indifferent to the storm winds which whistle down the campuses of lesser institutions. It has given battle to local authorities on behalf of youths apprehended *in particeps criminis* with the full resources of its wealth and legal battalions. During the World War when German measles and cabbage were being fatuously known by the name of Liberty, Harvard retained its German department and the teaching of its culture in the face of the mutterings and dornicks of the rabble, and when the strong voice of Abbott Lawrence Lowell said, "There will be German at Harvard," it was there as irrevocably as daylight followed an earlier *fiat lux*. By and large, Harvard moves with the Churches and with the Commonwealth of Massachusetts, but when it finds its roads departing from them it has never hesitated in its attitude of "go your ways and be wrong if you want to." As a whole Harvard doesn't give a damn for anybody and its aristocratic indifference is its supreme characteristic.

A man who goes to Harvard may devote his time to theology, Indic verb roots, the Communist doctrine or the taverns of the town. All that is required of him, if he is an undergraduate, is that he maintain an average of creditable mediocrity in his studies and keep out of the papers. He may attend an absolute minimum of lectures, may carry a green cloth bag, wear polo shirts in January, drink before breakfast, illustrate his rooms with red velvet and sing black masses, speak to anyone, be Whig, Tory or flat-earth prophet and nobody will care or molest him. He may consort with the derelict schoolma'ams of the Summer School once characterized by Professor Charles Townsend Copeland as the sexually unemployed, or he may confine his social

195

activities to the drawing-rooms of Beacon Hill where, in the Corona-scented library of his favorite debutante's father, he will discuss the better things of life until after the fifth brandy when *"The Apthorp Hymn"* will be sung. But he must remain anonymous in the public prints. That is the first and great commandment in Harvard Yard.

At home, Harvard is principally notable for its undergraduate activities, its courses in the liberal arts and sciences, its tolerance of all and any doctrine, its football teams and its accent, which is mistakenly supposed to resemble that of the youth of Oxford. In foreign parts it is one of the very few American universities whose name, even, is known at other seats of learning, and its graduate schools of law, medicine and the more profound humanities are accorded the respect and admiration of scholars and the practitioners of professional callings the world over. Any immediate contemporary view of the institution must concern itself for changes and events, such as "house plans" and "elective systems," appointments of new presidents and spectacular contributions to exact or liberal knowledge, but these are, at best, minor incidents in the progress of what is at once a body of learning and a proud tradition. Harvard is old, as American foundations go, and change and individuals, like movements and sects and schisms alter but little its determined purpose.

Harvard College was founded in 1636 by the settlers of the Massachusetts Bay Colony. John Harvard willed 779 pounds, 17 shillings, and twopence and 320 books—mostly theological—to perpetuate learning in the wilderness. The place selected was "Newtowne," now the overcrowded and grimy city of Cambridge, where the students might be at a reasonable remove from the more active life of Boston. For two centuries it remained little more than a theological seminary, although the behavior of many

HARVARD HALL, HARVARD YARD

Valor and the Humanities

students and some faculty members was not always characterized by overmuch piety.

John Harvard himself was a young graduate of Emmanuel College, Cambridge, who had crossed the seas to reside in Charlestown and who died two years after the incorporation of the still anonymous "School or college" of New England. He was assistant to the Rev. Z. Symmes in the First Church of Charlestown and a respected citizen, and the institution which benefited by his generosity was named for him with almost universal approval. Today, in front of University Hall, there stands the famous statue of Harvard, and visitors who stand beneath it to be photographed amidst the culture and traditions of Cambridge are fond of commenting on the serenity of expression and the broad brow of the young man. As a matter of fact no likenesses either in bronze or on canvas of John Harvard survive and the statue is purely a putative image, but it serves well enough.

Modest though an endowment of four thousand dollars would seem today, John Harvard's gift was magnificent in the poverty of the early Colony. The record of other bequests to the college is a touching index of the desire of all the citizens to have a seat of learning in their midst, and the youths who unfeelingly today dwell in million-dollar structures with every refinement of comfort and luxury at their disposal would do well to read of the humble gift to an earlier Harvard by a Colonist of a pewter flagon worth ten shillings, and of another, a quantity of coarse cotton valued at nine shillings, and of the pathetically generous donations of household treasures, modest volumes, articles of clothing and furniture, which started Harvard on its way.

Harvard's first "schoolmaster" was Nathaniel Eaton who seems, from the records, to have been the very archetype of Puritan harshness and brutality. It soon became apparent that Mr. Eaton's notions of discipline bordered on the emphatically sadistic, although the term had not then come into being, and upon one occasion he took to task a member of the faculty, Nathaniel Briscoe, beating him for upwards of two hours with "a walnut-tree plant big enough to have killed a horse and a yard in length." Outraged public opinion rallied to the contused Mr. Briscoe; Eaton was discharged from office and forced to pay thirty pounds' fine, and a litigious gentleman of far more amiable temper, Henry Dunster, was placed in his stead.

Dunster, a far more popular man, who fell "into the briers of Antipaedobaptism," was forced to resign in 1654, but during his term the College developed a character. The rule book for 1654 forbids tobacco and military bands. The curriculum consisted mostly of Latin, Greek, Hebrew, Chaldee, and Syriac. Students studied and shivered by the flickering light of the "public candle." And the first of the many College scandals occurred in 1645. James Ward and Joseph Weld burglarized two houses and were whipped by President Dunster before the assembled College. They were not at all bad boys, however.

George Downing who was a member of the first graduating Class in 1642 returned to England, curried Cromwell's favor, betrayed several regicides after the Restoration, and was made a knight.

These were thin times for the students. The freshman had to fag, and do such chores as cutting the President's hay and beating the one College carpet. They in turn were ministered to by goodies, that institution peculiar to Harvard. Mrs. Eaton, the first goody (a syncopated form of "good-wife"), wrote fondly, "And that they made their beds at any time, were my straits never so great, I am sorry they were ever put to it." She was given the title of

Valor and the Humanities

"Regina Bonarum," and this title passed to succeeding generations of leading goodies.

Second in importance were the janitors, or "Sweepers and Bed-makers," as they were more elegantly called. Of these the first, Matthew Abdy, was the son of a Boston fisherman. He was dwarfish in stature, twisted of face, and continually drunk, but popular with the boys as bootlegger and purveyor of forbidden delicacies. More famous was Daniel Barnett, of whom Jeremy Belknap wrote, "His Inwards were almost consumed with drinking RUM, his summum bonum." Barnett's epitaph attests to the truth of this:

> Under this Stone there lies the Trunk
> Of one who lived & died Drunk.

It is no exaggeration to say that the two things most frequently mentioned in the annals of the College in the seventeenth century were liquor and the Bible.

The Mather tribe of New England is famous for its grim Calvinistic theology and innumerable tedious literary endeavors. Increase Mather was the victim of "meltings," a kind of divine inspiration, and did not like didactic theology. He was supposed, by the College laws, to expound several Bible chapters to the students daily, but being more interested in politics and theological controversy, he preferred to live in Boston, and so neglected this duty—for which the students were truly grateful. During his administration William Stoughton, the famous "hanging judge" of the witchcraft trials, added the first building bearing his name to the College. Its successor stands, next to Hollis, in the green Western depths of Harvard Yard.

About this time the "high table" was instituted in the Commons. Here the sons of the wealthiest families were privileged to dine, often eating with their hats on to keep from catching cold. From the beginning students were listed

199

in order of their social importance, and this gave rise to much ill-feeling. No one dined very well. Stews and puddings were the main diet, with a common can of cider or beer to wash down the fare. Many students played hookey from the Commons and went to nearby taverns for sustenance.

One, Samuel Gibson, played host to these renegades in the seventeenth century. He had a house near the College and opened it wide for the students' revels. He also arranged midnight snacks in the students' rooms. According to Cotton Mather, the *pièce de résistance* of these feeds was turkey which was often "left stinking in some of the chambers and studies of the students." Gibson was later fined by the General Court for "entertaining persons of all character." In 1760 a law was passed forbidding students to dine out.

The College butler presided over the cellar and the buttery. He frequently dispensed liquor on the sly; indeed it was said of the earliest Harvard classes that cirrhosis of the liver was an occupational disease of scholarship. The students made up for the food they couldn't eat with rum and molasses. Each carried his own knife about with him; forks were unknown until 1707. There was no worse meal than breakfast; the crafty students affixed meat the night before to the underside of the tables with their pocket knives, and this and a small beer made a good morning meal. Many students skipped breakfast. Jones, the first College Bellringer, never varied a second the ringing of the dread bell.

The real College gaieties began under President Leverett, who came into office in 1707. He set down rules for behavior at Commencement, chief of which was one stating that a student must henceforth "have no preparation nor provision of either Plumb Cake or Roasted, Boyled or Baked Meates or Pyes of any kind, nor any distilled Lyquors in his Chamber." Such injunctions invited revolt, and got it. Nor were

200

the miscreants always students. While Holyoke was president, Isaac Greenwood, Hollis Professor of Mathematics, was dismissed amid vast public indignation for falling on his face in what was not generally conceived as a fit of vertigo during divine services.

The student in the eighteenth century was a dandy. He wore, when he could afford it, gold or silver lace, brocade, silk nightgowns, and even jeweled bracelets. He was constantly in need of discipline. The heaviest fine was imposed for card-playing, while similarly stiff ones followed such offenses as "going upon the top of the College," as walking the ridge pole was conventionally known. Freshmen were forbidden to wear hats, were obliged to run all the seniors' errands, and had to supply footballs for the use of all students.

An example of Harvard independence is furnished during the Revolutionary War. A few blue-blooded Tories brought India Tea into the Commons shortly after the Stamp Act, and were publicly rebuked by President Langdon. In 1769 several students organized the Marti-Mercurian band and paraded all over Boston in blue coats, nankeen breeches, white stockings, and cocked hats. During the war barracks were raised in the College Yard. Harvard gave Washington its first LL.D.

Shortly after the war occurred the worst scandal in the annals of the College. John Hancock, who had been treasurer of the College under Langdon, was called upon to account for the use of the College funds, and refused to do so. Moreover he ordered all the College bonds to be brought to him in Philadelphia where he was presiding at the Continental Congress. Later he was elected Governor of Massachusetts and still he would not account. Finally he admitted that he owed the College some thousand pounds which his disgruntled heirs later had to pay.

Boston and the Boston Legend

After the war, too, several innovations were introduced into the College. Before 1800 both the Institute of 1770 and the Hasty Pudding Club were founded for the sons of the aristocrats. In 1786 uniforms for all classes were prescribed, the classes being differentiated by the number of frogs on the cuffs. Another great uprising marked the turn of the century, when students, protesting against watered milk, poured tartar emetic in the kitchen-boilers and poisoned the whole College. Public nausea was suddenly universal.

The last century began auspiciously under the presidency of the liberal John Kirkland, who used to send each student a basket of pears before his oral entrance examination. One story characterizes Kirkland: he had often heard of the excellent brew at Porter's Tavern, and decided to sample it. Having done so, he made the brief comment that it was "excellent stuff! I should think the students *would* like it!" This same tavern was the scene and origin of another Harvard scandal. Emerson's class of 1821 once went there en masse, got their skins full, and then did an Indian dance around the Rebellion Tree that shocked all Cambridge.

The Rebellion Tree had been "instituted" during the war. It was regarded as the center for all caucuses, and in 1818 there was a freshman-sophomore riot which John Adams, James Otis, and Josiah Quincy started by throwing plates at the freshmen in Commons. The freshmen replied in kind with a crockery barrage at a practically flat trajectory which drove the Messrs. Adams, Otis and Quincy to cover behind a barricade of overset tables. The glad news of the tumult circulated about the Yard and adjacent taverns and the chivalry of the College rushed to the scene armed with cord wood, paving blocks and miscellaneous available hardware, joining one embattled side or the other with fine impartiality. Blood flowed and war-whoops resounded, and

Valor and the Humanities

across the Charles River in Brighton citizens reached for their fowling pieces under the impression that the Mohawks were again pillaging and burning. It was one of the most magnificent and outrageous of all Harvard disorders and the instigators were exiled from Cambridge for half a year and burned in effigy under the Rebellion Tree as they departed.

The 1800's were a period of gentlemanly presidents and famous characters. When Joseph Choate was a Freshman in '52 he received the following rebuke from President Edward Everett's secretary:

Mr. Choate, the president has directed me to inform you that he observes with great regret that you passed him in Harvard Square yesterday without touching your hat.

Everett Peabody, '49, was rusticated for making a bonfire on the steps of University Hall, and ran away to hide in a Boston tavern.

At this time, too, there was "Cap" Fosdick who ran the horse-car from Bowdoin Square in Boston to Harvard Square, and who generously gave free rides to the midnight revelers who had been absorbing musties in the Bowdoin Square bistros. There was Herb Foster of Holyoke Street who presided over one of the earliest snack emporia in Harvard Square. He always wore a straw hat and eyeglasses attached to a striped shirt with a pink string, and he fed hundreds of ham sandwiches daily to the avid undergraduates who rebelled at the food crimes of Memorial Hall, named for Harvard's Civil War dead. "Mem" Hall, sprawled out over half an acre and monstrous with barbaric pseudo-Gothic protuberances, has always been a white elephant. Students wouldn't eat there, nor dance nor study there. They are forced to graduate from its portals, and graduation, registration and general examinations are the only times they see the inside of it. Otherwise Sanders Theater, Memorial Hall's terraced auditorium, is used for infrequent concerts and the regular "Thursday nights" when the Boston Symphony carts its luggage to Cambridge.

The Yard swarmed with personalities. There was Doctor Charles, the negro porter, who, by collecting odds and ends from the students, became the richest negro in Massachusetts. Indigent professors used to borrow from him frequently. There was "Pogo," the old-clothes man, who started the gyp tradition among the Cambridge pawn doctors. He was later succeeded by Max Keezer, the friend of every student and a Semite of untold wealth. Nigger Lewis sold spruce gum and ginger-beer in the Yard. Jimmy O'Neill was famous because he sold candy and hated all freshmen. Best beloved was John the Orangeman, who greeted all Freshmen cheerily with the same exclamation, "I knew y'r father, fri'nd!" It was he who deciphered the Harvard motto *Veritas* to mean "ter hell wid Yale!" He was ex officio a member of every team, and was always accompanied by a cartful of oranges drawn by a donkey.

Then began the era of resident graduates, of whom the most conspicuous and tenacious was Jonathan Dabney. He lived in a loft over the old College House and was popularly referred to as "Sourbelly." He made a daily habit of going to the reading-room before anyone else could get there, taking off his shoes, and sitting on all the newspapers, reading them at painful leisure. There might even have been a cow in the Yard—the Boylston Professor of Rhetoric and Oratory was allowed one by his appointment—but that seems never to have happened, despite its inevitable projection as a witticism by every incoming group of freshman roisterers. Actually to purloin and pasture under Professor Copeland's windows a live cow, and to decorate with a cross bar the two tall power-house chimneys that used to stand

BOSTON MUSEUM OF FINE ARTS

Valor and the Humanities

by the River so as to form a gigantic H were invariably discussed by first-year men for generations as gestures of what they conceived to be almost incredible originality. They never were carried through.

From the occasions of uproar and atmosphere of hurrah recorded here it must not be supposed that Harvard's history at any time has been overwhelmingly devoted to pursuits clerical and alcoholic. As a matter of fact, it is well to bear in mind that her sister university of Yale was founded at Branford, Connecticut, because, even in its early years, Harvard had become too little a theological seminary for the tastes of the Puritan divines, and an index to the piety of Harvard scholars in after years is found in the university library which, when it was burned in the middle of the eighteenth century, was the most wonderful in the New World, and which, since that time, has doubled the number of its volumes once every sixteen years.

More perhaps than any of the great libraries of the world, that of Harvard commands the allegiance of an almost fanatical group of friends and patrons to whom the augmenting of its resources is as pious a work as was contributing to his favorite cathedral to a medieval prince. The tale is told of Archibald Cary Coolidge who met a friend in the Ritz bar of Paris immediately after the World War in a high state of excitement. "Do come to Budapest with me," he cried. "The Bela Kun revolutionists there have just seized and put on sale the finest Magyar library in the world and I'm going through on the next train to buy it for Harvard. Buying libraries is the best fun in the world. Do come!" The friend did, and Coolidge bought the library intact and forwarded some 50,000 volumes to Cambridge, making Harvard's representation in this field of literature finer than any other occidental library.

Chapter XX

GROVES OF THE ACADEME

THE latter nineteenth century in Harvard Yard was the era of President Eliot and the reforms he effected in the academic routine of the University. In its decades began the Harvard which is today recognizable in the general outline of the institution, although most of the details of his long administration have vanished in the mutations devised by subsequent academic hierarchies and something of the personal stature of the man himself was diminished by his bumblings and letters to the editor after he had been retired to private life. The Democratic party, the holy joys of prohibition, and other curious minutiæ of existence fascinated his nonogenarian years, but it was Charles William Eliot who transformed Harvard from a college to a university.

Dr. Eliot was thirty-five when he became president at Cambridge and it was during his first year in office that he threw in the faces of presumably wiser and certainly more

Groves of the Academe

conservative scholars such a statement as that "the whole system of medical education in this country needs a thorough reformation." From that time until his death, fifty-seven years later, reformation was his watchword and, almost single-handed, he accomplished the metamorphosis of the colleges of America from mere erudite high schools into universities and seats of mature learning. On his ninetieth birthday he told an assembly of scholars gathered to do him honor, "I have always liked a fight," and his life was full of fighting. Under Dr. Eliot Harvard achieved a breadth of intellectual scope, a liberalism of academic viewpoint strangely at variance with the straitened classical and scientific requirements which had prevailed during the previous two centuries of the College's existence, and the intellectual opulence of his spacious years is their distinguishing characteristic just as the economic opulence of Dr. Abbott Lawrence Lowell's administration was to succeed it.

The era of plutocracy and the visible and tangible university of the present time came into being during the presidency of Dr. Lowell. Lowell was a builder of buildings. He took pleasure in the physical manifestations of the institution of which he was the head and, should there be no patron forthcoming to foot the bill for a structure he had in mind, he wrote a check for it himself. The New Lecture Hall and several of the newer residence halls at the west end of the Yard were built at his private expense, although this was never made public at the time. He loved the traditions and souvenirs of the old times that abounded in the atmosphere of Cambridge, and one day, when the overseers were gathered in solemn annual conclave in the president's room in University Hall, word was brought to him that workmen in the Yard had, while excavating for pipes, uncovered fragments of the original Harvard china whose design had been lost for more than a century. Passers-by were treated to the spectacle of the President of the University, his silk hat on the back of his head and his lavender trousers daubed with clay, on his hands and knees in an excavation assisting workmen in the recovery of the treasured bits of pottery. The entire pattern was, at length, reclaimed and is in universal use once more at Harvard after having lain buried since the time of Andrew Jackson.

The details of the origin of the "house plan," which was destined to become the accepted system of living at Harvard, have been vague. It seems, however, that Edward S. Harkness, of Standard Oil fame, had always been an admirer of the groups of small colleges into which the great English universities are subdivided. A loyal Yale graduate, he wrote to the corporation of that seat of learning offering to finance a similar plan for the New Haven academe. Months passed and the Yale fathers showed insufficient interest even to reply to his letter. As a matter of record, they were busy at the moment, fobbing off on their *alma mater* a vast quantity of securities which, in the refining fires of the subsequent depression, were found to be something less than Sterling. Mr. Harkness was in a huff when it happened that the graduation of a favorite niece from Radcliffe brought him to Cambridge.

As an ambassador from the great realm of oil, Mr. Harkness thought it only proper to pay his respects to the Satrap of Harvard Yard and, without appointment, he presented his card to Dr. Lowell's chief secretary. Dr. Lowell had but remotely heard of Mr. Harkness, but a hurried investigation of the files of the *Boston Herald* brought back the magic telephoned words "Standard Oil" and "millions," and Mr. Harkness was shown in with suitable noises of welcome.

The conversation was at first general and then more specific, and Mr. Harkness, finding in Dr. Lowell not only

Groves of the Academe

a sympathetic pedagogue but also a builder in his own right, ventured to inquire what was his guess at the probable cost of the gift he had offered the uninterested men of Yale. Dr. Lowell opened a drawer, consulted a sheaf of papers, and announced the cost would be $11,500,000 plus or minus, depending on building conditions. Mr. Harkness swallowed hard and inquired further how Dr. Lowell knew so precisely, and the president, opening another drawer and, producing a complete set of architect's blue-prints, explained that he himself had long dreamed of just such a house plan and, just for the fun of it, had commissioned the Harvard architects to draw up an estimate together with an outline for the scheme.

Mr. Harkness knew the hand of fate when he saw it and presented Harvard, then and there, with the $11,500,000 plus or minus. It was not for more than a year that the mighty of the Yale campus began to realize that they had missed a very impressive bet and became polite to Mr. Harkness. He gave Yale the money for a house plan too, just for the sake of impartiality.

Individualists, be they clerical, secular, pedagogical or of the town, naturally abound in places of learning and breed like the fecund shad. Harvard throughout the centuries has enjoyed the performances of countless characters who have whirled and spun in their dervish dances down the years, but during the twentieth century no one became so much of a Harvard institution or was possessed of such a variety of amiable demons as Charles Townsend Copeland, Boylston Professor of Rhetoric and Oratory.

Copey, as he was known for more than forty academic years, was a little man of spacious influence, an enthusiast for letters bordering on the fanatic, a teacher of English in the literal sense of the word. He was not a professor of literature, and it was his boast that he was but little of a

209

scholar, but his reputation as campus ironist and classroom eccentric is known wherever Harvard men go, which is to the ends of the earth, and his little malices, his vanities and affectations provided a body of legend which achieved the importance of a Harvard saga.

Copey is still essentially a New Englander of the Puritan tradition, as is indicated by his speech and philosophy. Proud of his provincialism, it is his boast that he has never left New England more frequently than was absolutely necessary and only once during his life, and then for but a few petulant weeks, did he leave his native shores for Europe.

Starting his Harvard career as a corrector of English themes, Copey's academic progress was slow because of the distrust aroused in his more sedate colleagues by the informality of his teaching. Too, he had for a time been a reporter on the staff of Edwin Grozier's *Boston Post* and was reported to be a mighty fellow when whiskey doings were toward in the Bell in Hand in Pi Alley. But the Harvard undergraduates were aware of Copey and delighted in him at an early date, and the word that his talents transcended those of the mere pedagogical attracted a wide following.

Most of his instruction in the writing of English was conducted, not in the classrooms of Seaver and Harvard Halls, but in his own ancient chambers in Hollis. Here surrounded by a store of bibelots and antiquities fit to stock a wing in Boston Museum and in the light of outmoded gas lamps he inspired generations of students to the admiration of English letters as probably no schoolmaster has done in the history of academic America. Students were forced to read their work aloud to him. If the composition was not up to his requirements the little man would writhe in his chair. "Oh-h-h, my God," he would mutter faintly, "what have I done to deserve this!"

Groves of the Academe

If a period was ponderous and maladroit he would instruct the youth, "Write in the margin: 'March of the elephants.'" When a sentence was heavy with qualifying clauses and involved as one of President Harding's speeches, he would say with deceptive sweetness, "Write in the margin: 'Teacher says, eschew the swag-bellied sentence.'" Willard Huntington Wright, Kenneth MacGowan, Conrad Aiken, Heywood Broun, Walter Edmonds, Robert Benchley and hundreds of others who were undergraduates during the first thirty years of the century suffered under his almost sadistically sarcastic tongue.

Professor Copeland was famous also for his capacity for causing acute embarrassment to students who disturbed his classrooms. Even the most discreet cougher was summarily ordered to "join the birds outside in the Yard." "Peace, peace, perturbed spirit," was his admonition to an undergraduate who shifted from seat to seat throughout a lecture; and "What will you have with your tea?" once constituted his greeting to a fluttery youth who arrived late for a seminar. Copey's crusty manners, however, were universally recognized as the mask behind which he concealed an affectionate and at times even sentimental personality.

Copey's rooms on the third and fourth floors of Hollis Hall in the Harvard Yard were almost as famous an institution as Professor Copeland himself. On the third floor was his office, a drab room, barely furnished, which was used at infrequent intervals and only on the most formal occasion, but on the fourth floor was the mellow study in which visitors were received, themes criticized, and where many of his historic readings were given. With the passage of years, the informality in which these readings were conceived came to assume a ritualistic aspect of its own. Only the most privileged of Copey's protégés were allowed to sit admiringly on the floor, while celebrities, summoned by an invitation which amounted to an imperial command, occupied the posts of honor on chairs and sofas. The late Mrs. Minnie Maddern Fiske always attended these sessions when in Boston. President Lowell, Owen Wister and other men of letters were frequent visitors.

His favorite passages for reading on these occasions were from the Bible, Kipling, Dickens, Shakespeare or Robert Benchley, for whose humor his admiration was unbounded. He read rhythmically, with slow, clear accentuation of every significant word and phrase, and while he read the fall of a pin could be clearly heard. His hearers often wept when he recited "John Anderson, My Jo."

His classes were combination side-shows and instruction periods. They were seldom formal recitation hours. He would talk at length upon whatever subject at the moment interested him, and it was invariably of interest to his students. Professor Copeland partook of the natures of the actor and showman. His references were always perfect, his anecdotes ironic in the extreme. His fierce assaults upon the weaknesses of his students were often terrifying in their understanding of human vanities, and Alexander Woollcott testified that for years after he was out of Harvard, Heywood Broun, at sight of Copey, would shift uneasily from one foot to another, "like an elephant with something on its mind."

Professor Copeland's appearance in the lecture platform was diminutive, but partook of invincible dignity. His mild eyes assumed a purely fictional fierceness behind large, shell-rimmed glasses, and in his majestic passage from Hollis to the other buildings of the Yard, and even in the finest weather, he invariably appeared with a square crowned Derby hat and neatly furled umbrella. His boiled shirts, of an outmoded style with stiff collars attached, had to be specially laundered for him by August, and so consular was his deportment, once encased in one of these arrangements, that, as Witter Bynner once said of Henry Van Dyke, he could fairly strut sitting down. For years complete mystery surrounded his eating habits, although in the old days when, quoting Artemus Ward as he used to put it: "Harvard University was pleasantly and conveniently situated in the bar-room of Parker's in School Street," he frequently patronized that historic establishment. Tradition has it that his breakfast was daily hoisted to his window in a box with a pulley arrangement manipulated by a local restaurant runner, but nobody ever saw this machine in action.

He would never allow electric light or telephone connections to be installed in his rooms at Hollis, although as a concession to progress he tolerated steam-heat. For years his mail was brought upstairs every morning by Mrs. Sidert, his aged and faithful charwoman, because postal regulations forbade the delivery of letters above the second floor and Copey steadfastly refused to descend in search of it.

"I have the largest personal mail in Cambridge," he used to say proudly, although Kelley, the Harvard Yard mailman, was heard on occasion to state that it was largely advertising.

Although afraid of fire and professing to believe that Hollis Hall was a fire-trap, Copey would never abandon his rooms there, and after he retired, the University permitted him still to live in his historic quarters for several years before his doctor made him retire to a more modern but less flavorsome flat off Harvard Square.

"I can see the headlines now," he used to say. "One of these fine mornings all the Boston papers will read: 'Copey a Crisp.' "

As recently as the fall of 1929 a slight blaze did occur

in the next entry of Hollis, and Copey, awakened from his sleep and clad in a quilted bath robe, leaned from his window and quavered,

"Fireman, fireman, don't come tracking through my clean rooms with your muddy boots."

The residents in Professor Copeland's entry in Hollis lived in perpetual apprehension of his descents upon their studies in the interest of greater quiet. When Copey was entertaining and especially if he was reading, no water might be drawn for fear of noisy plumbing, no doors were to be slammed, and musical endeavors and singing were strictly interdicted. On other occasions he was impervious to any sort of uproar.

Copey's friends never forgot him after they had left Harvard, and he corresponded regularly with a large number of his former students. In New York an organization known as the Charles Townsend Copeland Association was formed of his more intimate acquaintances, and once a year a solemn banquet is still tendered him at the Harvard Club. On the day after the dinner, Copey will lunch less formally with his friends and read them selections from his favorite books. This is one of the few occasions upon which he can be induced to leave Cambridge, and he is very proud of his annual honor.

It must not be assumed, on the strength of the Copey legend, however, that Harvard Yard swarms with eccentric gaffers, or that the half religious reverence of the community for individuality is carried to wild-eyed extremes. There is a close parallel between the attitude of Boston and Cambridge toward their "characters" and that of the feelings of savages for the demented, whom they regard as the special children of God. The lunatic devisings of Copey, the militant latinity of Professor E. K. Rand, who has a penchant for delivering after-dinner addresses in the lan-

Groves of the Academe

guage of the Cæsars, and the irresistible urge which at times floods the being of Professor George Lyman Kittredge to knock off with a walking stick the hats of young men who fail to uncover in his presence are scarcely representative of the ordered academic atmosphere of the Harvard cloisters.

Although it has never been exploited in the name of democracy as has the club system of Princeton, and while the Porcellian is, perhaps, less synonymous with the high-minded *Sturm und Drang* idealism of undergraduate loyalties than Yale's Skull and Bones, Harvard's hierarchy of clubs is important both as a factor in College life and as a not inconsiderable influence in the latter world of Boston.

The two leading clubs, Porcellian and A.D., have of recent years contributed many of the most powerful members of the Harvard board of overseers and corporation, and the commercial and professional life of Boston is shot through with a skein of allegiances and prejudices dating from club elections in Linden and Mount Auburn Streets. Harvard clubs are gentlemen's associations and nothing more. They eschew the nightshirt and jack o'lantern rituals of adolescent societies on other campuses and confine their activities to the amenities of social intercourse, but the flavor of their essential characters survives graduation and they are more influential in the destinies of the University through their alumni memberships than might at first seem probable.

The Porcellian, dating from 1791 and ranking as the most important of student social organizations, is the beau-ideal around whose example most Harvard clubs have been founded and modeled, and A.D., at one time affiliated with the national fraternity of Alpha Delta Phi, but long since autonomous, is second in prestige and desirability. A lesser but still distinctive cachet of smartness derives from membership in the Fly, Phoenix-S-K, Spee and Delphic Clubs,

215

the last named of which boasts an impressive list of non-Boston graduates, including members of the Morgan and Stillman families of New York and a consequent solvency which enables undergraduates to drink its own mark of champagne at dinner nightly in its clubhouse in the shaded seclusion of Linden Street. Roosevelts have for several generations been members of the Fly, and other distinguished American families have favored various clubs with their patronage over a period of generations. Usually, although not of necessity, membership in a good Harvard club prerequires a certain financial standing. Their appointments incline toward the luxurious, and at one time joint members of the Porcellian and A.D. maintained an aged negro cab driver called Nappy whose sole duty was to ferry members from one clubhouse to the other, a distance of half a block, in the frequent event of their being unable to navigate it afoot.

One other Harvard club, the celebrated and outrageous Med-Fac, which still to this day exists with a secret membership of but three or four undergraduates each year, commands attention as an organization devoted to tumult and commotion. Early in the nineteen hundreds the Med-Fac forwarded to Tsar Nicholas of the Russias a handsomely engrossed certificate of honorary membership in their scientific sounding organization, and bestowed upon him all the rights and privileges thereto pertaining. The Tsar's chamberlain graciously accepted on behalf of his august master and, as a return token, sent the Med-Fac Society of Harvard University a complete set of the most approved surgical instruments cast in solid platinum!

While Harvard has never been, and very probably never will be coeducational, save during the summer school invasion of Copey's "sexually unemployed," there is Radcliffe close by to support the humanities upon the distaff side. A very low percentage of Radcliffe girls marry at all, but an astonishingly high percentage of those who do marry Harvard men. Radcliffe has the same faculty as Harvard and the President of Harvard signs Radcliffe's diplomas, but it has its own president, of consular rank, an office graced for many years by Ada Louise Comstock, whose name has become synonymous with the high intellectual standards of her university. There is little of the romantic about the Radcliffe "type," if such a thing may be said to exist, and if the young ladies of its cloisters yearn, at times, for a Lochinvar to ride out of the west, the trappings of his horse will assuredly jingle with Phi Beta Kappa keys.

Before Dr. Comstock's day, the President of Radcliffe was Le Baron Russell Briggs who, in a manner of speaking, made Radcliffe College for her to bring to its subsequent academic flowering. His tall, stooped figure, invariably topped by a battered brown felt hat (known as a Harvard hat and deriving from the shop of J. August, the haberdasher, they were vintage chapeaux and reached their best maturity after a decade of wearing) and carrying a green cloth bag of books, he was, somehow, the archetypal kindly, and in his last years, absent-minded professor. It was as Dean of Harvard College, however, rather than as President of Radcliffe that he achieved his greatest fame.

The Massachusetts Institute of Technology, Harvard's distinguished neighboring academy, was founded in 1861 by William Barton Rogers who was its first president and a scientist of distinction. From a small land grant college in Boston it has grown, architecturally, to an imposing array of structures regimented along the Cambridge banks of the Charles. Seventeen branches of scientific endeavor are taught within its halls and laboratories, including most known

Boston and the Boston Legend

fields of engineering, chemistry, architecture and biology, and it is generally regarded as the first of all scientific schools in America.

Tech, as it is locally known for the sake of brevity, occupies a somewhat less prominent place in the purely urban scene of Boston than does Harvard, if for no other reason than that its academic requirements are so exacting as to preclude most forms of extramural activity. But in engineering and other professional circles the reputation of being a Massachusetts Tech man is one of the highest recommendations available to an aspirant for such a career. In its social existence, as in its classrooms, Tech is a separate, self-sufficient unit, participating little in the life of the town and recruiting very few of its students from the rarified atmosphere of Commonwealth Avenue or Brookline. It does not contribute to the list of eligibles for dances at the Chilton Club, and only at infrequent intervals does it intrude upon the front pages with civic tumult and commotion. Once a year its leading physicists weigh the world with their laboratory apparatus for the benefit of the news photographers or determine the coefficient of expansion of the opera hat, but these are its sole gestures toward public suffrage. And unless the theory of values or the laws of ballistics should become subjects for popular discussion as manifestations of some yet unforeseen super-culture, Bostonians will continue to view the youths of Tech with the slightly startled respect they would accord a synthesis of Nicola Tesla and Merlin.

Elsewhere Boston teems with institutions of higher, lower and specialized education almost to the extent it teems with hospitals. There is Boston Latin School, the first public school, as the term is now known, in the United States, with a long and handsome record of scholarship and graduates of fame behind it; there is Tufts College, founded in the

Groves of the Academe

fifties near Medford by a group of Universalists, which today includes Jackson College for Women, schools of medicine, dentistry, theology and engineering and a number of other more or less precise sciences; there is Simmons College, where since 1902 women have been taught household economics, secretarial work, horticulture and nursing, and which includes in its academic economy the Boston Cooking School, whence stems Fannie Farmer's Boston Cook Book, established Bible of a hundred thousand American kitchens; there is Wellesley College in the more elegant suburbs, devoted to giving "young women opportunities for education equivalent to those provided in colleges for young men," and famous for its hoop-rolling, social superiority and contributions to the ranks of the country's more representative bluestockings. There is, too, a Conservatory of Music, a Portia Law School dedicated to the evolution of female barristers, and there are innumerable schools of law, elocution, medicine, nursing and accountancy. A modern time spirit may have dissolved a perceptible portion of the sweetness of classical erudition so earnestly recommended by Matthew Arnold, but it has by no means extinguished the light of learning in Boston. As the rustic exclaimed proudly at the dedication of the new district schoolhouse, "Booklarning, we sure have got it."

Chapter XXI

HARBOR-FRONT

The water-front of Boston is ancient without being whimsical, for it has never occurred to the shipwrights, chandlers, sailmakers and fishermen who for three hundred years have inhabited its precincts to contribute archness to their locale. Probably its salvation derives from the circumstance that, in spite of a few attempts to invest it with old-world charm, no one has ever been able to convince Boston that the harbor-front was an oddity. Town and city, all things have come to it from the sea: governors and churchmen and troops, fortune and the wealth of China seas, and tides and shipping, like time and the seasons, are an essential part of the record and the scene.

When Leif Ericson in his stout wave-walker first spanned the Atlantic whale road of the Norse kennings almost a thousand years since, the saga relates that he came upon

Harbor-Front

a river which flowed through a lake into the sea and that there were heavily wooded islands in the lake. It may well enough have been Boston Harbor, first port of call in the voyage to Vineland the Good, and a bronze statue in the mall of Commonwealth Avenue commemorates that hypothesis of the antiquarians. For Boston Harbor was once a pastoral study in green and blue, like the shores of Irish ports from the decks of liners, and after a bright and restless noontide in the history of commerce it reclaimed some of its earlier and less fevered qualities.

In its outer reaches there are still the islands, which may have heard the rowing songs of Leif's earls and seen the shield wall of his vessel as it shifted up the harbor on the flood-tide long ago, but they are no longer thickly wooded and some of them have been reduced by erosion to mere shoals. In the case of Nix's Mate where there once was room to hang pirates and accommodate a fair-size gallery of witnesses, there is no more than space for a channel beacon.

It is along Atlantic Avenue that the life of the water-front flows fullest and it is here that the record of the town's seafaring greatness seems most imperishably engrossed in a synthesis of traditions, associations, ship chandlers and a pervading and perennial odor of fish. It is along Atlantic Avenue that the great wharfs stood or to this day stand which brought the world's commerce to Boston in the past century and still bring a by no means negligible trade to her commission merchants. Many of the harbor-front buildings are raised on pilings, standing out into the harbor as the homes of lake-dwellers once stood in prehistoric meres, with galleries of small stores, offices and such, one above another in uneven courses, and reached by stairways sprawling up the outside wall of the structure itself. There are multitudinous tokens of the sea; here and there an old-fashioned

Boston and the Boston Legend

sign announcing "wharfinger," the prows of excursion vessels and coastwise ships moored within arm's reach of the sidewalk, their hawsers slack with the full tide, cargo hoists and booms swinging in arcs above the pier-sheds, shops filled to the windows with ship's stores, coils of hemp cable, compasses, sea boots, Gloucester oilskins, officers' blue jackets, handbooks of navigation, fish-forks, bale-hooks and marine equipment of a thousand sorts.

And there are the fishing boats themselves, not only the trim handsomely raked schooners fresh from the banks with their holds filled with cod and haddock, but the modest punts of Italians propelled by asthmatic two-cylinder engines, which bring their daily haul direct to the ultimate consumer and sell their catch from the deck or a shelter on an adjacent pier.

Ever a town for doing its own marketing without trusting to the agency of housekeepers or clerks, Boston comes to the water-front (when it doesn't go to Welch's in Charles Street) for its fish as it has for more than two hundred years. Epicures and Italian housewives in shawls prod appraisingly at the hake and weakfish, butterfish, tinker mackerel, flounders, sea-bass and red snappers, and bargain with Yankee shrewdness in a manner fit to addle the wits of the toilers of the sea. Here, too, is available that peculiar Boston sea-food, the scrod, which is in reality a juvenile codfish cleaned in a peculiar manner to emphasize the flakey texture of the flesh, and the swordfish, the first catch of which each season is chronicled at length in the public prints and attracts as much attention over Boston dinner-tables as the first Delaware shad does elsewhere.

The oysters which Bostonians will tell you are the finest in the world, despite the outraged anguish of Philadelphians for their seatags and Lynnhavens and of the French for their Biscayan and cupric shell fish, are known by the gen-

222

eral term of Cape Cod. They may come from Wellfleet or Oyster Harbor or Cotuit, the last of these being esteemed by connoisseurs the most delicately flavored because of the auspicious percentage of fresh spring water which flows in the salt tides where they are dredged. The oysters of the Cape come in brine-weeping barrels, along with huge hogsheads of eels, daily by the New Haven's fish trains, to be transshipped at Boston and raced by expresses over cleared tracks to the market centers of the country. Only Delaware with its shad, the Virginia Tidewater with its terrapin and the Florida gulf with its pompano can compare with New England as the gastronomic capital of the world of fish. Symbol of deep-water supremacy and of good living from earliest times, old Bostonians were accustomed to ornament their homes with codfish built into the wainscoting, and to this day it is associated with the civilization of New England as is no other distinguishing or characteristic hallmark. A few years since an enthusiastic commissioner of motor vehicles caused a white codfish to be incorporated in the license plates of Massachusetts automobiles, but a deal of innocent merriment at his expense followed and, after a single interlude, the custom was allowed to decline.

Few people viewing Boston Harbor realize that as part of its apparently limited expanse there is a navigable water frontage of eight miles with more than five times that distance of berthing space. The largest dry-dock in the world is located at South Boston and the most extensive of fish piers sometimes sees the daily loading of a million pounds of sea haul dredged from the uneasy water of the Grand and Western Banks and the nearer depths of the continental littoral frequented by sword fishermen.

Atlantic Avenue was laid out, as it stands today, along the line of the old Barricado, a sort of combination breakwater and bastion which was built across the harbor cove shortly after the middle of the seventeenth century. It extended from the South Battery, near Rowe's Wharf, to Scarlett's, near the Battery Wharf of modern times. In the early part of last century, when Long Wharf and T Wharf reached more than a thousand feet into the harbor, the Barricado bisected them in the middle of their extent.

The most famous of Boston's great piers, Long Wharf, has been a feature of the harbor-front since the first decade of the eighteenth century when the twenty-four proprietors of the project drew up a divisional deed of possession of the store lots along the north side of the structure. The first six hundred feet of the pier were finished by 1715 and the stores occupied by a variety of tenants, mostly, to be sure, proprietors of taverns. Alfred Anderson's saloon was a famous resort in its time and stood on the Atlantic Avenue corner. At the direction of the selectmen, one of the town's "watter engines" for fire-prevention purposes was stored on Long Wharf for many years. Governor Jonathan Belcher owned the first store on the wharf, the Crown Coffee House, whose landlord, Thomas Selby, combined the callings of host and the leading periwig-maker of the Colony.

The Crown Coffee House was very much a part of early Boston. It was the town's greatest gossip shop, and old man Selby retailed wigs, stone ale and information on the private lives of the citizenry with fine impartiality and a nice eye to effect. Sea-faring men who wanted a quick one might stop by at Anderson's, but the Crown was favored by the knowing, who absorbed stone fence, a beverage compounded in New England of hard cider and brandy or applejack, and backyard anecdotes by the hour. The Crown was also an auction gallery of some importance and Selby was forever thinking up sales. William Price, the undertaker, there inaugurated subscriptions for copperplate engravings of the town. It took a couple of years for delivery, since the

E H Suydam
Old T Wharf
Boston

ON T WHARF

pictures were drawn and printed in England, but they were highly admired by everyone, and a few of his various "prospects of the Town, curiously engraven by the best hand," are still in the possession of the historical societies. Somebody, apparently, stole Selby's best hat upon one occasion, as an advertisement in the public prints records: "Lately taken from the Crown Coffee House in Boston, a good new Beaver Hatt, never dressed, with a hole burnt in the brim about the bigness of a pea. Whoever brings the same to Mr. Selby at the Coffee House shall receive 10s reward."

Long Wharf throughout its history seems to have been a favorite location for tap-rooms, and it sometimes seems to antiquarians going through the records that half of Boston's archives consist of petitions allowing or disallowing the sale of strong drink there. In the nineties of the nineteenth century, the wharf policeman of the time asserted, there were more drunks on Long Wharf on a windy day than in all the rest of Boston. Bad weather drew water-front characters to the pothouses in droves.

The first trans-Atlantic steamers on regular schedules began sailing from Boston in the early forties, and it was upon the occasion of the departure of the first Cunarder in the Boston-Liverpool service that the vessel was icebound in the lower harbor. So great was the enthusiasm of the town for the innovation of steam that a thousand men were employed for sixty hours cutting a channel through the ice for her to the open water beyond.

There have, at times, been attempts, largely unsuccessful, to invest Boston's water-front with quaintness and a cachet of old world charm. During the years of prohibition the town's most fashionable night club was located in a loft at the end of T Wharf. It had the advantage of a narrow single staircase up which raiding federal agents could come but one at a time, thus providing ample opportunity for the disposal of illegal refreshments out the window and into the harbor below. Befuddled guests and members, however, were forever tossing themselves along with their pocket flasks into the midnight waters under the pier and a special guard was maintained on Saturday nights to fish the unwary from the tide before they should drown.

About the same time a small group of determined Bohemians decided that T Wharf would be an admirable background for life in a manner less conventional than that of Beacon Street. A lady artist rented a studio in the loft, and although it smelled forever faithfully of fish, the presence of the odor was, to a certain extent, compensated by the knowledge that Peter Faneuil and Stephen Minot had owned the place in 1718. Within a few years sixteen families had made the wharf their home. They pushed candles into the necks of bottles, hung fragments of seines on the walls, and wore canvas trousers and Basque fishermen's jerseys. They became accustomed, they said, to the fish, nor were they disturbed by the horns and whistles which made the waterfront a bedlam on foggy days. T Wharf developed a distinctly literary character and there was a lady novelist under every beam. The Sunday papers insisted on it. The precedent had been set by Nathaniel Hawthorne when he wrote his *Twice Told Tales* in the old salt house whenever he could escape from his odious job, weighing goods, at the Customs House up the street.

It would be a mistake to insist too harshly that T Wharf had lost its greatness. It is still useful. At one time fishing-boat center of Boston, it lost that distinction when the prodigious Fish Pier and refrigerating plant were built in 1916 at South Boston. There are, however, at the older wharf, a number of gaudily painted fishing schooners owned by Italians. During the day, the spot is agreeably filled with activity. In summer, the end of the wharf is crowded with autoists who go there for the best view of the inner harbor.

At this point the harbor is comparatively narrow, and on both sides is spiked with docks until it converges at the Charlestown Navy Yard, at the junction of the Charles and Mystic Rivers. From the East Boston side, which had only eight inhabitants in 1833 and is now one of the most crowded areas in the city, planes rise over the harbor from the airport, and cut across the city past the Custom House tower. The tower, of course, dominates the water-front, and Boston will never be indifferent to its height of five hundred amazing feet.

In one of the attic lofts, the Boston Pilots have their headquarters. There are twenty-four of these men and they cruise for a week at a time in a two-masted auxiliary schooner around Boston Lightship, seventeen miles out from the inner harbor. In the most violent weather they wait down there for incoming ships. They pilot, on an average, five vessels a day into port. In the fog they may hear the whistle sounded from a steamer. They go out toward her, send out a yawl with a pilot and two apprentice boys to do the rowing. The young fellows spend about eight years at odd jobs before they are allowed to take a ship into her berth.

Several other wharves, Constitution and Lewis, along Atlantic Avenue are interesting for their associations, although they are unprepossessing and grimy establishments.

It was from the Atlantic Avenue wharf, whose arc lamps sputtered fitfully in the famous late November blizzard of 1898, that the steamer *Portland* backed slowly into the strong running tide of the harbor on a voyage that was to scatter the bodies of her passengers and crew along half the beaches of Cape Cod before the next sunrise. The *Portland* ended in sixty fathoms of black water somewhere in Massachusetts Bay, and the only salvage, hauled in by a fisherman's trawl months later, was a piece of gingerbread work from her wheel house, an electric light fixture from her main saloon, and a woman's garter. Forty other vessels foundered that night between Newfoundland and the Virginia Capes, and the *Portland,* sailing against the orders of the harbor captain of the line, last showed her lights off Cape Ann. Somewhere in the night she went under, the water flooding her bunkers through the sprung half-ports, and rising to her decks and gangways as the dynamos failed and the lights went out. No single person survived to tell just what happened as the ultimate cascade of black ocean water swept down over the Turkey carpets of her main staircase while wan and futile signal rockets curved up from the smashed bridge, but a hundred and sixty persons drowned in a marine disaster which made the name of the *Portland* synonymous with dramatic tragedy.

No wires were able to stand the weight of ice and sleet on Cape Cod that night, and a special train was made up next morning at North Truro to bring in the news of the disaster. The New Haven's heavy Pacific-type locomotive battered for hours against the drifts to carry its chronicle of disaster to the newspaper offices of Washington Street.

Of the islands nearby, Castle Island is the most pretentious. There is a fortress on it, and civic greenery set out for mothers and fathers and babies who steam quietly together on hot summer afternoons. For two hundred years a chain was strung between it and Governor's Island, across the way, and could be raised on a windlass at the approach of enemy ships. The fort was used in the Revolution and as late as the Spanish-American War it was looked upon as a safeguard against a Spanish armada. Boastfully, the newspapers of the time announced that "Boston's coast defenses are in good condition."

Harbor-Front

There is today an easy serenity to the harbor scene. Rusty tramp steamers roll slowly up the channel. Tankers lie at anchor awaiting clearance. The snow-white vessels of the United Fruit Company arrive and depart on precise schedules. Cunarders and White Star liners berth in East Boston for a few hours each week.

The spacious days of Boston's water-front lapsed with the passing of the gallant clippers and the China trade, the bearded masters and the top-hatted merchants of Topliff's Reading Rooms, but the flavor is there, and the tradition, and the tides recurrently whisper about the piles of its piers of the brave times when all that was best in Boston went down to the sea in ships.

Chapter XXII

GOOD KING WENCESLAS

BOSTON, as the whole world is aware, is not without its Englishisms. They are as invariably associated with the town as its classic dish at Saturday night supper, its swanboats in the Public Garden or its established penchant for attending funerals at Trinity Church. There is the clipped accent of speech and the somehow interrogatory inflection with which even the most casual observation is vocally invested. There is the tradition which requires the name of Pierce, the grocer, to be pronounced to rhyme with hearse. There is the roast beef and Yorkshire pudding quality of Sunday dinner, served at noon, the belief in the sanctity of the family and the curious old-world habits of living within one's income and paying one's debts. And there is Christmas Eve and carols on Beacon Hill.

Nowhere else in America is there anything like this peculiarly Bostonian observance and few enough places in

230

Good King Wenceslas

England today where the established custom is so closely and, in its own way compellingly followed. Something more than forty years ago a youthful Unitarian clergyman named Shurtleff lived in his father's home in West Cedar Street. The Rev. Alfred D. Shurtleff took pleasure in the old customs and, although his friends across the narrow thoroughfare laughed tolerantly at him, he got into the habit of placing a welcoming candle in his study window to guide the way, not only for the Child of Christmas, but also for the awakening of the consciousness of an entire community to the old and beautiful observances of the season. In a few years, led by other clergymen of the neighborhood, scores of residents of the Hill lighted up their windows every year at this time and the custom spread through all quarters of the city, to little Italy on Copp's Hill and the homes of leisure and affluence on Commonwealth Avenue.

In was in 1907 that Ralph Adams Cram, Boston's distinguished architect and a faithful student of the customs of other times, persuaded Hollis French and a few other acquaintances to venture out into a snowy Christmas Eve and sing "Adeste Fideles" up and down the length of Chestnut Street, and it was in this way that Boston came to hear her first twentieth century carols. The following year the choir of the Church of the Advent followed Mr. Cram's example and sang "God Rest Ye, Merry Gentlemen," and "Good King Wenceslas" under the window of the rector, and from then till now Beacon Hill has always had its lights and its carols at Christmas.

Eight o'clock in the evening finds the Hill illuminated, populous and expectant. Traffic has been stopped on all its streets. Usually there is snow on the ground. Hundreds of sightseers in decorous holiday mood overflow Mount Vernon and Chestnut Streets, throng against the iron rails of Louisburg Square and jostle each other amiably in South Russell

Street. Here and there is an opulent sable wrap or gleaming dinner-shirt and top-hat, but largely the crowd is dressed less for a festival than for a semi-religious occasion. The atmosphere is by no means solemn but composed and respectful.

No self-respecting householder would fail to contribute something to the illuminations that night. There are candles in every window, real wax candles, some hand-dipped and bayberry scented, but all gleaming tapers. Neither the electric light company nor the fire department has been able to arouse much enthusiasm for a modern substitute. In some houses there are hundreds, rising tier on tier along the sills and sashes. In many homes they have been arranged behind holy scenes in colored glass panels or the house coat armor done in leaded panes. Apartment-dwellers have drawn back their curtains and wreathed their candles with holly and mistletoe.

The front doors of some houses stand open and liveried servants are on hand to receive friends and visitors. In such places it is often the custom to place the family treasures on view, and the best silver, Copley paintings, pewter ware and rare brocades brought home from the China trade by Great Uncle Handasyd in the time of Houqua are ranged around the front hall. There are probably refreshments, claret cup and iced cakes, cress sandwiches and Medford rum in the dining-room, and open house doesn't mean just old friends alone. The evidence of a knowing interest in an Asher Benjamin staircase or the desire to examine at close range the Staffordshire over the Holland brick fireplace will secure a warm welcome for the most complete stranger. The Hill and its possessions are a loan exhibit to the public this evening.

The warrant for all this hospitality and congress of townsfolk is, however, the carol singers themselves. In groups of ten or fifteen and under the leadership of some

Good King Wenceslas

experienced chorister, they wander through the streets, usually according to prearranged routes and schedules so as not to interfere with each other's programs or leave neglected any street or mall. If there are ill or aged who have specially asked for Christmas music the singers pause before their homes, but mainly the singing is for no individuals but for all to hear and enjoy.

All the old familiar tunes are to be heard, "The First Noel" and "It Came Upon the Midnight Clear," "Oh, Little Town of Bethlehem" and "Silent Night" and even a few in Latin and the older plainsong chants. The leader of each group carries aloft an ancient storm lantern upon a pole and sometimes the singers wear the long cloaks and steeple crowned hats of their ancestors. It is a solemn and memorable scene to strangers who have come long distances and to Bostonians who have come to consider it one of the most secure of their traditions. By and by the last measures of "Come All Ye Faithful" and "Star of Wonder" are carried down the midnight wind. The crowds disperse under the cold blue radiance of the arc lamps on the snow. The bell of the Church of the Advent strikes twelve measured notes and is answered across the muted city by the bell of the North Church, and Christmas Eve has come to Boston and gone for another year.

Chapter XXIII

SYMPHONY

THE story is told of a charming and cultivated woman, born and educated abroad as the child of Boston parents. A few years since she resolved to return to the city of her ancestors and take the place in the life of the Back Bay to which she was entitled by her birth and personal accomplishments. Established in the Mount Vernon Street mansion where her great grandparents had entertained Samuel Adams, she determined to invite the many Boston women who had been her parents' friends to an initial luncheon party, and sent out invitations naming a winter Friday for her hospitality. It took her a long time to live down the error and have it forgotten. For Friday is Symphony day in Boston and nobody ever entertains at luncheon the next to the last day of the week.

Symphony in Boston is ritual, an integral and venerated

234

part of the formal scheme of things and as essential to the social and spiritual well-being of Marlborough Street and Harvard Yard as the Arnold Arboretum or the lectures of the Lowell Institute. Friday afternoons during the season assume the aspect of local holy days dedicated to the classics and a vast craning of necks to be certain that the Hallowells and Forbses are in their accustomed stalls, and the conductor of the Boston Symphony Orchestra, *ex officio,* takes his place as a first citizen beside the Bishop of the Diocese and the President of Harvard University. To be allowed to contribute to the annual deficit of the concerts held in the bleak Huntington Avenue Auditorium is esteemed a privilege only ranked by the honor, successively accorded to each of the trustees of the Massachusetts Humane Society, of footing the bill for that organization's magnificent yearly banquets.

To see the most representative parade of the real Boston a visitor must go to Symphony on Friday afternoon. There is another concert each week on Saturday evening, but that is not the ritual observance, and no other regular festival in the calendar, neither the race days at Brookline Country Club in June nor Sunday church parade down the Mall of Commonwealth Avenue, nor even the mass meetings occasionally held in Old South Meeting House in the interest of some momentarily blazing humanitarian cause, has quite the authenticity of texture, the precise conviction of sanctification characteristic of the audience at Friday Symphony.

The winter season of 1881–82 in Boston was notable in more ways than most. For one thing, the first incandescent lamps to be seen in New England were installed in the public rooms of the Vendome Hotel in Dartmouth Street, where their glowing filaments were viewed with a mixture of pride and terror by the world of fashion which glided in a swirl of bustles, fringes, trimmings and flounces with outriders in Albert watch chains and weeper whiskers among its potted

Boston and the Boston Legend

palms, gilt mirrors and marble and ormolu splendors. Then, too, Thompson's Spa, the town's most celebrated ordinary and later the largest counter-lunch in the world, inaugurated its career opposite General Taylor's *Boston Globe* offices in Washington Street. It was the beginning of the quick lunch in a conservative, Bostonian manner. It was also the year in which Porfirio Diaz, the Mexican dictator, visited town. The precise matters which brought him there were never announced, but a singularly profitable flurry in mining stocks followed closely upon the auspicious event. And it was the season which welcomed the first concert of the Boston Symphony Orchestra.

Prior to this time music in Boston had been primarily represented by the Harvard Musical Association and the Handel and Haydn Society, the focal point of their endeavors having been the old Music Hall of the New England Conservatory of Music. But Major Henry L. Higginson, the Boston Maecenas of the era, felt that these organizations, supported at irregular intervals by wandering minstrelsy of uncertain antecedents, was insufficient for the then Athens of America, and, under his patronage, the Boston Symphony Orchestra came into being.

Since that time, under direction good, bad and altogether indifferent, through schism, strife and upheaval and in a generation that with mingled emotions found on its programs that Stravinsky's "Symphony of Psalms" had been written for its fiftieth anniversary, Symphony has been a *force majeur* before which all other obligations, engagements and musical allegiances in Boston have had to give way. It has become a legend almost every detail of which has its roots firmly imbedded in the soil of immutable reality. Seriously regarded by serious-minded people, it is perhaps Boston's most substantial basis in the twentieth century to claim to a cultural heritage.

Symphony

During the war its routine, until that time essentially Teutonic, was curiously revised to point in the direction of France. Dr. Karl Muck, the highly talented former Hofkapellmeister of the Berlin Opera, was hurled into jail at the clamor of the same rabble that howled that the dome of the State House should be painted a neutral color so as not to offer a target to German naval gunners, and an amiable mediocrity of French antecedents was installed in his place. During the reign of Pierre Monteux in the early twenties the celebrated musicians' strike at Symphony engaged the attention of a pop-eyed community. Upon one occasion the new radical spirit manifested itself to the horror of onlookers when the entire group of first violins refused to stand upon the entry of the conductor. Later that afternoon the managing editor of the *Boston Herald,* unaware of the cataclysm that had struck Huntington Avenue, overheard an angry muttering and bumbling from the office of Philip Hale, the *Herald's* music reporter. Mr. Hale was composing his review and endeavoring to express himself on the subject of the orchestral revolt in terms fit for a family paper. With a howl of anguish the managing editor dashed to the copy control desk and re-made his front page to include the dire intelligence of schism at Symphony as the leading local news story.

The retention, in 1924, of Serge Koussevitzky as conductor was, with the single exception of its actual founding, the most important event in the history of the organization. Finding the orchestra with its prestige seriously impaired by the Francomania of the patriots, its subscription list almost vanished, and its personnel verging on senile idiocy, Koussevitzky, by a series of radical executive and musical reforms, evolved from the lamentable material at first offered him a distinguished orchestra which, in a few short years, recaptured all the glamour of its vanished past.

Boston and the Boston Legend

Prokofiev, Stravinsky, Honegger and Copland appeared on the program. The subscription list exceeded all those of other years, and an extra series of concerts was actually added to the annual repertory. Boston still rather leans toward dead composers in the assurance that virtue alone can accomplish posthumous survival, but it knows at least that living composers exist, and Symphony, for all the suggestion of down-at-the-heels respectability of its audiences is, like the First National Bank, one of the vital going concerns of the town. Upon special occasions M. Koussevitzky himself has been known to perform concert solos on the double bass.

The shabby gentility of audiences in Symphony Hall is, as a matter of fact, only apparent. The right people who draw up to the Massachusetts Avenue entrance of a Friday in slightly faded and *démodé* motors of the most costly makes are dedicated to the perpetuation of low-heel shoes, Queen Mary bonnets, shirtwaists and chatelaine watches. Black broadcloth or modest tweeds have a decided edge on silver fox, just as the simplest of haddock chowder is established at the tables of affluent Bostonians who could easily, if they pleased, furnish forth Astrakhan sturgeon's roe on solid plate. The audience is largely feminine, what masculine element there is present deriving from the undergraduate and faculty ranks of Harvard or from the infinitely polite old gentlemen who spend the other afternoons of the week in the fastness of the stacks of the Athenaeum.

When the regular season of Symphony is over for the year and the members of the orchestra have retired to their studios where, almost to a man, they are engaged in the teaching of music, Boston's "little season" of May and June is celebrated in Symphony Hall by a series of somewhat less austerely classical performances known to the world as "Pops." These concerts are held in an atmosphere of beer

Symphony

garden informality which, while it may not recommend itself to the over-judicious, attracts capacity houses nightly for six or eight weeks to applaud handsomely for selections from "Rosenkavalier" and "Tales from Hoffman" and "The Bells of Saint Mary's" and "Overture: 1812." The orchestra itself is recruited from Symphony musicians and the concert master of the regular organization or a popular conductor is engaged for the season; the orchestra seats are torn up, and Verdi and Strauss are played in an atmosphere of cheer and beer and claret cup to patrons seated in fours and sixes at tables placed throughout the auditorium. Pops are an original Boston institution and vastly popular with the youths and maidens of local academies to whom the austerity of Symphony itself is something of a barrier. At Pops they may smoke and drink and visit from table to table in a *milieu* of decorous informality.

When Philip Hale was writing for the old *Boston Journal* (the date of this particular article is June 5, 1893), he saw the Pops with his usual indulgently satiric eye, yet with evident enjoyment of the scene and the music:

There was smoking, and there was drinking, and there was the sound of musical instruments of many kinds in Music Hall last Saturday evening. To change the bleak, shabby, cheerless hall into a "Dream of Elysian Delight," after the fashion of the final scene of a pantomime, would indeed be a hopeless task. Yet ingenuity had done much; and the scene, viewed from the balcony, was one of pleasing jollity.

The crowd was bent on pleasure, and the crowd was great. Mr. Adamowski was there. So were the faithful men under his baton. Marlborough Street sat by the side of Columbus Avenue. Neither was injured by the temporary proximity. The matron who at the strains of the waltz recalled the days of maidenhood was there. Governor Russell was there. The young man apparently created for the sole purpose of wearing this summer's broad and low straw hat was there.

The man with white whiskers was there, and he eyed approv-

Boston and the Boston Legend

ingly the beauty opposite, behind him and above him until he was reminded forcibly of the presence of his estimable wife. The lonely man was there, the man without friends, who welcomes a moment's chat with a waiter. The passing stranger who wonders at Boston and its inhabitants was there. And the mother and child was there. It was hot, and there was an unflagging demand for cooling drinks. The women drank strange, soft and sugary decoctions with pink, crimson and orange linings. If drops fell on their gowns, they laughed good-naturedly—that is, when there were men present. They did not object to tobacco smoke—oh, no, they were used to it; and they coughed violently from very delight.

There was a drawing of corks, and light wines cheered a little party. Young fellows with heavy sticks felt "real devilish" as they called for bottled beer. And the music accompanied the jest, the gossip, and business talk of those whom the black care follows everywhere, and mother's praise of favorite daughter, and daughter's timid answer and shy glance.

For lo, the winter is passed, the rain is over and gone, the flowers appeared on the earth, the time of singing birds has come, and the voice of the turtle is heard in our land; the fig-tree putteth forth her green figs and the vines with the tender grapes give a good smell; arise, my love, my fair one, and come to the Pops with me. And there be no talk of rubato and molto allegro, and dotted sixteenths, and temperament.

And Timothee, O son of long-oppressed Poland, look kindly this year, as in the past, on Strauss, Offenbach, Suppe, Waldteufel, Czibulka, and all other makers of gay, frivolous, heel-exciting, pulse-quickening, thirst-provoking tunes.

And to this day, interspersed among the youthful barbarians who actually laugh and light cigarettes during the *Eroica* can be seen a sprinkling of the real Bostonians, their tweeds, for the moment, shelved in favor of printed silks, their tailcoats for dinner jackets, cautiously ordering a half bottle of sauterne and appearing happy, in a conservative way, for waltzes and gaiety and springtime.

CHINATOWN

Chapter XXIV

ERIN GO BRAGH

FAMINE came to Ireland toward the middle of the nineteenth century. Not just the old accustomed failure of the crops, but famine that swept whole counties and countrysides with the potato blight which had first made its appearance in North America a few years before, and in many localities the entire harvests of 1848 were reduced to mere putrescent masses of vegetation. The British government instituted a dole of maize, and other relief agencies were organized, but the truth was growingly apparent that, during the past century and a half, the population of Ireland had far outstripped the facilities of industrial and agricultural production.

And so the Irish came to America, and because of the Queenstown-Boston sailing schedules of the Cunard Steamship Company most of them came to Boston.

241

Boston and the Boston Legend

A substantial Irish population in the Puritan town and city was nothing new. Fifty years before the Battle of Bunker Hill the Charitable Irish Society was a going concern, as it is today, but immigrating Irish by the steerage thousands was a new experience. They disembarked, the clay pipes of tradition in the green felt hatbands, at the great piers of the Boston water-front or at East Boston, as Noddle's Island was coming to be known, and they settled down, for the most part, within a stone's throw of the Cunard pierheads. As was natural with the various racial groups which arrived in Boston during the great waves of immigration, they clove strongly together geographically and socially as long as they were a minor element in the economic scene. They cared little enough for the countryside after the wasted fields of Kerry and Mayo and they had little enough curiosity about outlying reaches of the city, preferring the squalid intimacy of their shacks and tenements, so that the North End, East and later South Boston, became shabby, but joyous and at times riotous outposts of the Old Sod.

Few of them brought with them more than a pick and shovel—actually part of the baggage of early immigrants—a thick brogue and an epic capacity for work six days a week and tremendous whisky doings of a Saturday night. These and an unquestioning devotion to the Roman Catholic Church as represented in the person of the parish priest. But they were the new inheritors, and half a century later they had appropriated and adapted to their uses an impressive proportion of the Boston scene.

The first three decades of the twentieth century saw the Irish ascendancy in what was probably its fullest florescence, and the years after the World War found other races, deriving in background and ancestry from the Continent of Europe, making an increasingly successful bid for a place in the social, political and economic sun. Walking along Tre-

Erin Go Bragh

mont or Washington Streets today, three out of every four persons are either foreign-born or sprung from foreign-born parents. About half of these are of Anglo-Celtic stock, which means that about one out of three twentieth century Bostonians derives immediately from non-English speaking antecedents. This is a far cry from the entirely English community of the Puritan province, or even from the still essentially English city which emerged from the township in the early nineteenth century, but there are circumstances, peculiar to Boston alone of all American communities, which render these figures somewhat less conclusive than they may, at first sight, appear.

Two extraordinary circumstances from the beginning contributed to the rise of the Irish element in the midst of a community hitherto of almost purely British extraction. The Roman Catholic Church, which in the opening years of the nineteenth century was an almost negligible factor in Boston, found that in its rapid development and growth as the numbers of its followers increased, its ideals of human conduct were very closely parallel to those of the Puritan city itself. And the second and third generations of Boston Irish who found themselves successively in positions of power and authority in the municipal government and then in the business and professional structure of the city, far from aiming to destroy the social order in which they found themselves continually a more powerful group, were anxious to absorb and to perpetuate almost in its entirety the conservative creed of the sanctity of life and property and the dominance of religion which had always constituted its foundations.

Before the great wave of immigrations in the forties and fifties there had been no little persecution of Catholics in Boston, the most notable of the outrages being the burning in the early thirties of the Ursuline Convent in what is now Somerville. Relatively few members of the better element

Boston and the Boston Legend

in the community participated in the actual violence of the affair, but thousands of more or less responsible citizens looked on and lent the hoodlums their tacit approval.

The school had been established there amid beautiful surroundings on a slight rise of land and was attended almost entirely by daughters of Protestant families, but a whispering campaign was circulated against the sisters, and the burning of the convent followed. The Nativist movement, stimulated by economic conditions and fear of complete dominance of the Boston labor market by the rising tide of Irish, found its most extreme expression in the destruction of the school at Mount Benedict. There was no interference from the constituted authorities; the altar was profaned and the structure razed, while several nuns narrowly escaped with their lives. A number of first citizens, led by the Mayor, at once condemned the outbreak in a public meeting, but the damage was never repaired by the municipality.

The growing multitudes of Irish, however, as well as the Poles, Italians and French Canadians, lent their numbers to the support of the Roman Church, while the complete self-control of the Catholic clergy under incessant provocation served to widen their influence with all classes in the community.

No single figure in the history of Catholic Boston did more to assure the position of his church than Archbishop John J. Williams who, at the time of his death, had completed more than sixty years in the priesthood, forty of them in the episcopacy. Like Boston's first Irish Mayor, Hugh O'Brien, his successor in office, Patrick Andrew Collins, John Boyle O'Reilly of lettered fame, Thomas J. Garvin and Charles F. Donnelly and many other outstanding Irishmen of his generation, Archbishop Williams won his laurels of esteem and preëminence in the community on a basis of

WASHINGTON STREET, THE THEATRE DISTRICT

sheer merit. This first generation of Irish Boston boys had to measure themselves against the strongest Puritan competition and Yankee shrewdness in every field of endeavor, which is more than can be said for the generations that succeeded them.

It is the opinion of most informed students of the Boston scene that the cycle of Irish supremacy in Boston and Massachusetts politics has been completed and that new racial elements are already asserting themselves, notably the Poles and French-Canadians, both of whom have increased in vast numbers in the past twenty years. When they had overcome the Puritan opposition which forced them to put their best foot forward to achieve recognition, the Irish found they had lost their greatest incentive to enterprise. The strain ran thin and today, although it is usually the custom for large business and professional firms to take into their offices a certain number of the most promising young Irishmen as they graduate from Harvard or Boston College, the Irish element in politics and trade does not command the respect from their own countrymen that was accorded their predecessors of thirty years ago. The wheel has come, to a certain extent, full circle. Overmuch exploitation of race and religion brought into public and business affairs an element which had little or nothing else to recommend it, and the racial strains which, because they are underprivileged, are ever on the alert for advancement, have not failed to note and capitalize on this circumstance.

Socially the Irish long ago outgrew the lace curtain backgrounds of their fathers, just as they before them had abandoned the shamrock-planted shanties and Saturday night jigs and reels of the first immigrants. They moved up Commonwealth Avenue among the Forbeses and Searses and Paines, and up the slopes on Beacon Hill, until, in the persons of David Ignatius Walsh and James Michael Curley, they achieved the Massachusetts State House itself. The names of Phelan, Donnelly, Slattery, Giblin, Downing, Cahill, O'Hare, O'Donnell, Shea, Cotter and Madden have long been a part of the chronicles of the town's social doings, especially in the newspapers where the heads of these families, as executives in department stores, banks and utilities concerns, might control substantial advertising revenue. But it is not on record that such names as Mulvey or Flannery appear with any great frequency on the carefully checked invitation lists to débutante parties at the classic precincts of the ball-room of the Somerset, or that any but a Puritan Boston name is found in the membership list of the Myopia Hunt Club.

Illustrative, perhaps, of the rise to extraordinary political power in Boston of an ambitious and adroit son of Irish parents, whose beginnings as an orphan bootblack found him finally the wielder of complete control over the Democratic party in municipal affairs, was that of Martin M. Lomasney, the seventy-odd years of whose life saw the flowering and the first indications of impending decline of the Irish cycle.

With only the merest lick and a dab at education, Lomasney began as an errand boy, bootblack, messenger, laborer and finally as ward-heeler in the old West End district of the town in the sixties, the *cursus honorum* of the aspirant for political honors in the emergent Irish hierarchy. From city lamplighter to assistant to Michael Wells, Democratic boss during the Tilden-Hayes campaign in 1876, was an easy step, and when Wells died, young Lomasney already had the reigns of Democratic authority gathered in his capable and imaginative hands.

His famous Hendricks Club, named for the vice president

Erin Go Bragh

under Cleveland, became the source and fountainhead of all
Boston Democracy, and for three decades no candidate for
Congress from Lomasney's district was ever elected without
the sanction and endorsement of this organization. Lomasney, although he loathed the title, bestowed by a casual wag,
of The Mahatma, graciously accepted the post for his district in the Massachusetts Assembly every third term, just
to keep his hand in, and filled the intervening terms with
young hopefuls under his patronage. He held the balance of
power in most preëlection conferences and it was his strategy
to be non-committal as to his favorites until the last moment
before primaries. Ward, municipal and district politics were
almost his sole concern for fifty years and it is notable that,
unlike many other bosses of Irish antecedents, he contributed
neither wit, nor color nor spectacle to his delicate adjust-
ments of state. Uproar, ballyhoo and the spacious gesture he
knew not, and Boston was the less glamorous for his deficiency. Both John F. Fitzgerald who, because of his inevitable and unsolicited rendering of "Sweet Adeline" on
all public occasions, became known as "Honey Fitz," and
later, Mayor James Michael Curley, who made a very good
thing indeed out of the circumstance that he had once served
a jail term for taking a civil service examination "for a
friend," were more proficient in the art of self-exploitation.
When on campaign, Jim Curley, who was later to become, to
the amazement of all and the displeasure of many, governor,
was accustomed to cock an anticipatory ear for the inevitable
heckler who, from the crowd, would inquire the occasion for
his penal service. "I took an examination for the sake of an
old and beloved fri'nd, brother," and the candidate for office
would strike a martyred attitude amidst thunderous applause. There were those who asserted the heckling was a
preconceived campaign device to awaken sympathy in the

247

ever-loyal hearts of Kerry, Mayo and Cork among the electorate, and, in any event, it was a great success.

These were the figures in public view. Lomasney was the puppeteer.

Whether or not the Gaels will be able to hold their gains into the future, the Irish cycle has been one of the important phases of the Boston legend. It is indisputable in the light of the record that the twentieth century Irishmen in the public eye have been of less sturdy stuff than those of the seventies, eighties and nineties, whether in the field of religion, law, politics or finance. They have been impeached in public office. Since the failure of the Federal National Bank they have been more prone to trust their finances to others than to their own countrymen. It has been expedient in many cases for them to retain lawyers of Yankee origin, although Boston teems with Irish law practitioners.

Boston's City Hall politics have become synonymous with minor corruption and civic extravagance. It is common knowledge that an Irish mayor contributed materially to the subsequent collapse of one of the city's largest and oldest banks out of personal spite by causing a run on its resources during a financial crisis. The third generation of Boston Irish has, in an impressive number of instances, done much to justify the shirtsleeve adage.

But there has been little open cleavage between the Irish inheritors of wealth, position and authority and those with longer established antecedents. A "good front" has always been a Boston and Massachusetts tradition, and the Princes of the Roman Catholic Church, the Presidents of Harvard University, the Bishops of the Protestant Episcopal Church, and the Governors of the Commonwealth regularly occupy adjacent positions of honor at all public functions, subscribe their names as patrons to the same good works, and support very nearly the same causes and matters of public policy. An

Erin Go Bragh

Irishman who is a Knight of Malta was elected to the presidency of the $50,000,000 Boston Edison Company, after serving a mixed apprenticeship at Holy Cross and the very Harvard law firm of Ropes, Gray, Boyden and Perkins. There is another who is a director on the board of Boston's dominant financial organization, the First National Bank. A third, who is also the most enthusiastic of all Harvard football *aficionados* is the managing editor of the eminently conservative and old-school *Globe*. Harmony and serenity on the part of church, state and public institutions is one of the remarkable and refreshing aspects of the Boston scene.

All of which, because it is in this particular field of endeavor that the sympathetic bond between the Puritan tradition and the natural allegiances of old Bostonians on one side and the moral tenets of Catholicism on the other, leads to the widely heralded, much ridiculed, but still peculiarly illuminating subject of censorship. For, in the matter of Christian morality, at least in its outer and more tangible aspects, there is more agreement between the intellectual prejudices of the Yankee long acclimated to the New England midst and the strict Catholic outlook of the Cardinal Archbishop of the Diocese, than even upon the subject of sanctity of property and the justification of the accumulation of personal and corporate wealth.

Speaking generally, the work of protecting the not too receptive minds of Boston's middle classes against the contaminations of godlessness, subversive social policy, and immoderate sex stimuli has divided itself into two fields: the printed word and the spoken one. The Catholic Church, directly and indirectly, has concerned itself largely with the sins of commission of the theater, while the Watch and Ward Society of New England and various other agencies of militant reticence have attempted to purify Boston's book-

stalls and libraries. Of the two, it may be said, the only infrequent gestures of interference by Catholic interests with
the showing in Boston of plays not entirely to its approval
have had vastly more justification, if only in the essential
dullness of the banned works, than the fantastic and sometimes odious idiocies of the Watch and Ward.

For many years the office of city censor of plays in Boston was almost completely in the hands of an earnest former
trap-drummer named John M. Casey who operated as Chief
of the Licensing Division of the Mayor's Office. His function, pure and simple, was to preview plays, either in re-
hearsal or in their New York production and, if he found
them in part offensive, to warn the management that, unless such portions were deleted or suitably corrected, no
theater license would be granted for a Boston production.
As preparation for his high calling Censor Casey had for
twenty years controlled the percussion in orchestra pits of
vaudeville and burlesque theaters. He pattered snare-drums
and whanged the basses, rolled the kettle-drums, jingled tri-
angles, made a joyful noise before matinee audiences with
tambourines, and operated bird calls, train whistles and
bazoos. The loss of an arm resulted in his retirement and,
by a process of not too intricate political evolution, he was
delegated Boston's theater conscience for successive generations of Mayors.

By and large he was a tolerant and even amiable fellow,
and if he gagged at *Sappho* and *Salome,* so would a large
proportion of Boston audiences at the time of their presentation. *The Easiest Way* and *The Girl from Rector's* were
more puzzling as to their potential turpitude, but the greatest hubbub of his career was aroused by his rejection of
Strange Interlude. The intellectuals, pseudo and authentic,
harassed him and made his life miserable, and the O'Neill
drama played to crowded houses by removing from his

metropolitan jurisdiction to nearby Quincy. The liberal youths of Harvard and Bohemians from the back side of Beacon Hill might be outraged by Censor Casey's activities, but, generally speaking, he received the same basic approval from conservative Protestant elements as from the Catholic clergy, and retired after twenty-five years of play editing without having done any very material damage to the arts as represented by the serious stage. The circumstance that he tolerated the broadest sort of gaiety in variety and burlesque shows, seems, in retrospect, to have been beside the point.

A youthful Irishman appointed as his successor confined his activities over a period of several years to a refusal to permit the showing of a work by another Irishman, Sean O'Casey, called *Within the Gates,* and, since the drama had proved puzzling to the intelligences and vaguely soporific to the nerves of the New York audiences, few or no pulses were quickened to the boiling point.

The business of prohibiting the sale and circulation of books in New England in general and Boston in particular as undertaken by the Watch and Ward Society was largely a Protestant undertaking, although it can scarcely be doubted that in some instances it benefited by the tacit support and commendation of the Catholic hierarchy. The suppression of supposedly serious literature was never the primary objective of the Watch and Ward Society when it was founded in the nineteenth century. It was originally concerned for the detection and eradication of actual vice conditions and the prosecution of those circulating unquestionable and inexcusable obscenity, but it came into national prominence as an organization of book-baiters with the notorious Dunster House case in 1929, and came perilously close to losing its charter as a result of the exposure of its methods at that time.

Boston and the Boston Legend

The prosecution of a Harvard Square bookseller was based on a reported sale of a volume entitled *Lady Chatterly's Lover* to agents of the society, whose operations later caused them to be denounced by Herbert T. Parker, a former Massachusetts Attorney General, as "detested types of procurers and falsifiers lingering within the somewhat withered vineyards of the Massachusetts moral prohibitory laws." As a result of the activities of hired *agents provocateurs* by the society in its attempts to secure evidence in this case, the Rt. Reverend William Lawrence, Episcopal Bishop of the Diocese of Massachusetts, resigned as an officer of the Watch and Ward and his example was followed by so many other influential members of its board as virtually to render the organization impotent and discredited.

At a recent date the list of books which Boston bookdealers, whether they were such old established institutions in the community as Goodspeed's in Ashburton Place or the highly modernized Old Corner Book Store, might not sell under pain of possible prosecution included the following humorously assorted list:

Theodore Dreiser, *An American Tragedy*
H. G. Wells, *The World of William Clissold*
John Dos Passos, *Manhattan Transfer*
Elinor Glyn, *Three Weeks*
Beverley Nichols, *Crazy Pavements*
Michael Arlen, *Young Men in Love*
Babette Deutsch, *On Such a Night*
Maurice de Kobra, *Madonna of the Sleeping Cars*
Thorne Smith, *Dream's End.*
Sinclair Lewis, *Elmer Gantry*
Warwick Deeping, *Doomsday*
Ernest Hemingway, *The Sun Also Rises*
Sherwood Anderson, *Dark Laughter*
Conrad Aiken, *Blue Voyage*
Bertrand Russell, *What I Believe*

CATHEDRAL OF THE HOLY CROSS IN
MALDEN STREET

Erin Go Bragh

Jim Tully, *Circus Parade*
William Faulkner, *Mosquitoes*
Carl Van Vechten, *Nigger Heaven*
Lion Feuchtwanger, *Power*
Count Keyserling, *Twilight*
Julia Peterkin, *Black April*

Like many other manifestations of the social conscience the censorship of the stage and literature in Boston tends to advance and recede in alternate waves of intolerance and comparative liberalism, and at no time has it the slightest appreciable effect upon the tastes or inclinations, moral or esthetic, of the community. Its existence, however, stands as an index of the close similarity of viewpoints between the two most important groups in Boston's organized society: the Puritans of the established Yankee tradition and the Catholic Church, and only a person unfamiliar with the Boston scene would read in their somewhat casual gestures in the direction of books and plays any indication of their very real power and authority. The realities of life, not its illusions or pictured images, are the concern of the industrialists of Federal Street, the politicians of Beacon Hill and William, Cardinal O'Connell, who is one of the most vigorous and forthright princes of America's Catholic Church.

The original traces of the Old Sod in Boston, the shanty Paddies of the cartoons whose symbols were the shamrock and the brogue, have long since been supplanted by a generation whose hallmark is the Philomatheia, the Catholic equivalent of the Junior League, and a genuine participation in the most important communal activities. Upon one occasion a year only does South Boston revert to the epic forays and sanguinary safaris, the bottle tossing, nose-pasting and happy howling of a less inhibited time. Evacuation Day, a local festival celebrating the departure in

253

Boston and the Boston Legend

Revolutionary times of the British, falls, by joyous chance, upon Saint Patrick's Day, and the two, synthesized and sublimated into a sort of super-Gaelic Walpurgis Night, provide good South Boston Irish with the occasion for a jollification, the remorse and headaches from which last until it is nearly time to tank up again. On the seventeenth reporters and camera men from Boston papers prefer to witness the parade which is part of the celebration from the vantage points of neighboring roofs. American Legionaires and firemen find it expedient to wear their steel helmets into the streets, and a municipal official, whose duty it was to appear in the reviewing stand, once hastened to Brooks Brothers' shop for a hunting silk hat with reënforced, shock-proof lining before taking the salute. The barrage of bottles and other handy projectiles ranging from the intimate chamber utensils to cord wood is prodigious. It is the last happy souvenir of the lovely, rowdy days of the past for Boston's Irish.

Chapter XXV

THE BOSTONIANS

THE true history of Boston, it has been said, is essentially
biographical, the history of Bostonians. Nothing, whether
it be the chronicle of the town's past, the survey of its
present, analyses of its economic structure or charts and
graphs of its farrago of racial strains, can eclipse the legend
of its families, their emergence from history, and their
presence, assured and unhurried, in the immediate here. This
might not be true in many other American cities and could
not be so in most, but in Boston the names that appear
as signatories to the Cambridge Agreement are still to
be found in the *Directory of Directors* and the financial
columns of the *Herald,* and Saltonstalls and Winthrops, as
families, have survived from the times of the Mathers to
flourish undismayed in an era of more or less triumphant
Phelans and Lorettos and Tchapitoulases.

And in seeking to understand the essential Boston scene

Boston and the Boston Legend

it is necessary to know that, despite the rise of newer inheritors and despite the undeniable decline of Boston's
commercial supremacy, a very large portion of the wealth,
professional prestige, social dominance and standing in
the community is still held by Lowells, Amorys, Hemenways, Frothinghams, Searses, Adamses, Gardners, Higginsons, Stocktons, Coolidges, Forbeses and Perkinses, and
other characteristic Bostonians deriving from English antecedents whose names have been associated with authority,
affluence and commercial success for from a hundred to
three hundred years of Boston's history. The list of the
directors of any of the city's important banks or engineering firms, clubs, or fine arts institutions will indicate that,
far from having been submerged by time and tides of new-
comers, old Boston families have done exceedingly well for
themselves in an era when popular misconception pictures
them as fading from view. Their occupations and means of
livelihood have, indeed, strayed from the robust expansionist
pursuits of the nineteenth century, when Boston financiers
were the most powerful single agency in the development
of the West and in the commercial markets of the world,
but the Puritan stock persists and continues to dominate
the high places of State Street and Harvard University,
the Boston Museum of Art, the Athenaeum, Symphony and
the Humane Society, and all that these imply. And there
is no suggestion that it inclines toward abdicating its heritage.

But it must be admitted that the Puritan hierarchy in
Boston has been willing to abandon its leadership in a number of fields where once it supplied dictators, prophets and
arbiters. It has, with little or no battle, surrendered its
supremacy in the various associated branches of cultural
endeavor. Once the source and fountainhead of the best that
American letters had to offer, twentieth century Boston
has not added a dozen names familiar to amateurs of first-

256

THE FIRST CHURCH OF CHRIST, SCIENTIST

The Bostonians

rate literature. A distinguished editor or two, a literary biographer, a half dozen mildly adroit fictioneers, and a handful of Harvard versifiers are all that the generation since the war has produced. Boston is still a book-buying town to warm a publisher's heart, but few of the volumes on its library tables are any longer written by New Englanders.

So far as the theater is concerned it is still a Gilbert and Sullivan town, and one which for years welcomed the more saccharine musical comedies, but drama in the Boston Museum and Booth's *Hamlet* tradition simply no longer exists for audiences with a distinct predilection for the farces of Avery Hopwood and George M. Cohan's musicals. Only in Symphony is the proud legend of a distinguishing culture preserved among the first families of the community. Patronage of Symphony is still largely dominated by gentlefolk.

The Yankee families, having abandoned the pulpit, the editorial desk and the opera box as they relinquished the financing of Calumet and Hecla and the monopoly of the Fayal trade, turned to more passive activities in the fields of commerce and the humanities, allowing leadership to become a matter of antecedent record and the present to bask reflectively in the profit and prestige of the past. In some manner, accountable to the chemistry of the Yankee fiber alone, the families whose names are generally accepted as representatively Boston have contrived to retain a better foothold in the shifting sands of finance and commercial enterprise than they did in the world of letters and thought. The vein that ran to such high-test intellectuals as Thoreau, Emerson and Hawthorne proved, at best, a short cropping.

The ideal careers of leading Bostonians in the past, when specialization was less of a requisite in any field of endeavor than it later became, was a nice balance between public service and dividends. Perhaps in this respect the archetypal

Boston and the Boston Legend

Bostonian was Paul Revere who combined the talents of artisan, silversmith and prominent merchant with a flair for king baiting and patriotic endeavor. The fortunes of the Adams family were founded by men who managed to participate successfully in business, diplomacy and letters, while the most representative, perhaps, of all Boston families, the Lowells, have contributed merchant princes, mill owners, privateers, magistrates, astronomers, presidents of Harvard University, poets, architects and philanthropists with a nice and catholic impartiality. Of consular rank with the Lowells, the Cabot family has been represented by sea-farers, actors, surgeons, sociologists, manufacturers, judges, and shrewd investors of their own and other people's resources. The best Yankees, while maintaining a geographic unity as Bostonians and a sanguinary unity as hierarchical families, have been able to spread their talents over the entire social and economic scene, providing professional men, financiers, adventurers, artists and empire builders as the time and exactions of circumstance required. Some of them first asserted themselves in the era of Governor Winthrop, when Mr. Blackstone's orchard was still bearing fruit where now the Common stands, and some emerged from comparative anonymity when Bulfinch was laying out Park Street or when Donald McKay's shipyard in East Boston was launching clippers for Enoch Train. But two characteristics dominated the typical Bostonian; an integrity which determined his course in all affairs public and private, and a powerful sense of property. He knew the value as well as the cost of everything upon which he touched.

Few of the great Yankee families of Boston derived directly from aristocratic sources. A few years since, when a new structure at Harvard was named in honor of the Lowell family, Charles Francis Adams, rising in heraldic wrath against the architect's inclusion of the Lowell arms in a wainscoting, asserted that to his positive knowledge the only families north of the Mason-Dixon Line entitled to armorial bearings were the Winthrops and Saltonstalls. Most of the first settlers of the Massachusetts Bay Colony were yeomen, and many were gentlemen, but the peerage was sparsely represented. The evolution of family supremacy was almost entirely against a background of commerce.

That, until very recently, there were Boston families which quite refused to acknowledge the existence of any but the government of English kings is something more than a humorous legend. The city's most noted architect for many years, Ralph Adams Cram, followed the lost cause of the Jacobins and drank nightly to his king "over the water." The Winthrop family has always been stanchly Royalist in some of its branches, and there is the anecdote which still causes polite laughter in Beacon Street drawing-rooms of a prominent Winthrop who was engaged in showing Mr. Cram through his picture gallery. As they paused before a contemporary portrait of George III the descendant of ten generations of Boston Winthrops proudly remarked, "My king, sir." The distinguished corresponding member of the Royal Institute of British Architects snorted. "George the Third may very well be your king, sir," he said stiffly, "but my monarch is His Majesty, *King Charles the Third*."

It has been advanced by commentators on the Boston scene that one reason for the decline in the Irish in public life has been the absorption by the Catholic Church of the best youth of the race. Watched from parochial school-days, the most promising intellects and personalities have been marked for service in the priesthood where, celibate, they have failed to perpetuate the qualities with which they are endowed.

While the condition of celibacy is normally absent in the

first families of Puritan descent, it is, however, true that a very large part of the best energies of Boston have, in the twentieth century, been devoted to protective and conservative rather than productive enterprise. Where once there were merchant princes, capitalists and entrepreneurs of vast commercial undertakings, there are today an astonishingly high percentage of specialized trustees, investment bankers and others professionally and exclusively associated in the administration of estates and trusts of such amazing complexity as to make their guidance a highly technical occupation.

The effect closely parallels in the commercial community the celibacy of the priesthood. Creative vitality and impulse are supplanted by merely passive careers of conservation and administration. Hardly a Boston family of consequence but numbers one, perhaps several, trustees whose sole calling and source of livelihood is the leisurely but infinitely detailed guardianship of entailed estates, estates hedged and perpetuated by a labyrinthine maze of "spendthrift" clauses, mortmain devisings and legal barricades fit to addle the wits of a layman. The city is one of the most opulent securities markets in the world.

The commanding initiative and commercial impulse which directs Boston's dominant industries, as a matter of fact, has derived largely of recent years from a group of bankers and business men who, while many of them are Yankees, are scarcely heirs to the traditions of the city's more venerable families. Perhaps the dominant financial organization in the community, for example, the First National Bank, which, in effect, is controlled by the United Shoe Machinery Company and which controls in turn the Old Colony Trust Company and influences, through elaborately interlocking directorates, United Fruit, General Electric, Boston Edison and First National Stores, maintains a board of directors

The Bostonians

which includes a full half score of nationalities. The guiding genius of its rise to power, Daniel G. Wing, was born an Iowan, and its directorate has included such names as Olsen, Rooney, deMenocal, Le Fevre, Pousland and Semenenko. There are Forbeses, Winslows, Bancrofts and Beals in the high places of State Street, but there are many names which do not derive from Anglo-Norman antecedents.

When one speaks of proper Bostonians, that is to say of persons who to the world represent the prestige, tradition, insular Britishisms and economic sufficiency of families who have achieved wealth and distinction during the three hundred years of the community's history, he speaks ever increasingly of persons associated with the City of Boston professionally, commercially or historically, but not residentially. Most proper Bostonians actually live in Brookline, Milton, or in Prides Crossing, Beverly, Nahant, Magnolia and Marblehead Dedham, the Newtons or Chestnut Hill, maintaining at the most a town house or apartment within the city limits for brief winter occupancy. There are a few great mansions still occupied along Commonwealth Avenue such as the Sears, Ames, Baylies, and Phineas Sprague houses, and the Bigelow home and a great number of more modest red brick and brown stone homes in Beacon Street, Marlborough Street, Bay State Road or on Beacon Hill, but the impressive residences of Forbeses and Mandells are in Milton or within easy drive of the Myopia Hunt or Essex County Club. The motor-car delivered all but a few and straitened sections of the city to tenements, shabby apartments, or the uses of trade, and, like representative Philadelphians, Bostonians pursue their professions or administer their commerce from the metropolitan midst but seek suburban villas for their permanent habitat.

The typical Bostonian of today may be a Federal Street bank executive, or a lawyer with a Beacon Street office in the old Ticknor mansion facing the red brick façade of the State House, or a shrewd buyer for Filene's or Jordan, Marsh or one of the other of the most profitable department stores in America which line the narrow way of Washington Street. His outside interests will lie in the activities of the Union Boat Club, in drag hunting along the North Shore, or in raising dahlias in the shadow of Blue Hill, but he will contribute to Boston charities, such as the Massachusetts Humane Society or the Charitable Eye and Ear Infirmary (Mrs. Jack Gardner remarked that she had never heard of a charitable eye or ear in Boston) with pious regularity, attend the exhibitions at Fogg Museum at Harvard even though his understanding of the fine arts is limited merely to knowing what he likes, and he will wear galoshes into April even though the crocuses are already flowering along the lawns of Commonwealth Avenue. He may attend Emmanuel Church with the Baylieses and Hallowells and Hollis Frenches and drop his offerings in a plate passed by Hooper Hooper, Boston's senior dandy, or Trinity in Copley Square, or the Church of the Advent where, as has been previously recounted, Mrs. Jack Gardner, moved to an episcopal and holy frenzy, was accustomed to scrub the front steps during Lent. It is unlikely, however, that he will attend the First Church of Christ, Scientist or one of the numerous churches owing allegiance to the Cardinal Archbishop of Catholic Boston. And while on the subject of churches in general, it is impossible not to touch on the very remarkable ascendency achieved in a few decades by the Christian Science faith.

The Christian Science Church, the medium for the propagation of the "scientific system of divine healing," was founded in the latter years of the nineteenth century by Mary Baker Eddy. In 1875 Mrs. Eddy published in Boston *Science and Health,* which, in revised and clarified form, is the textbook of the doctrines of the Church of Christ, Scientist, and until her death in Chestnut Hill in 1910 she initiated every step in the progress of a faith which proved remarkably persuasive and achieved a world-wide following. The dominant feature of Christian Science is its clear-cut distinction between what is real and what is apparent or seeming, but actually non-existent, and this is the basis not only, as is widely believed, for a system of faith healing, but for an entire scheme of living based on a harmonious spiritual existence.

Mrs. Eddy herself was a product of the purest sort of New England background, her parents and forebears having been Congregationalists and countrymen, and a woman of remarkable vigor, as may be imagined from the circumstance that she organized and directed an entire religious movement from what amounted to a monastic seclusion. The First Church of Christ, Scientist, came into being in Boston, and it was natural that here should be the heart, *fons et origo,* of the religion. In 1908, two years before her death, she founded the *Christian Science Monitor,* a daily newspaper specializing in selected and edited news of a non-sensational nature, the circulation of which, varying from most urban journals, is largely outside of the city of its publication.

An amusing sidelight on the practices of the followers of Christian Science lies in the fact that, although, as a general rule tolerant of the comforts and common solaces of the flesh, they scorn the mild stimulus of tea and coffee. Their tables groan with most of the good things of the world, excepting always these beverages, and mortification of the flesh is not one of the requirements of their creed.

The actual influence of the followers of Christian Science in Boston is so intangible a factor in the life of the community as to be, essentially, inestimable. That it exists, to a certain extent, is undeniable, but Christian Science followers are not prone to emphasize their faith for political purposes or to be regimented, in general, on the side of conservative interests, as are the members of other Protestant sects. They are intensely sensitive to any possible misrepresentation or criticism of their faith, but their church membership reveals but few names of individuals representative of public affairs in the city. The sphere of influence of the followers of Christian Science is a latent rather than a discernible one, but it is apparent from the substantial and responsible element of the community which acknowledges their creed that it cannot be inconsiderable. Since the time of the emergence of Emerson's transcendental philosophy at Concord, Christian Science is the only considerable intellectual and spiritual movement to have had its origins in Boston.

Two Boston events during the twentieth century served, more than any others, to call attention to the peculiar temper of the community's conservatism and the attitude of proper Bostonians toward economic and social manifestations of changing times. The police strike of 1919, quite incidentally, brought into being the legend of Calvin Coolidge and made him President of the United States, and the Sacco-Vanzetti controversy focused the attention of a large portion of the world on the potentially fallible aspects of Massachusetts judicial procedure, but each of them, in its way, illustrated the passionate and essential conservatism of the Puritan tradition of New England. And in neither of these crises was there any indication that authority in Boston had passed from the hands of the Anglo-Norman inheritors.

In the case of the police strike the issue was clearly defined; a patent situation in which the moves of the contending forces, the motivating impulses and the progress and evolution of an unprecedented grouping of allegiances were at all times plainly visible and undistorted. There was no subtlety in the attempt on the part of the rank and file police of the city to form a union and there was neither evasion nor hesitancy on the part of authority in the community in discharging the entire force and recruiting another to replace it. Every action of the episode followed logically upon every antecedent move and, as far as diligent research after the event can discover, there was no basis for the rumors of disagreement in high places which accompanied the tense week or so of that hot autumn.

The issue concerned the formation, in defiance of the ruling of Police Commissioner Edwin Curtis, of a patrolmen's union, and the two days of chaos that followed the walkout of the department's roundsmen served momentarily to focus the attention of the world upon Boston as it had not been since the fire of 1872. The city, devoid of uniformed protection save for that of the ranking officers of the police department, who remained at their posts, seethed with riot, tumult and violence, and resembled, after the first few hours of total dishevelment, an armed camp. Merchants and householders appeared on the streets with Winchester express rifles under their arms. Retail shops were barricaded, and automatic rifles in the hands of private police were substituted for the customary "persuaders." Armed bands of hooligans and toughs, heartened by the absence of authority and in many cases actually recruited by the striking officers, smashed windows in the shopping district, broke open warehouses and assaulted women. The sound of gun-fire was a commonplace by night. When, on the second day of the strike, Governor Coolidge called the State Guard, order could scarcely be said to be restored, but at least the mob was under control. The militia, including in its numbers members of the Union and Somerset Clubs, Harvard gradu-

Boston and the Boston Legend

ates and professional men, swept the lawless element back to its kennels with a blaze of gun-fire that killed half a score and wounded hundreds. In the South End when a young lieutenant gave the threatening command to a platoon to "load" and "aim" a rowdy in the mob at bay sarcastically cried "fire" and six hoodlums were blown to ribbons in the ensuing blast. Gamblers shooting craps on Brimstone Corner were bayoneted by the hard-boiled military and the business of being disorderly in Washington Street was a capital offense. Boston was a chastened city and the striking police were discharged to a man. Few persons outside of Boston ever heard of Commissioner Curtis, a conscientious and honorable citizen, but Governor Coolidge was well started on the road which led from Frank Stearns's table in the restaurant of the Touraine Hotel to the White House at Washington.

It is conceivable that had the guilt or innocence of Nicola Sacco and Bartolomeo Vanzetti remained a local issue the homogeneity of the Boston scene might not be of the quality it is today. As it was, however, the Sacco-Vanzetti trial, more, probably, than any other event of the twentieth century, served at once to illustrate and to emphasize the cohesion between all the groups and individuals who comprise the responsible element of the city and the Commonwealth of Massachusetts. There were self-styled liberals in Boston who allied themselves to the cause of the defense, but they were few and lacking in influence, and the projection of themselves onto the scene of a considerable number of unaffected Bostonians, who were without exception concerned either for self-exploitation or for the exploitation of the case as a source of social dissatisfaction, inescapably altered the entire fabric of the controversy. It most certainly accomplished the electrocution at Charlestown Prison of the accused men, and it welded together in a curious man-

The Bostonians

ner the opinions of groups and individuals not commonly in absolute emotional sympathy. For once the conservative burghers of Bay State Road and Beacon Hill found themselves in complete agreement with the citizens of South Boston and allied against the blackguarding of the community by the associated sentimentalists and camp followers of "liberal" causes. Whatever Boston thought of the judicial conduct of Judge Webster Thayer it had, by and large, unimpeachable faith, backed by a wealth of emotional prejudice, in the integrity and findings of Governor Alvin T. Fuller's commission of inquiry, made up of President Lowell, Judge Robert Grant and Dr. Samuel W. Stratton of Massachusetts Institute of Technology. The ordered and associated forces of the city and the state moved more or less ponderously about the business of disposing of a case which assumed the proportions of a major nuisance value. The average Bostonians never regarded it as anything else but that.

The structure of twentieth century Boston is by no means either unprofitable or uninteresting to the Puritan inheritors, but it tends increasingly to deprive the community of their native sagacity and integrity, their potential talents for the arts and humane professions, their political and, in its wider sense, their social leadership, and their personal presence. It is not so much a case of the disintegration of racial strain and fiber, for these have been maintained intact in the first families of the Yankee succession, but of a graceful retiring from the scene of combat in the same spirit that Walter Savage Landor wrote, "I strove with none, for none was worth my strife." To continue the quatrain's sequence, the essential Bostonian loves nature first and, after nature, art, but having conquered the elements and the Pequots, the king's men, the ocean seas of the world and the Transcontinental Divide, he feels that he may retire to the cultivation of the nature he has vanquished and the enjoyment rather than the practice of the arts.

The British life of his soil-sound forefathers runs strongly in him, and at Southborough or North Easton, Wayland, Hamilton or Wellesley he retires to what are probably the finest, if not the most pretentious gentleman's landed estates in North America. There may be vaster gardens and more magnificent mansions in North Carolina, in Westchester or at Newport, but the Yankee homesteads reflect what, to a certain extent, they have never lost, a quality of spacious simplicity, usefulness and hospitality. For three centuries the tides of migration and change have flowed back and forth in New England, the emigrations of the nineteenth century pouring into the mill towns, the gold of '49 and the opening of the West calling the farm boys out of the green hills and the meadows of Arundel. Now the Bostonians, both those stemming from the Puritan colony and those who emerged upon the tidal prosperity of ante-bellum times, are rediscovering the countryside from which the great majority of them first emerged.

Chapter XXVI

EATALLS AND TOSSPOTS

THE history of gastronomy, the legend of gourmandism in
Boston, was inaugurated the day that Julien evolved his
soup. The precise date of this event can only be left to conjecture, but it was either three or four years before the
end of the eighteenth century.

Scrodded codfish, brown bread, baked kidney-beans and
Cotuit oysters are, naturally enough, universally and rever-
ently associated with the tradition of Boston table fare. They
are characteristic, indigenous dishes to the region, deriving
from its setting, the tastes of its inhabitants and the genius
produced by their early necessities and resources. It comes
as a surprise, however, to learn that such an essentially
Gallic contriving should have as its source, *fons et origo,*
within the precincts of Yankee Congress Street as that arrangement through whose agency Julien became known to
fame. Consommé, somehow, is not as patently a Down East
derivative as, say, quahogs or salt-rising bread.

Jean Baptiste Gilbert Payplat *dis* Julien came to town

Boston and the Boston Legend

in 1794, a refugee from the Paris terror. He had at his disposal, it appears from the records, the sum of $6,000, and with this he undertook to introduce to an as yet strictly home-faring Boston an authentic French restaurant. Up till then people had eaten in public at cook-shops and taverns, but Julien's "Restorator," as he called his enterprise, set diners out by the ears with its Parisian elegance of fare, its new and foreign dishes and their cachet of fashionable smartness. His modest frame establishment at the corner of Congress Street and Milk became the resort of the town. The Restorator thrived. Gustatory symphonies were prepared to the accompaniment of a leitmotiv of clattering dishes and tinkling crystal. Hogsheads of fine Claret washed down firkins of Strasbourg *foie-gras*. Crêpes a l'orange came into ambrosial being over flaming spirit-lamps. Truffles from Perigord appeared to ornament galantines of grouse and cold sides of Restigouche salmon. The proprietors of the Hat and Helmet and the Green Dragon waxed vainly apoplectic.

And then one day Julien created a new consommé and fame and fortune hovered over the tureen of its birth. Overnight Jean Baptiste Gilbert Payplat became the toast of gastronomes, a veritable prince of soups. The recipe for Julien flew out of town with a hundred galloping stage coaches, and from far and wide eatalls and epicures converged on Congress Street in hungry hundreds.

Rumors of this gastronomic Klondike reached Hartford and the most distinguished gourmet of all time simultaneously. Claude Anthelme Brillat-Savarin, whose *Physiology of Taste* was a few years later to become a classic of good living, was on a wild turkey shoot. He hung up his fowling piece and engaged passage on the first stage to Boston. The Field of the Cloth of Gold palls beside the meeting of those two mighty monarchs of the saucepan.

Eatalls and Tosspots

In return for the boon of a new consommé, Brillat-Savarin taught Julien the secret of cheese fondue, and the proprietor of the Restorator found that in inventing one new dish he had acquired two. Cheese fondue, a sort of lineal antecedent of our own rarebit of Wales, became the favorite late-supper dish of Boston, and when Brillat-Savarin went back to New York on his way home Julien sent him a fine roe deer which, the father of transcendental gastronomy records, was vastly appreciated at a party he gave on the eve of his sailing. No reigning sovereigns could have exchanged more princely tokens of their mutual esteem.

When Julien died his wife inherited the property and the recipe for the consommé and held forth at the old stand a decade before she sold it to Frederick Rouillard. This estimable boniface, unlettered, perhaps, in the subtleties of Continental cuisine, ran the Restorator as a chop-house, as the following verses, penned by an anonymous patron, survive to indicate:

Julien's Restorator

I knew by the glow that so rosily shone
Upon Frederick's cheeks, that he lives on good cheer;
And I said, "If there's steaks to be had in the town,
The man who loves venison should look for them here."

'Twas two; and the dinners were smoking around,
The cits hastened home at the savory smell,
And so still was the street that I heard not a sound
But the barkeeper ringing the Coffee House bell.

"And here in the cosy 'Old Club,'" I exclaimed,
With a steak that was tender and Frederick's best wine,
While under my platter a spirit blaze flamed,
"How long could I sit and how well could I dine!"

By the side of my vension a tumbler of beer
Or a bottle of sherry how pleasant to see,

271

Boston and the Boston Legend

And to know that I dined on the best of the deer,
That never was dearer to any than me!

The Restorator, apparently, like other taverns and ordinaries of the time, held with the old custom of naming its various apartments and dining-rooms, and the Old Club must have been one of these.

Julien's was torn down in 1824 after three decades of service, but the name was evidently too valuable a one to be allowed to perish, as is attested by an insertion in the *Boston Advertiser* in 1831 which informs the public that at the Julien House in Congress Street "Gentlemen and ladies from the country who are in pursuit of board and pleasant situation will be most thankfully received."

Until the third decade of the century the various taverns, ordinaries and stage-coach inns of Boston were sufficient, both in numbers and appointments, to accommodate the transient travel of the city, but in 1828 it appeared that there was a real need for more spacious and impressive facilities for the entertainment of visitors, especially of distinguished foreigners, who were flocking to town in ever-increasing numbers. To meet this need a group of public-minded citizens pooled their resources to build, in the Tremont House, the earliest first-class hotel in America.

The inaugural dinner of this establishment, the distinguished guests at which included Daniel Webster and Edward Everett, was indicative of the manner in which meals were served in public restaurants at this period.

The waiters [wrote a contemporary] filed into the upper end of the room where the landlord, Dwight Boyden, stood with a long white apron around him, and carving knife and fork in hand; and at the sound of a bell one seized upon a quantity of plates, another knives, a third forks, a fourth a lot of large soup spoons, and a fifth the smaller spoons. At the second sound of the bell they moved into line, and at the third marched with sedate steps behind the chairs of

UP FEDERAL STREET

the guests, and simultaneously the bearers of plates, knives, forks and spoons, with a flourish of the hand, placed the various articles upon the table before the guests, and then gracefully stepped back into line ready to carry out their orders. In the meantime, the landlord was carving.

Such was the ritual of the host's dinner, a ritual which obtained until the first à la carte bills of fare made this pleasant regimentation of service a thing of the past. The Tremont House was for many years the wonder and glory of American hotel-keepers who came from far and wide to study its crystal chandeliers, Turkey carpets, French ormolu clocks, its free New Years' Day dinners to all guests and its innovation of free slippers provided for guests while their jack-boots were being cleaned and returned to the long row of gleaming footgear in the front office. It was the Boston residence of celebrities including Charles Dickens, President Van Buren, the Prince de Joinville, Edwin Forrest, Daniel Webster, William C. Macready and President Tyler.

Boston's next great hotel, constructed during the fabulous forties some score of years later, was the Revere House, then considered a palatial caravanserai, which in its time sheltered Jenny Lind, the Prince of Wales, the Grand Duke Alexis, the Emperor Dom Pedro and General Grant. A tattered railroad guide of the fifties in the possession of the writer recommends that voyagers who have safely survived the perils of the train brigade trip from New York by the Long Island and New London ferry route may with confidence put up at the then new Adams House, the American House, the Revere House, the Tremont House or the United States Hotel.

It was Harvey D. Parker, however, who made modern history in the Boston world of hotels. Parker House rolls were to bear his name and renown throughout the world. Parker's Hotel was to become a Boston institution almost as representative of the town as the proverbial codfish, whose image hangs in the State House, and second only in fame to the Athenaeum, the *Transcript* and the uncontrolled passion of authentic Bostonians for attending funerals.

Mr. Parker, whose seaman's beard, innocent of mustaches, and sturdily handsome profile you can still see hung in the up-to-the-minute Parker House of today, came to Boston from Paris, Maine, and served his apprenticeship as coachman for a lady of circumstance living in Watertown. His cockaded topper bravely set over one ear, his top-booted feet planted firmly against the dash of a lurching coach which swayed in a seagoing manner over the roads on cantilever springs, young Parker drove her on shopping trips into the city at frequent intervals, and it was his custom to lunch in a modest Court Square restaurant kept by one John E. Hunt.

Whether it was because he found the orders short and indulged that almost universal hanker to be proprietor, some day, of an establishment in which one has received a fancied slight, or because he saw a more secure and affluent future as boniface than as groom must be a matter for conjecture, but in any event, in 1832, he bought Hunt out for the sum of $432, and some notion of the shrewdness of the trading involved may derive from the circumstance that items as small as a ten-cent lemon squeezer were listed in the bill of sale.

Parker's restaurant, in the conduct of which he interested as steward John F. Mills, prospered because of the perfection of its service. The Jacks and Pats and Timothys who were its waiters practiced all the little attentive touches long since bequeathed to a Gallic race of Henris and Marios in the restaurants of the land. The Tremont Restaurant fairly coined money.

In 1854 Parker bought the old John Mico house, hung

Eatalls and Tosspots

a simple shingle with the word "Parker's" over the busy sidewalk, and set out to test an idea he had harbored in the back of his head for some time: namely that perhaps hotel patrons might like their meals at other than specified hours. Heretofore, even amid the almost Babylonish elegances of the Tremont House, meals had been served at fixed hours, and he who was late went without. The American plan, as it is to this day known, and continuous dining-room service came into immediately popular being at Parker's.

Subsequent additions to the original Mico house carried the School Street façade of Parker's to the corner of Tremont Street, opposite King's Chapel, and almost as far down the hill as to be opposite the stone and iron gates of City Hall. Parts of its exterior suggested a Georgian mansion, others the Chateau of Chambord. Its corridors, as most Bostonians recall, resembled gas-lit catacombs carpeted in Turkey red and full of improbable angles, turns and levels. The chances were heavily against a late diner's ever getting to his own apartment, even if the lift deposited him in its approximate vicinage, and one gay old dog used to recall that he slept more frequently in linen closets than in his own bed. Its lobby, with its black and white marble floor and mahogany-fitted desks and offices, was one of the sights of the town, and the writer's father was fond of recalling how, as a boy in the sixties, he used to be brought to Parker's for the heavenly experience of seeing the famous wall-paper, gay as it was with steeple chases, departing coaches and huntsmen galloping across the rolling and perpetual countryside of its pattern.

What the Brown Palace was to Denver, the Planters to Saint Louis, the Saint Charles to New Orleans, Brown's to London and the Windsor to Montreal, the Parker House, as it became formally known after the death in 1884 of Mr. Parker, was to all New England. It was the meeting

place of countrymen, with chin-whiskers and carpet bags,
of the sort known as Silas on every comedy stage in the
land, of mutton-chopped bankers over from New York in
George Pullman's new plush and maple walnut palace cars,
of white top-hatted sports who matched their trotters of a
Sunday afternoon on the "Mile Ground" as the stretch of
Commonwealth Avenue was known that lay beyond Cottage
Farm Bridge. The whiskered and Tattersall waistcoated
blades of Harvard arrived and departed, refreshed, on the
hourly horse-cars to Cambridge that stopped at the little
waiting-room on the corner of Bosworth Street. State Street
merchants had their first Scotch grouse of the season, washed
down with Perrier Jouet extra sec in its sober dining-rooms.
Drummers, literateurs, the unspeakable Mr. Dickens who
returned America's gracious hospitality with a vulgarian's
churlishness, *bon viveurs,* all the world of travelers for a
third of a century made their rendezvous there.

It was as the meeting place of The Saturday Club that
Parker's inspired Dr. Holmes to his well-known lines:

> Turn half-way round, and let your look survey
> The white façade that gleams across the way,—
> The many windowed building, tall and wide,
> The palace-inn that shows its northern side
> In grateful shadow when the sunbeams beat
> The granite wall in summer's scorching heat.
> This is the place; whether its name you spell
> Tavern or caravanserai or hotel.
> Such guests! What famous names its record boasts,
> Whose owners wander in a mob of ghosts.

For many years Parker's bar-room made more than $100,-
000 annual clear profit, and now that common sense has
again been incorporated into the Constitution it is possible
that the new Parker House may approximate this handsome source of legitimate revenue. Heaven knows the place

Eatalls and Tosspots

was dismal enough during the great dry spell, and the writer recalls the horror registered on the face of a waiter captain when, in a private dining-room, a bucket of ice was commanded for the cooling of a couple bottles of wine at a dinner for a prospective bridegroom.

The Parker House roll was, of course, the most famous of the contributions to the tradition of gastronomy in School Street, but other things, especially game, were notable as specialties of the house. The following menu, that of a private dinner given in an era of less Spartan table fare than is currently fashionable, gives a fair index of what a Bostonian of the seventies might expect at Parker's when he had, with anticipatory forethought, unbuttoned his Albert watch chain and smoothed his napkin into the folds of his white linen vest.

Château Yquem Grand Vin
Little Neck Clams
Yriarte Pâle
Clear Green Turtle aux Quenelles   Pôtage à la Reine
Schloss Johannisberger
Soft Shell Crabs, Sauce Tartare
Spanish Mackerel à la Maitre d'Hôtel
Pommery and Gréno "Sec"
Filets of beef à la Triano
Green Goose Purée of Chestnuts
Sweetbreads à la Toulouse   Broiled Fresh Mushrooms
Supreme of Chicken aux Truffles
Pâté de foie gras à la Bellevue
Roman Punch
Château Mouton Rothschild
Upland Plover   Doe Birds
Parisienne Soufflé   Opera Biscuit
Chantilly Cream   Petits Charlotte
Roquefort and Camembert   Olives, ripe and green
Hamburg Grapes   Apricots, Cherries
Strawberries   French Fruit
Ice Cream Sherbet

277

Boston and the Boston Legend

Pousse Café
Café Noir
Cognac 1811
Liqueurs

These casual snacks would not, of course, have been considered anything suitable for a formal occasion. The terrapin, saddle of mutton, canvasback, mongrel goose, grouse and other essentials of true dining were omitted altogether, but the bill will indicate what was esteemed proper for a small supper tendered to an eminent barrister on the occasion of a notable legal triumph. The rapid whirring sound audible in the direction of the Granary burying ground is doubtless the Puritan father who watered his family's soup lest they should enjoy it overmuch, turning over in his grave.

No account of the annals of dining in Boston would be complete without mention of the old Bell in Hand, of Jake Wirth's immortal resort of beer and song and of Billy Park's, beloved of Harvard students, but space compels us to Winter Place.

The brass sign on either side of the door reads Locke-Ober's Winter Place Wine Rooms, and it is here that an entire school of Boston eatalls and tosspots of enduring fame for more than half a century have resorted. For here, in a narrow alley, scarcely a long stone's throw from Brimstone Corner, is a true shrine of the culinary art in its robuster moods, and like pious incense the savors of its service drift through the open windows into the tranquil evening of the city around it, complemented by an amiable leitmotif of laughter and clinking crystal.

Early in the eighties Louis Ober hung out his bush in Winter Place. Eben Jordan, the great merchant, ate there and drank deep and was pleased, and his patronage brought a prosperity to the taverner. Twenty years later Frank

Eatalls and Tosspots

Locke, a rival boniface, established a similar place of business next door, and the substantial citizens of the community found it agreeable to drink a whisky sling at Locke's before having a Medford rum at Ober's, where the food was admittedly superior. Sometimes these potations were retroactive in effect and the doors between the establishments were kept in a state of abrupt oscillation by customers hurrying from sling to rum and, conversely, from rum to sling. On such occasions the food consumption was practically negligible, but everyone agreed that Locke's and Ober's were essential one to the other, and in 1894 the party wall between them was torn down with what amounted to a public demonstration. The two taverns were merged as Locke-Ober's Winter Place Wine Rooms and the brass sign in the alley still announces this cheerful circumstance.

Prosperity has always been associated with Winter Place tavern, as it is commonly known. Even during the years of the great drought, when its bar was dedicated to oysters alone, the bright youth and chivalry of Harvard thronged its tables and were careful of the disposition of their feet so as not to disturb the bottles under their chairs. The long carved mahogany bar with its French mirrors, imported from San Domingo at great expense and installed with public rejoicing, the steam dishes of the free lunch with their intricate system of chains and counterweights for lifting the covers, the magnificent bar-room nude at the end of the room with a crystal goblet in her hand and vine leaves in her hair, all are symbolic of physical well-being dating from the days when the burgesses in frock coats and top-hats lined the bar and invented the Ward Eight.

The invention of this arrangement was unquestionably the high point in the history of Winter Place. The precise details of the epochal event, together with the name of the pioneer in bar-craft of its first designer, are shrouded in

Boston and the Boston Legend

the mists of antiquity, but word of the phenomenon spread rapidly and it was shortly after this that Locke and Ober jointly participated in a ceremony which consisted of throwing the key to the front door into Boston harbor. The Ward Eight is a sort of whisky sling based on ancient Bourbon and served in a highball glass. Compared with it a bolt of lightning is a very mild form of stimulant. The tinkle of ice in the glasses appropriate to this toddy became louder than the traffic in Temple Place hard by, and if the secret of its composition had not become generally known it is probable that excursion trains from all over New England would have converged upon the common goal of Boston filled with thirsty enthusiasts. Locke and Ober, as a result, got rich.

The increased patronage of the house called for a revision of the menu, and Emil Camus, who succeeded to the property when Locke and Ober took the Ward Eight with them to the Elysian Fields, and Nick Stuhl, the manager, designed a bill of fare which became famous for its fish and game, sweetbreads Eugenie, lobster Savannah, monumental filets of beef and distinguished cellarage full of hocks. Theodore Roosevelt invariably patronized it when in Boston. Thomas Lawson, between moments of frenzied finance, projected his urbane personality and inevitable gardenia upon its festive scene. Thomas Bailey Aldrich and Henry Cabot Lodge were members of a regular patronage and Enrico Caruso could hardly be dragged away when it was curtain time at the opera house up in Huntington Avenue. As a matter of fact, Louis H. Mudgett, oldtime manager of the opera house, used to detail a special agent who was to cut off the great man's supply of edibles when it was becoming apparent that if he consumed one more entrée he might have convulsions on the stage in the midst of "Aïda."

Nor has the passing of time dissolved in any appreciable

280

degree the flavor of authenticity which pervades this substantial ordinary. The man who has fared there on Cotuits and grilled Scotch grouse complemented by a bottle of Rudesheimer Oberfeld of that greatest of years, 1921, the whole served by Charlie, dean of waiters, has dined indeed. By custom the older patrons of the establishment who are dining alone are seated together at a long common table. There H.T.P. of the *Transcript* was for many years the arbiter of its conversation. Professor John Livingston Lowes of Harvard has been no stranger to its board, and at one time a mysterious undergraduate organization known as the Michael Mullins Chowder and Marching Society put in a not too reticent appearance, arriving in horse-drawn herdics and, for the earlier part of the evening at least, immaculately attired in silk hats and tailcoats. Neither chowder nor marching gave its members very much concern.

Only masculine persons are permitted in the restaurant proper or at the oyster bar presided over by the ingraciating Jacimo, but there are *cabinets particuliers* upstairs, upholstered in the crimson satin of tradition, dating from the period when drinking champagne from the slipper of a dancing lady was considered the very smartest, if slightly daring form. Under its florid and ornate electroliers Winter Place has seen much of Boston history. For more than half a century it has dispensed sound food and mellow liquors and it is possessed of the worn quality, the patina of useful age which only time and good cheer and the passage of stout eaters and happy drinkers can impart.

It will be apparent, perhaps, from the foregoing memoranda on the most important of the arts devised for human comfort and delight that neither as a Puritan community nor as a latter-day Tyre of the Western World was Boston an undernourished citadel of lean fare or languishing trenchermen. And private entertainment was not accustomed to

Boston and the Boston Legend

lag behind that at public functions if one is to judge by the catalogue of the fare set before the guests of William Gallagher a century or so ago with all its lavishness and occasionally frightening Gallicisms intact.

BILL OF FARE

CENTENNIAL DINNER

Exchange Coffee House, September 17, 1830

Mock Turtle Soup	Perdrix au Chou
Boiled Bass	Dindons a la Gallentine
Baked Cod Fish	Fricandeau aux Tomata
Auguille a la Tartare	Lobster Curried
Boiled Hams	Roast Beef
Boiled Corned Beef	Roast Leg of Mutton
Boiled Tongues	Roast Mongrel Geese
Boiled Legs of Mutton	Roast Tame Ducks
Boiled Turkey, Oyster Sauce	Roast Chicken
Beef Alamode	Roast Larded Wild Pigeons
Beef Bouille	Roast Partridges
Chicken a la Suprème	Roast Wild Ducks
Vol au vent au Huitres	Roast Wild Gray and Black
Vol au vent de Volaille	Roast Woodcocks
Vol au vent a la St. Lambert	Roast Plovers
Vol au vent Wild Pigeons	Roast Quails
Poulettes a la Conti	Roast Snipes
Puddings, Pies, Custards	Turks Caps, Ice Creams, etc.

Dessert

Nor has the passage of time diminished the capacity of the town's gourmets, who celebrated the first year of repeal and the arrival of André Simon, President of the Wine and Food Society of England, with libations whose echoes must have reached even to the vault on the Common where Master Julien dreams of vanished triumphs. At the dinner accorded him in a private home on Beacon Hill, M. Simon

282

Eatalls and Tosspots

was able subsequently to recall that with the hors d'œuvres was served a very old Madeira, a Cossart Gordon's 1826 Rainwater; a Batard Montrachet with the soup; a century-old pale Sherry with the fish; a hock with the entrée; Burgundies of three distinguished years ranging from a Clos de Vougeot '87 to a Grand Chambertin '15, with the roast (a Mallard duck per guest); a sweet hock with the soufflé; and then, said M. Simon, the real drinking started.

Coffee was supplemented with six brandies; two kinds of Armagnac, two Charentes and two Cognacs of 1820 and 1848, respectively. After these came a couple of bottles of wonderful old Medford rum, described by the celebrated diner-out as "a steel fist in a velvet glove," and finally a very rare old Bourbon and a hundred-year-old Rye out of the cellar of the host's grandfather. M. Simon later told newspaper reporters he did not expect to meet such hospitality elsewhere on his grand tour of the United States.

An amusing sidelight on the Puritan caste of thought which has animated the Boston licensing authorities down to the present day is the requirement that the entire interior of taverns must be visible from the street. By this device it was hoped citizens would be shamed from standing up to bars and drinking in full view of the populace. But the result has, happily, been the reverse, and strollers, until then quite unconscious of their need, have viewed the happy topers through the window and dashed inside to get themselves in similar case.

Warmed by the genial fires of third-proof rum, Boston has always been a town of eatalls, but it required Julien and Brillat-Savarin to make it a city of gourmets. And the coot stew at Haussman's in Avery Street, like the inimitable cream cheese and bar-le-duc dear to old gentlemen at teatime in the lounge of Clark's Hotel next to the Adams

House, are as much a part of the Boston legend as the elusive accent of its inhabitants, the First Corps Cadets, or the tradition of John L. Sullivan, the strong boy of Roxbury and the wonder and glory of an entire generation of sporting Americans.

Chapter XXVII

OLD LANDMARKS IN THE MODERN CITY

FRIDAY in Boston is market day. Other cities may long since have ceased to regard any designated day of the week as a special occasion for shopping, but Boston puts a basket on its arm and sets out to buy its bread and meat every Friday and so perpetuates an observance as old as the world's earliest urban community where countrymen sold their first produce in the agora. On Friday the newspapers carry a greater volume of trade than on any other day; commuting trains are heavier, and cinemas record their best grosses of the week. Those to whom the missing of Symphony would be unthinkable are usually finished with their marketing in time for one o'clock lunch.

Boston's market-place is one of the famous bazaars of the world and the surrounding precincts are some of the most characteristic and colorful of the town. Faneuil Hall dates back to 1742 when it was presented to the town by Peter Faneuil. The Old-Market house had stood in Dock

Square before it as long as anyone could recall, but in 1736 there was a great schism of popular opinion as to whether the purchase of edibles should be made at a recognized center or at one's door-step from itinerant vendors. Feeling ran high. Oratory flourished. Mugs were smashed for emphasis in the Old Cocked Hat across the way in North Street, and one day, inflamed by a veritable Demosthenes of non-market persuasion, a mob fell upon the ancient hall and proved the heresy of its opponents by quite demolishing it. The rabble, says a contemporary observer, "were disguised as clergymen." Boston's mob a few years later was to reaffirm its taste for combining violence and costume parties in the famous episode of the tea.

When, a few years later, a marketless citizenry repented its rashness the generous Peter Faneuil gave them a new market. Many changes and additions have been made to the original structure during the past century and a half, but a grasshopper still visible as the weather vane was for a long time thought to be part of the Faneuil crest. It seems more probable, however, that it was executed by its designer, "that cunning artificer," Deacon Shem Drowne, in imitation of the celebrated grasshopper vane on the Royal Exchange at London. (Deacon Drowne also made the vane so famous atop the Province House—a poised Indian representing the arms of Massachusetts.) From time to time the grasshopper has received repairs, and on one such occasion a paper was taken from its innards with the following inscription:

Shem Drowne made it, May 25, 1742. To my brethren and fellow grasshoppers. Fell in ye year 1753, Nov. 18, early in ye morning by a great earthquake by my Old Master above. . . . Again like to have met my utter ruin by fire, but hopping timely from my Public Scituation, came of with broken bones and much bruised. Cured and fixed. . . . Old Master's son Thomas Drowne, June

Old Landmarks in the Modern City

26, 1768, and though I promise to discharge my office, yet I shall vary as ye wind.

Faneuil Hall grasshopper is as much a symbol of Boston as the gilded dome of the State House or the lion and the unicorn of the Old State House, and Samuel Cooper, when he was American consul at Glasgow reports that he once used it to test some sailors asking him for fare home to Boston, which they claimed as their native town. As proper Boston identification he asked each what was on Faneuil Hall vane. One said a fish, which wasn't so bad a guess, one a horse, and the third named the grasshopper. Mr. Cooper very justly threw the first two out as impostors and gave ear to the complaints of the third.

Faneuil Hall is as inseparably joined with the public life of Boston as it is with the cause of American liberty. Designed by its donor (whose name is properly pronounced to rhyme with flannel) as a meeting place for all classes of citizens, the first public oration delivered within its auditorium was, unhappily, the funeral eulogy of Peter Faneuil himself. James Otis made there his celebrated speech on liberty in 1763. During the occupation of the city by the British army General Howe's officers turned it into a handsome theater. Later the merchants of Boston gave a splendid banquet in its great room for Lafayette, and from that time until the present its walls have looked down upon a long succession of public meetings, receptions of distinguished strangers and other civic functions.

Today the lower floor is rented to merchants whose stalls display almost every table luxury known to the palate of man. The great hall is as it always was, available for any public occasion or the pleading of any cause, and its walls are decorated with valuable portraits of notable Americans. There are Copleys of John Hancock, Samuel Adams and Joseph Warren, a full length Washington by Gilbert Stuart,

287

Boston and the Boston Legend

Lincoln and Rufus Choate by Ames. And upstairs is the armory of the Ancient and Honorable Artillery, the oldest military organization in the land, and sharer in Boston's military affections with the celebrated Battery A of the First Battalion of Field Artillery.

Application to form a military company for the protection of the Massachusetts Bay Colony, from which came the charter of The Military Company of Massachusetts, now The Ancient and Honorable Artillery, was first made to the Colonial government of Governor Winthrop in 1637 by a group of Boston citizens. The petition was turned down in the belief that danger to the state lurked in a standing body of armed men, but the year following this the request was granted. The incorporators were Robert Keayne, Nathaniel Duncan, Robert Sedgewick and William Spencer, and the charter gave them the right to choose their own captain, lieutenant and all other officers. Keayne was the first captain.

After assembling elsewhere for a time the company was assigned to a headquarters in Faneuil Hall in 1746 and from that day to this they have been inseparably associated in the public mind with the historic structure. The earliest uniforms of the organization have been forgotten, but in 1754 the members voted to appear on training days "in white silk hose" and two years later members were required to provide themselves a blue coat and gold laced hat as became a crack company. Spatterdashes of white linen and a leather cartridge pouch were added. Wigs and hair were clubbed, and since then there have been but few changes, and those minor, in the dress attire of the Ancients.

Anniversary day is held the first Monday of every June and the ritual follows that laid down in 1638. After breakfast in the armory the company files downstairs to the tolling of the bell in the cupola, and is marshaled into parade formation by captains bearing espontoons and sergeants armed with swords and halberts. Through a populace dazzled by such martial finery and usually generous in applause they march to the State House and escort the governor and his military staff to church service at the Old South Church in Copley Square, not to be confused with the Old South Meeting House. There is a drumhead election on the Common and the day concludes with a monster banquet at a suitable hotel.

The late Frank Ward O'Malley of the New York *Sun* inclined toward an impious levity when writing of the Ancients and once referred to them as "the bottle scarred veterans," and indeed, a few years since, the service of spirits at breakfast was discontinued in favor of getting up the hill to the State House. Nobody has ever denied that the banquets of the company were gala affairs and during the great foolishness the annual October dinners were held in Toronto, but valor on the field of battle has never been wholly unallied to valor with the pots and, as the flower of Boston's war-like chivalry and certainly the dressiest military company north of the Mexican border, the Ancients are privileged people.

The thirteen toasts which, from time immemorial, or at least for the past century or so have always been drunk by those Ancients who survived their banquets to the point where the toastmaster was assisted to his feet are as follows:

The Governor of the Commonwealth
The United States
The States which have adopted the Constitution
Speedy completion of the Federal edifice (This toast has from time to time been thought to mean a new post office.)
Louis XVI, Our Illustrious Ally and the friendly powers of Europe
The Day
General Washington
The Militia of Massachusetts

Boston and the Boston Legend

May our citizens prize the honor of being soldiers and our sailors never forget that they are citizens.

Our illustrious ancestors who first laid the foundations of military knowledge in America by the institution of this company.

May benevolence and peace so far influence the world that the implements of war may safely be converted into tools of husbandry.

The President and University in Cambridge

Freedom and Peace to all mankind

The actual market facilities of Faneuil Hall have long since been inadequate to a crescent metropolis of notable trenchermen, and early last century the adjacent and far more extensive Quincy Market came into being. Here, lining a central mall which runs almost the entire length of the two Market Streets, is a seemingly illimitable vista of good living. Butchers and fishmongers, poultrymen, fruiterers, game merchants and importers of herring and caviar, pomegranates, birds'-nest soup and shark-fins, each immaculate in white and wearing, even in dead of winter, the marketman's straw hat of tradition, they stand before their stalls soliciting trade.

There are festoons of sausages, pyramids of Northern Spies, whole mounds of rabbits en route to hassen-pfeffer mit kartoffelkuchen, sirloins of prime, heavy beef, shoals of halibut, sturgeon and Delaware shad, parterres of Indian Runner ducks, regiments of crated eggs. There are cheeses from Melton Mowbray, Montreal melons, pompano from Florida waters, firkins of good New England creamery butter, alligator pears and smoked salmon and braces of grouse, a fragrant and eye-filling farrago of table fare, a gustatory epic.

Bostonians like to do their own marketing. To some extent they have, with the passing of the years, come to accept the institution of delivery service, and a market basket is a comparatively rare sight, but they insist on selecting themselves what they are going to eat. Women in Stearns hats (like Queen Mary's) who arrive in expensive town cars from Brookline poke cynically at the sirloin or sniff the Gorgonzola with all the knowing appraisal of a French pension proprietor. Scholarly lecturers from the precincts of Harvard Yard and hard-headed bankers from adjacent State Street like to find their own Irish bacon or fresh smelts, and it is a Boston ritual for the head of the family personally to select the turkey at Thanksgiving. Then, most Boston shoppers, having checked off the last item on their marketing list and bought a bunch of Hamburg grapes simply because they looked so fine, cross the street and climb the stairs to Durgin and Park's dining-room.

Durgin and Park's is not a restaurant; it is a dining-room in the old New England manner, and nobody raises an eyebrow if his neighbor tucks his napkin in his collar and blows on his coffee in its saucer. It is a marketman's eating place and anyone not in straw cuffs and white apron is there on sufferance. There are a few small tables, but mostly patrons sit at long boards as in an ordinary, and in the center of the room the cooks do things with meat and fish and vegetables directly under the professional and highly critical gaze of experienced dealers in these very commodities.

You do not dine in the gourmet's sense there, but you feed magnificently. The bill of fare is long: there are about fifteen cuts of steak, and the food simple. An impressive baked potato, buttered and salted to perfection, and a kind of hot tea cake—the specialty of the house—come with every order whether a patron indicates them or not. Usually he indicates a preference for more.

Durgin's closes early, toward eight in the evening, because it opens at four in the morning to serve breakfast to the marketmen who come to town by night, but many substantial citizens make it a point to be caught late at the office about the time the first shad comes north or venison is in season so as to have dinner there. The waitresses are great blowsy girls, all good teeth, smiles and affability, with notions of their own as to what patrons ought to eat and ideas of table service that would make the hair of a French waiter captain stand up on his head. Durgin's is old New England eating at its worst and best, and the hallmark of its authenticity is the pie on its breakfast list.

The Old State House, located a city block south of Dock Square and the market district, was known, until the Federalist era in Boston history, as the Town House, and, in part, at least, it is older than Faneuil Hall since the walls of the structure as it stands today date from the year 1713. Forty years after it was originally set up it was gutted by one of Boston's frequent eighteenth century conflagrations, but its façade and the lion and unicorn of Royal England, which still face State Street from its gable, have seen nearly two and a quarter centuries of Boston pass and vanish. The Puritan town in its earliest simplicity, the crescent seat of Colonial government, the youthful stronghold of freedom in a newly organized land, the dominant Boston of Victorian times; they have all left their marks and their patina on the Old State House. The accession of George III to the throne was the last proclamation of the succession of an English king to be read from its balcony, but the heraldic devices of the crown, brave in red and gold, have survived like so much else of Boston into the latter day of a dubious democracy.

MASSACHUSETTS GENERAL HOSPITAL

Chapter XXVIII

WISTFUL SOUVENIRS

MORE austere in its associations than Faneuil Hall, the Old State House has been the object of a deal of rhodomontade, having been termed by John Adams the site "where Independence was born," and by numerous successive orators as another "shrine of liberty," largely because of the circumstance that a casual street brawl known to the pretentious muse of history as the "Boston Massacre" was staged within its shadow. For the matter of that the shooting took place right outside the Exchange Coffee House, but that admirable institution was never known to posterity as a "shrine" because of it.

In British Colonial times the Town House was the scene of the ceremony of proconsular rule, and it was the custom to read the commissions of royal governors there in the midst of the contrivings of ermine and scarlet, of smashing artillery salutes and bursting maroons so pleasing to the

Boston and the Boston Legend

good folk of the time. In less formal moments the common council sat in the eastern chamber upstairs, while the lower floor, with doors thrown wide, or at least as wide as their straitened construction would permit, was free of the townspeople as a meeting place for business and promenade for pleasure. The faded walls and nice but elusive traces of Dutch design in its dormers and belfry and squared front make it easy to imagine a time, long before the sullen roar of metropolis overflowed it, when the Town House was alive with the talk of molasses and rum (and ankers of smuggled brandy) of blue-coated merchants, and when its floors re-echoed to the tread of spurred king's men, the stout shoes of countrymen from north of Boston in town for the day, and the red-heeled London pumps of the dandies of the Old Colony.

A decade before the actual outbreak of the Revolution popular indignation against the Stamp Act found an outlet in front of the Town House in the form of an orgy of burning of stamped paper in defiance of king and Parliament three thousand safe miles away, but for all the efforts of the rabble orators of the time and sentimentalists since, the "massacre" of 1770 remains, after a century and a half, an indifferently stirring exchange of musket balls and the more provocative Anglo-Saxon monosyllables. To compare it in significance with the thoughtful and deliberate resistance to England and authority of established patriots is patently an essay in idealizing the facts of history.

After the Revolution the Town House actually began to be known by the name it bears today as the first seat of the Massachusetts Legislature. The building has undergone many metamorphoses since then, having been a lottery office, a fire station and the editorial rooms of a short-lived newspaper, the *Repertory*, along about 1805. In its way it is really a pathetic memorial to the past. Hedged about with

Wistful Souvenirs

gloomy office buildings, undercut by the caverns and turnstiles of the subway, the Old State House is a repository of memories but not of glamour. On the Fourth of July, now, a high school youth, usually a son of a city hall "solon," as local politicians are known to the press, mounts to the balcony where once Washington saluted the people and where the appearance of royal governors was the signal for field pieces to crash throughout the length of the town. There, in a rented Colonial costume with the wig askew and suffering from a severe attack of stage fright, the unhappy boy reads the Declaration of Independence. There are sometimes as many as twenty auditors, counting relatives, to applaud him where once the thousand cheered.

The Old South Meeting House, whose present structure is another two blocks south along Washington Street, is among the richest in Boston in historical associations and, in spite of its non-secular character and origin, it has somehow kept abreast of the changing times since first the congregation met in 1669, so that, so far as atmosphere is concerned, it is quite the reverse of the Old State House.

In the very heart of the life of the city, it has stood with its present form scarcely altered for more than two hundred years, and seemingly drawing strength and vitality from the flow of time and events around it. The Old South Society, or Parish, was less than twenty years old when Sir Edmund Andros, the royal governor, arrived in Boston and commanded Goodman Needham, the sexton, to ring its bell for services "for those of the Church of England." But the Old South Meeting House, breasting the tide and traffic of an alien era, is still a factor in the daily business and public life of the city.

Although unmoved on its foundations since the last course of brick was laid, the Old South has had the paradoxical opportunity of standing in five streets since it was built.

Boston and the Boston Legend

It has faced on Cornhill, Marlborough, Newbury and Orange Streets (names not lightly abandoned, but used elsewhere again) and finally upon Washington Street, these being the nominal versions under which the same street has passed under its slender steeple. Benjamin Franklin, among others, was baptized there, the fifteenth of his mother's seventeen offspring, and, in a robust age which had scant time for extended accouchements, was brought to the font in a hand-me-down christening dress the afternoon of the morning he came into the world.

When Boston was invested by the British, as every schoolboy knows, the Old South was turned into a riding academy for the pleasure and exercise of the king's officers. Dean Hubbard's silk upholstered pew was carted off to become a pigpen and the rest of the interior chopped up for firewood, while a number of valuable records of the early colony, stored for safe-keeping in the steeple, were scattered to the winds by the callous soldiery. What grieved Bostonians most when they once more took possession of the Meeting House was the loss from its archives of that invaluable item of Americana, the manuscript and only copy of Governor William Bradford's *History of the Plimouth Plantation.* The history was the record of the Plymouth Colony through 1646 told by the man who himself had been governor of the Pilgrims for thirty years, and its loss was utterly irreplaceable, either as an object of sentiment or as an historic document.

Fifty years later, however, the English Bishop of Oxford, as a form of episcopal relaxation, set about compiling a history of the Church in America. As a best-seller it was no rival of Lord Byron's *Don Juan,* a near-contemporary, or of the novels of Mr. Dickens, but ecclesiastical historians and students of Colonial times, when they got around to reading it, were electrified to discover in it references which

Wistful Souvenirs

could only have derived from the long missing and supposedly destroyed Bradford history. Train and Company's packets bore feverish inquiries across the Atlantic, and with maddening British composure the answer came back that the manuscript was indeed in the stacks of the library of the Bishop of London at Fulham Palace. But return it to Boston? The Bishop of London was agreeable, but the Archbishop of Canterbury didn't think it was proper. While concerned for the propriety of returning the stolen goods, however, the Archbishop was gathered to his fathers and the affable Bishop of London succeeded him in office. He sent the manuscript back with his best wishes, and today the yellowing parchment, illustrated with the uncertain holograph of Governor Bradford, can be seen in the vaults of the State House on Beacon Hill, one of the prized possessions of the Commonwealth of Massachusetts.

Another episode in the history of the Old South Meeting House and usually spoken of as its "near-desecration," despite the circumstance that it has never been consecrated to the service of any faith, set Boston by the ears a number of years ago when the same vulgarians who are forever suggesting cutting the Common up into business lots proposed that the structure occupied real estate that might far better be put to commercial advantage. The yahoos got their campaign well under way before civilized citizens were aware of what was toward, and in the end it was Boston's old friend and sister city Chicago that came to the rescue. Chicagoans said that if Bostonians didn't want their own historic monuments the Middle West knew a good thing when it saw it, and did, and a move was started in the Chicago papers for funds to transport the Old South Meeting House, brick by brick, and set it upon the shores of Lake Michigan. Such earnest piety in the despised hinterland was wormwood and gall triple distilled, *absinthia tetra*

297

thrice over, to Beacon Street. The sum of $400,000 was raised by public subscription to preserve the Meeting House in perpetuity and all talk of skyscrapers was promptly relegated to the discard.

Of the narrow streets that, even in the modern city, bring to this section some flavor of the past, it would be impossible not to mention Cornhill. When Faneuil Hall was built it was christened Market Street, for the excellent reason that it gave access to that section, but later, when the demand for its original name was increased in the immediate vicinage of the Hall itself, it received the name that had formerly been applied to what is now Washington Street. It still has about it the atmosphere of a more leisurely century, and for many years its principal attraction was the open air bookstalls similar to those of London before the great fire or of the banks of the Seine in Paris today. The most famous of these, Bartlett's, has passed from the scene, but there are still a few proprietors outside whose premises there are sidewalk counters of tattered volumes, back numbers of magazines and paper-bound *romans policiers*. There is, too, a coffee-shop famous for its three- and five-cent cups of fresh brewed Java and Mocha. It is generally considered a little showy to order the nickel cup, two three-cent servings being considered more conservative.

Around the corner in Court Street is the famous steaming kettle above the sidewalk which advertises another coffee-stall, and next door a huge Meerschaum announces a pipe-maker's shop to all who pass. Umbrella repairers, gunsmiths, scissor grinders and watchmakers, too, still hang out appropriate symbols of their callings, and Boston is one of the few remaining American cities where old-time artisans and tradesmen still proclaim their crafts with representative street signs.

Wistful Souvenirs

Antiquarians and pious Bostonians will turn down an empty glass for one landmark, for a century and a quarter familiar to this quarter of the town. The Bell in Hand, at the time of its passing a few years since, was the oldest tavern in the city and its pewter mugs and extraordinarily varied clientèle made it a tap-room which, had it boasted a George Bellows to immortalize it in lithograph, would have rivaled the fame of John McSorley's ale-house in midtown Manhattan.

Along the year 1795 "Old Jimmy" Wilson, the town crier, found himself, somewhat to his own surprise, of a mind to retire from the vagrant and stentorian manner of life which constituted the art and mystery of his calling and, like all men in their right minds, he wanted more than anything else to be a tavern proprietor in his old age. But a lifetime on the streets had taught him that strong drink raged indeed and he was divided between the holy joys of temperance and the charms of the life of a boniface. In this hideous dilemma somebody suggested that he start a tap where only brew and cider and such light beverages should be stocked and Jimmy, enchanted with the idea and mindful of his honorable past, started the Bell in Hand. From then until the most fearful years of Prohibition the old sign, a crier's bell grasped in a man's hand, hung out, first next door to the Exchange Coffee House and after 1851 in Pi Alley, a a straitened lane running off Washington Street to the mews back of City Hall, which derives its name from the proximity of the publishing office of the *Boston Post* and the consequent traffic of printers in its limited precincts.

There were three low-studded, wainscoted rooms, the floors of which were daily strewn with fresh sand, and the beer pumps were old-time arrangements with long wooden handles imported from England. Mostly the place was so

299

Boston and the Boston Legend

dark that it was necessary to strike a match if one wanted to see the time, and, while there were some really valuable Hogarth prints, theater bills and such on the walls, they passed quite neglected in the pervasive but cheerful crepuscule. If a patron fell down among the cuspidors he was likely to go undiscovered for days and, as the chances were that he was a reporter from one of the adjacent offices of Newspaper Row, his acquaintances would pool their intellectual resources in the front room and send in to his office reasonably convincing dispatches fabricated over his byline.

The patrons of the Bell in Hand were as varied as those of the London cabmen's shelters affected during the nineties by Ernest Dowson and other exotics of the period. Along with the hackmen and teamsters there often entered a Harvard professor and with the "bibulous riffraff of no particular identity" the young Charles Townsend Copeland and the dignified General Charles H. Taylor, founder of the *Globe,* could be seen standing manfully up to their pewter mugs of lager. Quiet business and professional people absorbed their brew and departed, and top-hatted youths on the way from the Old Howard to the Racquet Club stopped their herdics in full career and ran in for a quick one just before closing time. The Bell spanned at once the gap between the eighteenth and twentieth centuries and that between the glittering American saloon and the more intimate British pub.

Although the crier himself died in 1841, his legend is still green in Washington Street, and if Wilson should suddenly, some noonday, appear in his cocked hat and skirted coat, bronze bell in one hand and script of news in the other to harangue passers-by, there are old-timers who would instantly identify him. He was a valiant fellow at rhetoric and could move hearers to grief, amazement or alarm like any actor. The sound of his bell invariably collected a group

BIG BUSINESS IN FRANKLIN STREET

Wistful Souvenirs

of solid citizens mingled with the town's gutter-snipes who paused open-mouthed at his eloquence and to laugh at the jokes he would sometimes include in his announcements for their special benefit. Deacon John Sullivan, who was fond of children, once detailed him to make the rounds of the town's public schools and invite all the scholars over to the Common to roll in the hay, new-mown that morning. When Master John Tileston, a first citizen and public figure of note, departed the scene Wilson announced the sale of his effects so movingly that his hearers wept wherever he went. "They were a good old couple," he proclaimed of the jolliest and most patriarchal of schoolmasters and his spouse. "They lived together sixty-six years and never quarreled. Now come, good people, do come and buy." The auction was an overwhelming success and many a scholar whom Master Tileston had soundly birched purchased a snuff-box or candlestick for his memory's sake. Wilson was an inimitable raconteur and is credited in Boston tap-rooms to this day with having first told the story of the two gentlemanly stews who were standing against his bar when one of them suddenly nudged the other and commanded him, *sotto voce,* "Don't look around now, but there's somebody just going out the door with your hat and coat."

There is a French proverb to the effect that everything gets broken, everything eventually passes away, and all things become a weariness, but the Bell in Hand, while it succumbed to a barbarous and intolerant time spirit and passed from the scene, never became, for Bostonians, a weariness. The spirit of the town crier haunted the depths of Pi Alley where Rufus Choate, apprehended one day by an acquaintance while wiping suds from his whiskers, remarked, "Ignominious, but convenient." On winter nights when the snow drifts deep in Pi Alley and the late city

301

edition is off the presses in the *Globe* and *Post,* homeward bound wayfarers sometimes still imagine they hear the hospitable clanging of a ghostly hand bell, and they know that Jimmy, the town crier, is walking his old route and ringing the news of yesteryear.

Chapter XXIX

BEACON HILL BOHEMIA

Disillusionment, Bohemia and beautiful letters arrived
with nice precision in Boston after the World War and immediately became associated with real estate promotion on
the slopes of Beacon Hill. Greenwich Village in New York
and the bistro civilization of Montparnasse in Paris were
the products of a gradual evolution of kindred spirits into
geographic and social entities, but Boston's Greenwich Village sprang, by a process of unpredicted and emergent evolution, into sudden, raucous and boozy being with the arts
for an indifferent warrant and garret to garret hey-hey as
a leitmotiv. Overnight large numbers of previously rational
and plausible youths and maidens discovered James Joyce,
the artistic temperament and the formula of synthetic gin,
and the feature writers of the Sunday editions hinted cheer-
fully at a mode of life in Joy and Pinckney Streets characterized by something less than the "middle course" of the
Greeks. Liberation from the conventions was manifested by

Boston and the Boston Legend

eccentricities of conduct and verse structure which drew sniffs from substantial citizens comparable to the sniffs which, in the previous century, had greeted the smocks and ideology of Brook Farm. It was all very strange to Boston and would have been tolerably alarming in any other ordered community. It produced neither letters nor paintings from whose internal evidence its likeness can be reconstructed and Beacon Hill's Bohemia of the twenties can be chronicled only by an archeologist who is also a connoisseur of the fatuous.

It may have been an urge to continue in the fevered tempo of the war years; it may have been the Russians who, in the form of the Moscow Art Theater and Balieff, were already introducing a vogue for batiks, samovars and lugubrious river songs, it may have been any one of a number of things that started a section of the Hill off on its career of abandon, but it certainly was not the Boston tradition of letters that lent it impetus. In the offices of the *Atlantic Monthly* Ellery Sedgwick was stirred to no fever of enthusiasm by the intelligence that the Hill was suddenly crawling with unrecognized writers. Marc Antony deWolfe Howe, the community's leading biographical call fireman, kept right on doing family histories for those who could afford his stiff fees. Amy Lowell in her Brookline home recognized the existence of Elliot Paul, but was more concerned for her cats, Tampa-wrapped claro-cheroots, and the more orthodox verses of Foster Damon and Robert Hillyer, who were just emerging from the green and anonymous fastnesses of Harvard Yard. There were no evidences that the blood pressure of the curators of the Fogg Museum had achieved Union Club proportions over the flowering of a local and Puritan Athens. The Joy Street Police Station, however, put two more roundsmen on night duty, and an imaginative bootlegger who specialized in rush bottle de-

Chestnut Street
Boston

E H Suydam

CHESTNUT STREET

Beacon Hill Bohemia

liveries acknowledged the influence of the New Theater by devising a code for telephone calls in which "two balcony seats" indicated as many quarts of gin and "an orchestra" was a symbol of Scotch whiskey and comparative affluence. There was a surprising rush of theater ticket purchasers noted by druggists who had pay phones in their shops, but few folk from the North of the Hill were ever observed at the Shubert or Hollis playhouses.

Perhaps the first harbinger of the impending descent of the muses was the inauguration, with suitable ceremonies, of a tea-room which became locally famous as "The Green Shutters." A short, stocky vassal of Gasterea named Billy Paul hung out his bush in Cedar Lane Way, a street so difficult to discover that even mature Hill residents are sometimes unaware of its existence. It was a tiny place, seating but thirty patrons at its tables, although on special occasions some of his guests preferred to sit on the floor as merely anticipating the time when they would find themselves there anyway, but The Green Shutters became symbolic of the New Art in Boston and was the first of a vast number of similar chintz and candle-light salons to be licensed under the Boston law, dating from the eighteenth century, as "common victuallers." Paul had a partner in the enterprise, Alan Wallace, who managed the establishment and presided over the congresses of the devout which assembled there when Paul was on one of his *safaris* to London to inquire into the state of the British stage, excursions which were comparatively frequent and mostly led to the stage door of the Gaiety Theater.

Thespis followed in the footsteps of Gasterea and was from the beginning wooed over heroic portions of gin and vermouth discreetly furnished forth at The Green Shutters in tea-cups. Her principal suitors were several in number, and in person so distinguished of appearance as to excite the

305

Boston and the Boston Legend

stares of the curious when they ventured into the uninitiated and vulgar reaches of Tremont or Washington Streets. Viola Black had been known as a figure in Greenwich Village in Manhattan when the Provincetown Theater was first exploiting the talents of Eugene O'Neill and Robert Edmond Jones, and as an authentic Bohemian of experience and standing she was the arbiter in all matters of smocks, foot-long cigaret tubes, the little theater movement and general conduct among the intelligentsia. John Melvin Perkins hailed from Chelsea and will be known to history as the first man ever to wear a béret in Boston. Larry Bolton was a shy and wide-eyed youth who had come to town from a summer occupied as a singing waiter in a Maine resort hotel. He was looking for a position in a choir and gave the impression, somehow, of having been laundered too much.

Elliot Paul, who later made a not inconsiderable name for himself as a novelist, was the Hill's most authentic Bohemian. Hailing from one of Boston's drearier suburbs, he inaugurated the reign of shiny black suits, broad-brimmed black felt hats, wide Basque belts and Van Dyke beards. He had actually been to Paris and had seen James Joyce and Gertrude Stein plain, sipping Pernods on the terrace of the Dome, and was regarded with all the veneration of a prophet of the true faith who has made pilgrimage to Mecca. He possessed a vast stock of exotic lore, knew the uses of "reefer" cigarets and made few or no concessions to the bourgeois scheme of things which prevailed off the Hill. Paul's constant associate was a rangy youth named Prescott Townsend, whose strictly accountable background and actual supply of ready cash were not particularly held against him even in the most enlightened circles. Townsend emerged from Harvard Law School, possessed and wore a raccoon skin overcoat that was the envy of Cedar Street, and could talk informatively on any given subject for the

306

space it required his auditor to consume precisely a quart of gin.

The other moving spirit of the Boston Stage Society was Catherine Huntington, granddaughter of a bishop and frequenter of circles which ordinarily would know little and care less for the New Enlightenment. She threw in her lot, however, with the esthetes of Cedar Lane Way, and subsequently found herself associated with some of the most curious dervishes ever to whirl and scream their ways through the dusty anterooms of art.

In Myrtle Street the ancient mansion that had belonged to Moody and Sankey of hymnbook fame had for years been uninhabited save by a family of rats of undoubted fecundity. Without so much as by your leave to the executors of the hymnal estate, Paul, Bolton, Perkins, Viola Black and a chance acquaintance, Creighton Hill, moved in and took possession. Paul took over the best room for a studio. Bolton was elected janitor by acclaim and Viola Black was awarded the ground floor in which she promptly opened a dressmaking establishment. There was another tea-room called The March Hare, across the street by this time, and meals and Tom Collinses were ferried back and forth while the Moody and Sankey windows were pried open for the first time in decades and the rat family was being stalked by Bolton with a stout broomstick. The rental agents didn't know what to make of it and for a time inclined toward tossing the invaders into jail for breaking and entering. In the end the eloquent Hill persuaded them to allow the drama colony to remain in possession rent-free, on the basis that it was better for the premises to be occupied even by stage people than falling into ruin for lack of a caretaker.

Townsend, who was, perhaps, the only strictly solvent member of the early Bohemians of '22 and '23, was induced to invest in a parcel of real estate on the steep slope of Joy

Boston and the Boston Legend

Street which included a barn of considerable proportions in a fair state of preservation, and here the muse of the drama was solicited to take up her permanent Boston residence. Expeditions throughout the adjacent countryside for purposes of loot and pillage were organized in Townsend's Model T Ford, and outraged lumber dealers, stone-masons and artificers in Malden, Quincy and Watertown witnessed the rape of various unattached portions of their stock in trade which vanished down the road in the hands of persons whom they usually described to the police as having donned fancy dress for purposes of disguise. Upon one occasion Elliot Paul put in an appearance with a thousand of red glazed brick and a vague tale of having come upon them out near Medford, and at another Townsend dragged into admiring Joy Street behind his car the main steel strut of the proscenium arch of the Cort Theater, then in process of demolition. It was his notion that it might come in handy, although the structure of the Barn Theater, as it was by now known, would not have supported a proscenium arch of papier-mâché, let alone a two-ton I iron. Principally, however, the loot seemed to run to geraniums and flower boxes for the windows and properties that might have been useful had they decided, for instance, to present "Monte Cristo," and the grand opening was postponed for a year.

Meantime the slaves of Thespis had again transferred their allegiance to a new café, The Brick Oven Tea Room, run by Reginald Lawrence, a comparatively civilized Princeton graduate. Townsend decided that the group should do its own printing and propaganda, and two ancient presses were established in the cellar near the cache of gin. It was this gesture of economy that was later responsible for the charges by the police that counterfeiting was being practiced on the premises. The print shop was in charge of Laning Humphrey, a feature writer on the *Post,* on the theory that, being a newspaperman, he should know all about the mechanics of publishing. He was terrified of his new assignment and used to bang a dishpan loudly before going through the trap-door to the cellar to scare off the rats that were dining off his printing ink.

The Barn opened in November, 1922, with a production of *The Clouds* by Jaraslov Kvapil, a Hungarian who had been chosen because nobody on the play committee, far less the Boston public, had ever heard of him before. He must be good. Much time had been spent shoring up the floor of The Barn so that the audience would not be precipitated into the basement, and little thought had been lavished on provisions for more than its bare safety. The cash patrons sat on boards strung between barrels and had to stay awake or fall to the floor. A high degree of nervous tension was perceptible on opening night, and Elliot Paul subscribed to the theory that the Shuberts, in jealousy and desperation, had spread the rumor that the place was a fire-trap.

H. T. Parker of the *Transcript* did not occupy the barrel end reserved for him in the front row, nor were the other first-string critics in evidence, but a brief paragraph in the *Herald* the next morning reported that the "only action in the drama was the paint drying on the backdrop." That, of course, was just what was to be expected from a reactionary organ whose *beau idéal* of the drama was probably Dion Boucicault, but it helped keep business away from The Barn.

A meeting of all the Bohemians associated with the Theater Society was called at the Moody and Sankey mansion next day. Lawrence closed The Brick Oven and brought all his liquid assets. The proprietors of The Green Shutters did likewise. Laning Humphrey told his managing editor he had to bury a relative in Springfield. Billy Paul, who was in no way related save by common sympathies to Elliot, turned up with six bottles of Holland gin in stone crocks. All the beards, black hats, jade earrings and long cigaret tubes of the Hill were in solemn conclave under one roof, deciding the fate of the drama.

The second day the supply of potables ran out. Everyone was broke. Not even Townsend had the price of a "balcony seat." It was a major crisis, met in the end by Reggie Lawrence, who, with his wife, went up the street and opened The Brick Oven for lunch. Three or four customers appeared, were fed, and were amazed, upon reappearing at dinnertime, to find the doors locked again. In this manner the drama conference was supported for what is still recalled by Beacon Hill residents as a week of the most emphatic esthetic endeavor of history. When the gin ran out The Green Shutters or The Brick Oven or The March Hare would be opened on a purely temporary basis. As soon as enough patrons had dined to put the management on a cash basis with the rush bottle purveyor, down came the shades, the door was locked, and life began anew in Elliot Paul's studio. Nothing of moment was uncovered during the deliberations except by Laning Humphrey, whose managing editor had taken no stock in the burial at Springfield and had docked his salary during his absence. The drama on Beacon Hill was temporarily suspended.

About this time John Murray Anderson was busy presenting to the audiences at the Boston Metropolitan Theater the first of the unit stage performances which later became so popular with film audiences everywhere. Somebody, probably Billy Paul, introduced him into the more uninhibited salons of the Hill and, in return for their gin and courtesy, most of the Theater Society were made free of the Metropolitan's backstage. Vestoff, the first dancer under Anderson, and Leonidoff, his stage director, became familiar figures in the Hill studios and lent a gratifying foreign atmosphere

Beacon Hill Bohemia

by their presence. Lady artists appeared stalking through the smoke and havoc of soirées in slinkier gowns than ever, and cigaret tubes achieved eighteen inch proportions overnight. Somebody imported a leopard skin evening gown which was in tremendous demand, gracing the person of first one siren and then another on successive nights, while heavily painted eyelids became requisite costume among the female released thinkers.

Into the tumult and esthetic delirium of the Beacon Hill scene outside personalities were being constantly projected for brief exposures to the influence of the muses. Many of them retired hastily, their wits and kidneys in a state of grievous disrepair, but a few flourished for protracted periods. Robert Hillyer, then newly appointed to the Harvard English faculty, had an apartment in a mews off Charles Street and occasionally lent his presence to more decorous levées. James Gould Cozzens, who had his first novel published as a Harvard freshman and took up white linen spatterdashes and wing collars on the strength of it, sometimes would turn up in the midst of a bizarre brawl declaiming Swinburne's "Triumph of Time" or Dowson's "Cynara" for those still in a condition to listen to him. There was Dudley Fitts, an accomplished medievalist with high Episcopal leanings, who wrote all his communications in excellent classical Latin to the bafflement of most of his friends and all his business associates. Kenneth McCaleb, then one of the editors of the *Boston Telegram,* a low and joyous chronicle of local infamies which never let a day pass without using the word "orgy" on the front page in 72 point Caslon, inhabited a sixth-floor flat in a dolorous mall off Joy Street. The climb was such a long one that "balcony seats," ginger-ale and other refreshments were customarily hauled up the façade of the building to his window in a basket on a string. Upon one occasion he apprehended a stout Amazon being

Boston and the Boston Legend

sought by the authorities and kept her handcuffed for a week
to his radiator while the *Telegram* ran her memoirs under
the title "Loves and Adventures of the Bandit Queen." Her
language when he eventually handed her over to the police
is remembered in the precinct station to this day with reverence and admiration.

Cynthia White, archetypal Bohemian of New York's Village, came over to Boston to engineer an artists' ball at the
Copley Plaza. The affair was such a howling success that
the patrol wagons were drawn up in a thick rank along
Dartmouth Street an hour after it began and Sergeant
French, on the desk at Station 16, was packing the screaming Bohemians into his jailhouse, six to a cell. A wretched
youth named Alan Burke, who for years had threatened
suicide to the boredom of his friends, accomplished it one
night by accidentally discharging a loaded gun at himself.
A poet named Harold Vinal started a slim feuilleton called
Voices in which he was accustomed favorably to review his
own volumes of verse as they came from the Harold Vinal
Press. Robert Lincoln O'Brien darkly hinted in the *Herald's*
editorial pages that while many of the boys and girls living
together on the Hill might be married in the sight of God
there were a number who had not applied for a license at
City Hall. There were hints of even more exotic practices,
and prominent Bohemians were apprehended in raids on
negro night clubs in the South End. The muses flourished in
an atmosphere of joyous poverty, uproar and outrage with
overtones of essence of juniper.

The Boston Stage Society loved art for its own sake and
sniffed in the general direction of Huntington Avenue where
Henry Jewett, with occasional obeisances in the direction of
the muses, was principally devoted to the presentation of
such plays as *Mrs. Partridge Presents* and other certified
Broadway successes. But audiences preferred Mr. Jewett

Beacon Hill Bohemia

and the company of E. E. Clive at the Copley Theater, and the Stage Society went into a decline. Billy Paul and Allan Wallace organized a new group of serious thinkers and occupied the premises of the Peabody Settlement House with such dramas as *The Deluge, The Tidings Brought to Mary* and *Sophie. Sophie,* having a situation or so in the script which might upset maiden ladies from Beacon Street had they thought to attend it, attracted the attention of City Censor John Michael Casey, and the Mayor, Aldermen and other city hall nabobs flocked to see it. Boston seethed with the cheerful tidings that a drama of unredeemed lechery and fancy talk was in progress. Peabody House couldn't handle the throngs of customers who arrived waving unaccustomed cash, and the Stage Guild became a going concern to the surprise of its organizers and the distress of rival entrepreneurs. It lasted a full year on the proceeds of *Sophie,* and such was the affluence of the proprietors of the venture that a dreadful and powerfully emetic parody of Scotch whiskey made its appearance instead of the familiar dollar gin.

The Brick Oven outgrew itself and, on the strength of the circumstance that Reginald Lawrence had unearthed an appropriate sign at a rummage sale, a new one called the Saracen's Head was opened, in defiance of all fire regulations, above the Barn. The Brick Oven was taken over by Effie Jordan, a tea-room proprietor of experience, who, in her gone but remembered youth, had played in vaudeville, and, when the orchestra started, would now and then absent-mindedly go into a buck and wing routine and achieve the swinging doors to the kitchen with a wildly applauded "off to Buffalo." The back of her bistro was turned into an art gallery and the surrealists of the Hill, who had not yet heard of Dali, guardedly admired each other's conceptions of a discordant universe upon its walls by the hour, hanging their canvases at angles and occasionally turning them quite upside down for better effect.

More puzzled by its art colony than even the old established residents of the Hill were the Gaelic police officers of Joy Street Station. Unenlightened as to Scriabine, surrealism and the dramatic opera of Kvapil, their suspicions turned to more familiar channels and the studios of Myrtle and Mount Vernon Streets were subjected to frequent and fearful raids by embattled roundsmen who visioned counterfeiting, cocaine vending and worse wherever a bayberry candle glimmered in the neck of a discarded whiskey bottle. Usually, however, when they had discovered nothing worse than a temporarily decommissioned playwright or Harvard Latin instructor under the bed they joined the party, and an assortment of abandoned nightsticks, firearms and belts was always dutifully forwarded to Captain McDevitt's desk the next morning, along with their owners.

Schism and strife with the aid of the sheriff finally routed Beacon Hill's art colony, at least as a moderately cohesive unit. A last frenzy of vitality overtook it during the winter of '25 when Creighton Hill and Mrs. Huntington presented a series of dramas enacted, successively, by troupes of negroes, Chinese, Burmese and Polynesians. Psychoanalysis raged through a final crop of tea-rooms where earnest youths and maidens stared fixedly at each other and exhorted themselves to abandon their uncompensated inferiority fixations. Studio parties turned out to be brawls of Scott Fitzgerald proportions and there was a tidal wave of erotica which surged through the bookshops of Mount Vernon Street in tide-rips of *Fanny Hills* and crosscurrents of *Memoires of a Birching Beauty* and *Only a Boy*. Frank Harris's *My Life and Loves* appeared, dog-eared and spine-broken, and it was apparent that art had reached a final and imperial decadence in Boston's Bohemia. Mrs. Huntington

Beacon Hill Bohemia

was clapped into jail during the Sacco-Vanzetti trial a season or so later. Elliot Paul disappeared in the fog of Dadaism and controversy surrounding the Rotunde in Paris. Viola Black returned to the sand dunes of Cape Cod. Larry Bolton lingered longest of all in the deserted temple of Thespis in Joy Street. The *Telegram* folded and Ken McCaleb emigrated to Manhattan and the *Daily Mirror*. Robert Hillyer retired to the grove of the academe and received the Pulitzer Poetry Award. The public works department swept up the torn bérets, Gordon's gin bottles and withered vine leaves that had graced the hair of vanished poets. Dust gathered on the sills of Mermaid Taverns closed by order of the sheriff, and the ancient tranquillity that it had known in the days of the Mount Vernon Associates returned to Beacon Hill.

Chapter XXX

THREE-CENT TEA AND OTHER CLUBS

CLUB life in Boston is a thing above and apart from similar existence in any other city on the face of the earth. It is austere, eminently respectable and largely non-interlocking. A New York or London clubman may belong to as many as twenty different associations and societies so that every other door in Fifth Avenue or Pall Mall is open to him, but few Bostonians boast more than three clubs or are closely concerned for the affairs and internal economy of so many. Nor is existence behind the portals of Boston's gentleman's clubs very gay. Gambling for other than the most conventional stakes is frowned upon. With two or three exceptions the art of gastronomy receives only the most casual attention, and serious drinking, as practiced in many resorts of masculine relaxation over the face of the globe, while tolerated, is hardly encouraged. Uplift and good works, how-

ever, are the reverse. Benevolence flourishes, light is dis-
seminated, and a high moral tone pervades the general
premises. The only laugh that has been heard in the Union
Club in recent years was when an irreverent member (who
was promptly shushed) discovered a sign in the reading-
room saying "Only low talk permitted." But club life is, as
the newspapers say, "exclusive" and flourishes soberly in an
atmosphere of morning coats, scrod, and Sunday afternoon
concerts by string quartets of undoubted proficiency.

Whether the Somerset Club of Boston or the Union of
New York is the most British club in America has been a
matter of long-standing dispute. Certainly, however, the social desirability of the Somerset is demonstrated by the circumstance that fifty New Yorkers maintain full residence
membership on its books even though they only use it twice
a summer on the way to and from Bar Harbor.

The Country Club, at Brookline, America's No. 1 association of this sort, is, of course, so distinguished in its field that
it is simply and universally spoken of as *The* Country Club,
and the Massachusetts Humane Society is so conservative
that it maintains no clubhouse, indulges in such frivolous
activities as dinners but once a year, and, according to popular legend, has no printed membership list as all members
know their associates anyway. Then, too, there is the Algonquin Club, with the best food, the handsomest mid-Common-
wealth Avenue location and the finest lilacs on its lawn
tended by a faithful doorman named Frank, and within the
Algonquin flourishes Boston's most admirable circle of gourmets, The Beacon Society, whose dinners are so delectable
that they are held but infrequently in the interest of the
health of its members.

Of the Chilton Club, Commonwealth Avenue and Dartmouth Street retreat of elderly bluestockings and matrons
determined that their daughters shall be launched at the so-

berest and least animated of debutante balls, the tale is told
of a New York woman prominent in good works who arrived there to give a lecture. As the interval between the
arrival of her train and the appointed hour was brief, she
telephoned for dinner to be sent to her room while she
changed her dress and rehearsed her more memorable periods. But when she answered the knock on her door, instead of the expected waiter, there entered a whalebone and
bombazine manageress whose hair, curled in the manner
known as *a l'Anne d'Autriche,* was complemented with black
mits and a chatelaine watch. With a disapproving glare she
scanned the visiting lecturer from earrings to ankles,
snorted disapprovingly, and finally swished herself out with
the ultimatum, "You are far too well to have dinner served
in your room."

But, although it is not strictly a club, the Boston Athenaeum is certainly the best known and in many ways the
most characteristic of the town's organized societies.

When the Athenaeum first opened its doors on what is
now Scollay Square, Boston was still a town, bounded on
three sides by water and boasting a population of 30,000.
The year was 1807. An appreciable amount of traffic in
the streets was composed of gentlemen on horseback and
there were everywhere hitching posts for the accommodations of their animals and mounting blocks for themselves.
Public transportation was accomplished by a bewildering in-
tricacy of stage lines which had their starting points at the
various taverns of the town. The water was supplied by
six miles of wooden pipes from Jamaica Pond. Public affairs were in the hands of the nine selectmen and everything
west of Charles Street was still marshland and vaguely
tidal water. Church life, banking and fire insurance were
the polite avenues of accomplishment for young men just
out of Harvard.

Three-Cent Tea and Other Clubs

Today the Boston Athenaeum is the finest gentlemen's library in the world. Membership, although based on the possession of purchasable shares (which once hit an all time high of 900) is very largely composed of men and women of culture and assured position, and its facilities for reading and research are reported to be far more comprehensive than those of any other private library known. Science in its technical aspects, current fiction and works relating to professions are not its concern, but belles lettres in the widest meaning of the phrase are its reason for existence, these and the association through their medium of an amiable convocation of Boston individualists. These constitute what is practically a family, and at the back of each volume on the Athenaeum shelves is a slip which reads: "Readers who care to express an opinion of this book for the guidance of others may do so below. An opinion should contain not more than five words and should be followed by the initials of the reader." Athenaeum readers do not, always, observe these very specific instructions, but it is notable that criticism slips are pasted in volumes of Shakespeare and Milton, Aristotle, Plato and the Hebrew testament.

The Athenaeum was founded in a day when letters were, perhaps, a more universal preoccupation of educated people than they are today. A group of public spirited litterateurs which included the Rev. William Emerson, father of a more distinguished son, formed in the early years of last century a modest circle known as the Anthology Club, which met once a week at dinner and discussed, over the turtle soup, the editorial contents of the latest issue of *The American Magazine* and, over the Port and walnuts, letters in general. The club possessed a modest library contributed by members, and from this grew the characteristically Boston institution, complete with a large part of the library of

Boston and the Boston Legend

George Washington, which is the Athenaeum of today.

Belonging to the Athenaeum, beside partaking of obligations almost those of membership in a family, is at once a rite and a distinction. The austere premises at 10½ Beacon Street are a shrine of the literate proprieties, and habitual communicants, distinguishable by their green cloth bags and general resemblance to the kindly absent-minded professor of fiction, assemble daily for services in the stacks and for three-cent tea in the afternoon. China tea and cakes for three pennies give inordinate pleasure to members, both because of the nice economy involved and by reason of the distinction of the tradition.

A great many distinguished Bostonians have been members of this Beacon Hill fellowship from the sagacious Theophilus Parsons, an early Chief Justice of the Commonwealth, down to the present, and first woman librarian, Miss Elinor Gregory. Thomas Appleton, Julia Ward Howe, Rufus Choate, Mr. Longfellow, James T. Fields, Charles Sumner, Mrs. Jack Gardner, Henry Cabot Lodge, Dr. Holmes and Charles Francis Adams are only a few names of habitues selected at casual random.

Charles Bullard Fairfield, who was assistant librarian at the Athenaeum many years ago, recalled the austere impression made by its benign atmosphere upon his boyish memory early in the nineteenth century:

The Athenaeum [he wrote], surrounded by horse chestnut trees, stood there in aristocratic dignity and repose, which seemed almost sacrilegious to disturb with the noise of our childish sports. There were a few old gentlemen who used to frequent the reading room whose white hair (and some of them even wore knee breeches and queues and powder) always stilled our boyish clamor as we played on the grass plots in the yard. To some of these old men our heads were often uncovered, and to our young imagination it seemed as if they were sages. . . . They seemed almost as much a part of the mysterious old establishment as the books on the shelves, the

320

MT. VERNON STREET UNDER THE STATE HOUSE

Three-Cent Tea and Other Clubs

dusty busts in the entries, or the old librarian himself. Sometimes I used to venture into those still passages, and steal a look into the reading room whose quiet was never disturbed save by the wealthy creak of some old citizen's boots, or by the long breathing of some venerable frequenter of the place enjoying his afternoon nap. In later years I came to know the Athenaeum more familiarly; the old gentlemen lost the character of sages and became estimable individuals of quiet tastes—but my old impression of the awful mystery of the building remains to this day. I mourned over the removal to its present fine position, and I seek in vain amid the stucco work and white paint of the new edifice for the charm which enthralled me in the old home of the institution.

The good old times when Dr. Bass, the librarian, sat on one side of the fireplace, and the late John Bromfield (with his silk handkerchief spread over his knees) on the other have passed away.

A pleasant picture of an age the harmony and repose of which, even in Boston, have forever vanished.

A long time ago, too, Lord Coleridge, Lord Chief Justice of England, visited the Athenaeum in company with Governor Butler of Massachusetts. The Englishman was startled to observe that in the reading-room there was a sign on every statue with the peculiar admonition "Feet Off." He had, he remarked, frequently seen signs saying "Hands Off," but that "Feet Off" was quite new to him. The attendant explained that some of the old gentleman who frequented the place were apt to doze a bit after luncheon and that recently one, in elevating his feet to the level of a statue of the Discus Thrower, had pushed the entire arrangement over with frightful damage, not only to the bust, but to the nerves of everyone present. Feet, thereafter, were warned off.

The appointment of the present librarian of the Athenaeum, an event second only in interest in Boston to the election of the new president of Harvard, caused some small flutter over the town's tea-tables. It was not so much that Miss Gregory was a woman, and the first ever to be elevated to that estate, so much as that she was a heretic. She was reported not to believe in the Athenaeum ghost. This particular Beacon Street hant is supposed to be the spirit of an elderly bluestocking who, years ago, lost her way in the stacks and perished miserably before a rescue party could come to her aid. Generations of Athenaeum members have piously subscribed to the legend, some even to the extent of swearing to encounters with the ghost, attired in other-world raiment closely approximating the poke bonnet, reticule and chatelaine watch in which she met her end, and naturally a scoffer was looked at somewhat askance.

In the Widener Memorial Library at Harvard there is a room secured with chicken wire and padlocks for the detention of erotic literature and known to undergraduates as the inferno. At the Athenaeum there is a similar section of books available only on special request famous in Boston as the "scruple room," because reference cards for volumes in this category are marked with a pharmacist's scruple mark for identification. Any member of the Athenaeum is free of the scruple room, but to get the key he must name to the librarian the book that has aroused his curiosity. The modesty even of Boston's most mature and supposedly informed citizens is attested by the circumstance that calls for the key, together with the nomination of a title from the works of Petronius, John Cleland or the Marquis de Sade, are forthcoming only at the most infrequent of intervals.

For all its legends, or perhaps because of them however, the Athenaeum is very much a part of the Boston scene. Its overtones of Brahminism, its associations with almost every New England man of letters for more than a century, its very consciousness of its own flavor of individuality make it one with the Latin name-plates on the trees of the Common and the awareness of courteous usage which prompts Bostonians to post signs reading "Newly Seeded Ground,"

Three-Cent Tea and Other Clubs

where, anywhere else in the world it would say "Keep Off."

Among its other distinctions, and they are several, the Tavern Club, located in the mews behind the Colonial Theater, has never really believed that Mr. Edison's incandescent bulb is here to stay and pins its faith in illuminating gas which has been around longer and is more prone to continue its service through thunder-storms. To be sure, some of the younger radical element of the Tavern have initiated electric illumination in the depths of the library, but even that concession to modernity and the machine age was made over the prostrate form of Professor Charles Townsend Copeland and others who viewed the innovation with alarm and allowed that such a mechanized way of life would end in nothing good.

Really Boston's most admirable of clubs, the Tavern includes in its membership authentic professional men, literateurs and almost anybody whose family or achievements may make him considerable for membership. Its list is distinguished by numerous Codmans, Coolidges, Cabots, Cushings, Otises and Thayers. William Dean Howells was a prime mover in its foundation fifty years ago. J. Pierpont Morgan stays there when in Boston, Dr. A. Lawrence Lowell (Cousin Larry, to half of Boston) lunches there daily, and Gardners, Hemenways and Sedgwicks converge about its round table upstairs for some of the best dinners eaten in Boston. Probably the annual dinner of the Humane Society, which is paid for in rotation out of the pocket of a trustee, is more magnificent in its champagnes and terrapin than any other gastronomic function of the town, but the fish chowder at the Tavern is archetypal New England food and its wine list, while simple, has been arranged by experts after long and scholarly consultation.

Visitors to the Tavern note with occasional surprise that the winding stairs of the clubhouse have, in addition to the customary outside banister, an inner hand rail along the wall. This was installed for the benefit of Alexander Wadsworth Longfellow, now unhappily dead. Mr. Longfellow, a descendant of the poet and a sea captain famous for his white beard and racy salt-water anecdotes, once fell the length of the stairs in a veritable avalanche of marine expletive after a club dinner. The absence of suitable safeguards to life and limb was universally lamented and the extra banister forthwith made its appearance.

Once a year the Tavern's members stage a play, an occasion when decorum is usually suspended, and once a year, too, there is a club dinner. The symbol of the society is an intelligent-looking brown bear who can be seen in various festive postures throughout the decorative scheme of the premises, and at the dinner the bear, personified by a stately member invested with an old fur rug, usually makes a speech. It is a relatively solemn moment.

Even more so perhaps than the Somerset, the Tavern is aware of the proper Bostonians to a degree that in any other community might be esteemed snobbish. A short time since the then Secretary of the Navy, Charles Francis Adams, was elected to membership and his name posted on the bulletin board. There is another Charles F. Adams in Boston, a highly respected Yankee merchant and organizer of a vast chain of commodity stores, but he is not of the Bourbon Adams stock, and under the posted name of the descendant of two presidents, three ministers to England and a somewhat esteemed writer, a wag scrawled the words "the right one."

The Saint Botolph Club, whose ancient premises in Newbury Street more closely resemble those of an old London club than any other in town, was founded in the early eighties with Francis Parkman as its first president. While not primarily a club of actors or writers, its home is closely

DOWN COURT STREET TO THE STATE HOUSE

suggestive of the celebrated home of the Players in New York's Gramercy Park and its membership derives from professional, artistic and educational circles rather than from those impinging upon formal society. It is a place of charm and souvenirs of a festive and bohemian past, and its oak-paneled dining-room is illustrated with a decor of flagons, magnums and other containers emptied upon celebrated occasions. Its overtones are those of things worn almost to shabbiness with homely use, of authenticity and mature tastes in the good things of the world.

As there is the Beacon Society within the Algonquin Club, the Saint Botolph, too, used to boast a club within its membership. The Bund was very exclusive, having, to be exact, but six members, but its Sunday night suppers were notable occasions. Every Sunday evening during the winter The Bund members met in a private room and prepared their own meal. Richard Borden, a Fall River industrialist, was a general dictator of the scene; Gino Lorenzo Perera, a genial Italian, inevitably built his masterpiece of baked oysters with special cheeses, known as oysters Perera. Dr. G. Howard Maynadier,* then of the comparative literature department at Harvard, was master of beverages, and Beth Vincent and Tom Fox, assisted by Dr. George Burgess Magrath, Boston's picturesque and astute medical examiner, were assistants at call. Dr. Magrath, whose bush of snowy hair, inseparable pipe and flowing Windsor tie are one of the town's oriflammes, has a brilliant record as a criminologist; has hanged many men and sent scores to jail as a result of his powers of detection which are at times almost fic-

---

* It was Dr. Maynadier who achieved fame with several successive generations of Harvard students in his courses for his celebrated theory of lighting woodfires with the kindling on top rather than on the bottom. His course in the English Novel was, not infrequently and to the invariable pleasure of his auditors, interrupted with brief lectures in the interest of this cause.

tional, and is an indefatigable raconteur. Founded to thwart the thirst which for a time threatened during the great drought, The Bund survived as a very admirable, if little known, Boston institution, into a happier and saner era and the memory of some of its historic foregatherings will haunt the dim chambers of the Saint Botolph as long as the memory lives of brave times and the company of heroes.

Two other clubs demand the attention of serious-minded observers of the Boston scene: the Union Boat Club and the Tennis and Racquet. The Union Boat members are actually leagued in the name and practice of rowing. They scull themselves up and down the broad reaches of the Charles even to farthest Cottage Farm and the Weeks Memorial Bridge. Gaffers of mature years array themselves in shorts and head swathings and whisk vigorously around in whimsical shells. Frank Buxton, editor of the *Herald* and a trustee of the Public Library, is a stanch paddler and would rather take guests to the Union Boat house than to the Park Street precincts of the Union itself.

The Racquet and Tennis, whose somber premises overlook the Boston and Albany's switching yards in Boylston Street and flank the Sixteenth Police Station, is the resort of the town's more gilded youth. Upholstered in easy luxury and heartened with rum sours, its members damn successive Federal administrations and tirelessly dispute the controversy over whether gentlemen should affect notched lapels or shawl collars on their dinner jackets. Its principal adornment is Willis P. Beal, for years Boston's most eligible bachelor and a man about town of amiable distinction. Mr. Beal achieved local immortality by espousing the cause of the notched lapel at a time when Brook Brothers still stocked only the shawl collar type in the belief that any other variety was fit but for waiters and musicians.

Chapter XXXI

HEEL TAPS

THERE are eight members of the Heel Taps Club, the rank-ing American association of breeders and fighters of game cocks. Their names are shrouded in august anonymity, but the legend of their organization is one of arbitrary domina-tion of fighting cocks and of strains as carefully registered and jealously preserved as those of Derby winners. Of the eight overlords of the oldest and most tenaciously ineradi-cable of American sports, five are Bostonians, and their country estates are the national center of activity of the eminently illegal, secretive and altogether gentlemanly sport of matching the forces of blooded game birds in battles where death in the ring is the ultimate sporting accolade. Boston is the cock-fighting capital of America north of the Rio Grande.

Always Boston has been, in a characteristically conserva-tive way, a sporting city. Its unabashed loves have been baseball, hockey and horses, and all estates of citizens have

327

shared a vast, profane and delighted enthusiasm for them.
Baseball is perennial; hockey, its *aficionados* attest, has
been a twentieth century emergence; and the kingdom of
the horse has opened new vistas of excited speculation with
the repeal of gambling restrictions in adjacent Rhode Island
and New Hampshire. Of the great American sport of cock-
fighting, however, which true Yankees share with the Cre-
oles of Louisiana, huntsmen of Virginia, Ohio rustics and
country gentlemen of New Jersey, little is openly said and
nothing is chronicled in the public prints. Unlike the breeders of the Deep South where the law knows better than to
hinder the pursuits of gentlefolk, New England sportsmen
have never achieved a satisfactory feudal immunity from
humanitarian regulation, so that, while cock-fighting exists
in the vicinage of Boston on a flourishing and impressive
scale, it is of necessity shrouded in reticence.

Invitations to mains held at the North Shore estates of
Boston's fighting bird fanciers rank on a par with invitations to dance in the private ball-rooms of Commonwealth
Avenue and, while they are entirely verbal and informal,
partake somewhat of the nature of a command among the
knowing amateurs of the town. The scene, on the Essex
County estate of a State Street broker who is also a hunts-
man and horse-breeder, is notable not only for its color
and circumspection of conduct, but because it represents a
long tradition of New England sport which has flowered
unabated since the first Puritan youths threw their birds
into a ring behind a forgotten seventeenth century haymow.
The line has been unbroken from the time when the Mathers were abroad in the land to an age of chrome and steel-
finished roadsters flashing up the drive of a gentleman's
farm and liveried house-footmen serving Scotch highballs
behind the stables. The faces are the identical ones, lean and
Yankee; the cries of the handlers have echoed down the

Heel Taps

centuries. Strip away the tweeds, Tattersall waistcoats and gleaming cordovan field boots for the fustian roundabouts and homespun of the Colonial farmer and the picture is still the same. Again and again New England returns to itself.

In the drive between the white-painted Colonial house, with its low-roofed kitchens and offices behind, and the green-roofed stables are parked twenty or thirty motor-cars ranging from sports-bodied Isotta-Fraschinis to the latest model Ford station wagon. There are a few chauffeurs in linen dust-coats, but largely they are owner-driven. The ring is in the tan-bark of the stable itself, between the rows of varnished boxstalls with the necks of hunters outstretched for patting and to see the excitement. There are a few women present, the familiar long-faced British country type, in cloth hats and low-heeled boots, but the greater part of the gathering is masculine, pipe smoking, smelling vaguely of Harris tweed and saddle soap. It is, in effect, the local hunt meeting, and, to heighten the parallel between Hamilton, Massachusetts, and a Sussex market town, there are a few tenants and farmers present, lean-jawed tobacco chewers in overalls and open-necked shirts with cropped white mustaches and a civil equality of speech and manner stemming from ten generations of Yankee yeomen. When there was but one mail coach daily over the Newburyport Pike and when pinks and snows were outfitting further north in Arundel to harry British shipping in '76 they were the same.

The handlers, retainers in the employ of the patrons of the ancient sport, have appeared with their birds, two teams representing the best blood of several "stables" maintained by amateurs of the North Shore region. The main is to include eleven matches between twenty-two cocks (the number of fights is always uneven) for a thousand-dollar wager between the contesting teams and any number of side bets

329

among the spectators laid in as many combinations of odds as there are to a horse race. There are a couple of professional bookmakers present with the consent of the host for the amusement and possible profit of his guests and they circulate among the sportsmen and rustics with impressive sheaves of bank notes folded lengthwise between their fingers soliciting trade. "Five to four on the Stone Fence in the first meet," they announce loudly. "Three two on the Irishman's team for the main." Stone Fences are not only a toddy peculiar to New England and the apple-growing regions of rural New Jersey compounded of a shot of spirits in a tall glass of hard cider; they are a strain of fighting cocks, and the Irishman is the host's trainer.

While the bets are being placed the handlers are shearing the comb and wattles from the first birds, clipping short their proud wing feathers that they may not trail underfoot, and adjusting the slender and curved Mexican gaffs to their legs. The weapons available to each bird are his gaffs, his beak and the clipped wing feathers which, when spread, present a fan-shaped array of quill points, but of these the two-inch steel spurs do the great execution. The birds have been weighed in so as to provide matches between cocks of a similar class, and, although it is doubtful if even an expert from the staff of *Game Fowl News* or *Grit and Steel*, official cock-fighting gazettes, could tell just how much Yellow Pile blood, how much Kansas Slugger or Crazy Snake is in each warrior, they are sure to be fighters. Long and patient breeding and selection has eliminated every trace of "dung-hill" in them.

Formalities over, wagers laid, and the spectators, most of them with highballs in hand, crowded about the ring, the main is on. The handlers face each other across a board which is sunk into the earth so as to protrude about an inch across the center of the ring. They are ruffling the crests of the birds to irritate them and pushing them to within a few inches of each other so that the fierce desire to kill which is the utterly dominant trait of fighting cocks may be aroused, and at a given signal they toss the gladiators together in the center of the pit. For an instant they engage each other with hostile stare, stepping warily sidewise, eyes never for an instant leaving their opponent, the quills of their necks erect and bristling with mutual and deathless hatred. Then suddenly, in a smother of dust and a violent whir of wings, they close, cutting, slashing, leaping, dodging with incredible rapidity, with necks out-thrust and silent fury. At times the two birds are indistinguishable in the mêlée; and even if the eye can follow a favorite cock it can never know precisely what occurs in the breathless moments of actual encounter, so swift are the cuts and parries. Indeed, veteran cock-fighters assert that very few telling thrusts or blows are ever seen by the spectators, only their results being apparent.

In the battle in progress it is impossible to distinguish which bird is which save when, at intervals, they break and retire a few inches, when it is patent that one, the darker cock, is suffering fewer wounds than his opponent, whose drooping wings indicate an advanced stage of fatigue. Cheers and groans, appropriate to the sympathies of the onlookers, greet each move of aggression or defense. Late bets, hedges are shouted back and forth as the odds shift and adjust themselves. Bank notes are waved in excited fists.

"Two to one on the red bird; two to one!"

"You're on for twenty dollars."

"The light one will wreck him yet."

"Ten says he doesn't."

"It's as good as in my pocket. I'm spending it now."

Only the birds in the ring appear oblivious to the uproar. Once the dark cock appears to be down; his wings flutter

and he stretches his neck out in the finely screened dirt. His
beak is open and the feathers on his neck are black with blood,
but time is called and the handler blows the clots from his
beak with his lips and smooths his ruffled feathers. In a
twinkling he is back in the ring, as vicious as ever. They are
in the thick of it, raising dust, hacking and stabbing, coming
together, breast to breast with audible thuds and furious
flutterings, leaping high and rebounding, game to the last
ounce of endurance. Then suddenly it is over. With a mo-
tion which only a speed-shutter camera could record, the
dark bird delivers a mortal thrust with his gaff into the neck
of his enemy. The spur is caught in the muscles and they
fall together, one stretched in the dust, his wings beating a
feeble tattoo, the other struggling to free his blade. The
victor is scooped up by his triumphant handler, brushed and
petted and a few drops of whiskey poured into his beak.
He lives to fight another day and eventually to die, magnificently and happily, pursuing the irresistible urge of his
being.

Highballs circulate; money changes hands with feigned
bad grace, it being a cock-fighting tradition to lose only
under protest; the handlers are clipping the second brace of
birds, and the bookies are making their odds afresh.

The next match is between a cock with a local reputation
of being a "killer" and an untried valiant whose owner as-
serts him to be in the direct line of descent from a famous
shuffler in the strain developed by August Belmont, a cock
fancier of note. The long end of the betting is with the
Whitehackle whose record is known and who has been vic-
torious in fifteen encounters, and the long money wins. For
within thirty seconds he has clashed with the scion of Belmont sires; stabbed a gleaming spur through his brain, and
strutted, a miracle of complacency, toward the edge of the
ring in search of further combat. The losers are stunned,

SCOLLAY SQUARE

and retire from active betting for all of ten minutes, at the end of which term they are evolving fresh financial stratagems to recoup their losses and slyly engaging the bookies in guarded converse.

And so the morning passes to the satisfaction of all. Of the eleven fights, five end in outright kills, a consummation as gratifying as a knockout in the prize ring. In the end tweeds and flannels depart in their cars with shouted farewells and a wealth of waving gloves, pleased with the prospect of another main of consequence that day a fortnight on a neighboring estate. In a few minutes the stable is again the domain of the mild-eyed horses and their grooms, and another chapter has been added to the saga of a venerable and classic sport that is nowhere more esteemed than by the gentlemen and touts, bookies and college youths of Boston.

Chapter XXXII

THIS BOSTON

IT is difficult to embrace what George Santayana, who was once himself a Bostonian, calls the "total vision" of any community in which the past and the present are so inseparably blended as in the city which arose on the site of Mr. Blackstone's garden. Boston's history has been essentially a record of paradoxes, of a search for religious freedom which ended in theological tyranny, of strife with the British crown while proudest of being a purely English settlement, or a redeeming liberalism inextricably blended with a proverbial conservatism, of a boasted Athens maintaining absurd reservations and pruderies. And the most notable of Boston's paradoxes is that while it is one of the most diversified cities on the face of the globe in point of social, economic, racial, religious and aesthetic interests, it has about it also a pervading homogeneity which baffles identification while apparent to every perceptive sense.

334

This Boston

In some manner, however, it seems more nearly possible here to achieve the "good life" that has engaged the attention of so many thoughtful people at so many periods in the world's history than in numerous other cities famed for their various attitudes toward the business of living. What constitutes the "good life" must, necessarily, be defined by the individual, but it must be apparent to any sensitive person that Boston is at once a tranquil, homely and in certain ways a gracious place. The swan boats that Robert Paget designed for the waters of the Public Garden when Martin Brimmer was Mayor are a symbol of it. The incessantly steaming tea-kettle above the sidewalk in Court Street, reminding of a more ingenuous age of advertising, suggests it. There is a reflection of it in the white kid gloves of the Harvard youths in crew haircuts who dance at the balls at the Somerset. The arcade of shade trees along the Mall of Commonwealth Avenue is a reminder of it. These are mere random visual tokens, but they stand as an index of a temper of existence, as witness that the "good life" somehow is there. It may not be a gay city, but Boston is one of the substantially happy cities of the world.

It has been remarked that Boston is in many ways characteristically Edwardian. There is more than a little truth in this and possibly when we revise our opinions of what is desirable in the way of world scenes it will be found that Edwardian times were rather admirable after all. Certainly Boston has changed but little physically during the twentieth century. There are, in the back alleys, the ancient cries of the town. The Paris of Villon's time echoed with the call of vendors of *"le bon fromage de Brie"* and *"à la mal tache"* for stain remover, but Boston's street cries are those of the rag and bottle man, the meat fat collector, the one-man ice corporation, "aye-e-e-e-ce"; of the fruit and vegetable dealers with the horses and covered wagons dangling

335

inevitable scales behind. There is the catnip man who has taken his stand these forty years outside the Granary Burying Ground with his stock of feline intoxicant; there are, in spring, hurdy-gurdy men, staring hopefully at upper windows while grinding their dreadful but friendly machines, and for generations there has been the head of a Neopolitan family, the balloon and windmill man, who sets down his basket outside the Webster's iron fence in Exeter Street for the delight of children. In the lower city there are flower stalls wherever an alley offers or there is a handy setback from the stoop line, and in the doorway of the Pierce Building in Copley Square there is the dignified newsvendor in a bowler hat and white walrus moustaches who knows all the limousined great of the town as they come for groceries.

Probably there are more passageways of exaggerated narrowness in the city than even the small boys of the town know about. It is possible, of course, to go vast distances in New York's underground footways, but Dr. Holmes remarked that one could "bore one's way through Boston," and that is as true today as when horse-cars ran down the center of Marlborough Street, stopping to deliver the blueing at Mrs. Endicott's or, if it were Friday, to remind Mrs. Peabody of Symphony. In many places, too, there remain street signs which tell the number of the Ward they are located in, surviving from a time when that geographic unit was of more considerable significance.

Like London, Boston is at its best in June, as is appropriate to a climate where fogs and sleet and thaws make galoshes requisite sometimes into April. Then the town flowers into a "little season" characterized by Commencement at Harvard, the races at the Country Club and a program of Pop concerts at Symphony. Spring itself has, of course, been heralded by the universal benison of bock beer and the reappearance of the swans in the Fenway, but June

336

THE GILDED DOME OF THE STATE HOUSE

This Boston

finds the lilacs in the stone urns in front of the Algonquin Club at their best and the crews, as nearly naked as is decent, raising their stroke up and down the basin of the Charles.

There are no longer any open cars, red for Norumbega Park, blue for Auburndale, in Kenmore Square, but the traffic jam in Bay State Road is worse at five o'clock, and in the cool courtyards of Cambridge clubs there is champagne cup on the tables and flannel trousers and copies of the closing stock edition of the *Transcript* on every hand. When there are horse races at Brookline on the seventeenth, Back Bay goes en masse as to a meet at Epsom Downs, white top-hats, rat-catcher suits and smart horse rigs dragged from the last year's moth balls and forgotten stables.

Harvard Commencement is of significant importance in Boston despite the relatively small number of people immediately affected by it. The governor arrives in his coach surrounded by outriders and lancers in scarlet tunics. The High Sheriff of Middlesex County, without whose presence or deputy no man may receive a degree, mounts the platform in his cocked hat and blue Colonial coat faced with buff, and raps three times with his court sword. Supplemented by the academic music of a German brass band concealed behind a grove of rented potted palms the ritual latinity of state is spoken, and suddenly—the season is over and Boston is deserted for the summer.

The Boston and Maine's Pullmans running in extra sections, bound for Dark Harbor and Wiscasset, New Brunswick, the White Mountains and the porch rocking chairs of a hundred profile and notch houses, are jammed to the guards. Every state-room on the Nantucket steamers is sold out for a fortnight, and the Cape, from Cotuit to Provincetown, opens its tea-rooms and bathing pavilions and sum-

337

mer theaters for the annual biggest season on record. And for the less pretentious summer commuters the Nantasket steamers are running again twice daily, and the cottage colonies of Lynn and Revere are alive with orchidaceous bathing attire flapping from unabashed clotheslines.

The Boston which is the essential core and being of an entity combining a scheme of living, an abstract in biography and a geographic quantity is a city quite divorced from any tangible or consciously exploited local color. Chicago, for example, is a product of its own environment, living up to a character it created for itself in the spacious years of cattle millionaires and the silver dollar bar of the Palmer House, and the same is true of many other American cities. They have come to assume the qualities expected of them.

But the hallmarks of Boston, from Thompson's Spa to spendthrift trusts, and from green cloth bags to membership in the Union Boat Club, are clues to a society that has evolved them. Curling at the Country Club in winter; women's low-heeled shoes and the Queen Mary bonnets perpetually stocked at the corner of Tremont Street and Temple Place, an anachronistic knowledge of bridge-whist and an intensive snobbishness on the part of the curators of the Fogg and Fine Arts Museums merely mirror the traits of the community; they do not dominate it.

The Boston accent, precise, articulate, and vaguely superior, is as implicit with confusion to outlanders as an Englishman's single eyeglass. As true Cockneys must be born within sound of Bow Bells, so to inherit an authentic Boston accent one must be reared within a certain indeterminate but limited distance of the Boston Stone, embedded in the wall of a Hanover Street structure and since 1737, the precise center of the city from which all mileposts throughout the New England countryside were measured. No suburban dweller from the faubourgs of Chelsea or Somerville, Belmont, Brighton or the baffling Newtons, from Arlington, Braintree or Malden may achieve it. It is a heritage like the habit of calling trolleys "broomstick cars" or being buried from Trinity Church.

Boston continues to do without a number of institutions deemed essential elsewhere. Its public architecture is of an order so generally low as to be sometimes positively frightening, the lore of building having been devoted by architects, from Mr. Bulfinch to Ralph Adams Cram, almost entirely to private dwellings. The formal delimitations of gilt-edged society, save through the agencies of the Vincent Club and the Junior League, are but little emphasized except among the newly affluent along the more horse-conscious reaches of the North Shore. Everyone knows everyone of social importance without recourse to formal directories and the local edition of the Social Register is scantily patronized. Night life is practically non-existent. There are but a handful of not too glamorous night clubs and only the last senile years of Prohibition saw three or four pseudo de luxe speakeasies in the manner of Manhattan. Gang warfare is of such a dismal and uninspired nature that even the *Record,* William Randolph Hearst's low and joyous chronicle of infamies, finds difficulty in sublimating its occasional violence to tabloid standard. Smart Boston dines at home or in the restaurant of the Ritz Carlton overlooking the Public Garden, and its after-theater supper is more apt to be laid out on the sideboard than served up, as in New York or London, amidst the smash of bands and the exhibited anatomies of diaphanously clad nymphs on a dance floor. Neither has Boston a Harlem, and seekers after the cocaine-stimulated carousing of epicene bagnios must look elsewhere. Traveling salesmen unite in the opinion that to spend Sunday evening in Boston is the worst fate that can befall a stranger, unless possibly it is a similar occasion in Philadelphia.

Boston and the Boston Legend

And out of all this traditional farrago of ancestors and integrities—Bulfinch houses, Irish mayors, the athletic essays of Miss Eleonora Sears, the most prosperous department stores in the world, fishballs, Frothinghams, fishing parties down the harbor aboard the *King Philip,* Christian Science, Crimmins, the waiter-captain at the Harvard Club, portraits by Sargent, hitching posts, Papanti's dancing classes, the legend of the great blizzard of 1717, a sort of curtain raiser to that of 1888, Ward Eights and Jacobite adherents—there emerges something approximating the "total vision" of Boston. The gold dome of the State House, a pronunciation of the word "cow" which gives it four syllables, Phineas Sprague's Rolls Royces, Saturday beans from Friend's, old ladies in frilly parasols and an allegiance to codfish are part of the traditional associations of the town. There are others. There is a sartorial scheme for men which prescribes an incredible soft hat turned up both front and back, a frequent and unsuspected classical erudition among life insurance salesmen, a charming sentimentality over the New Haven Railroad; which, having bankrupted half the first families, still ranks near the top in their institutional affections, there is a street sweeper in Copley Square who wears a morning coat to work and an eminent lawn mower and furnace tender in Newbury Street with Chester A. Arthur whiskers, trolleys known as articulated trams, the Uncle Dudley editorials on the *Globe,* and a tremendous and universal enthusiasm among all classes of citizens for professional hockey games. There is a handsome footway along the Charles known as the Esplanade, and the only Fellsway in this part of the world, there is a curious tendency to say "me" instead of "my" and "keh" for "car," there are old gentlemen whose cellars of Madeira were laid down by their grandfathers, there is a Gibson-girl lady who drives a 1908 automobile with brass lamps, an upright wheel and

340

This Boston

no windshield, and there is no Bohemia or Greenwich Village anywhere in the town.

And to all this there is a pattern, as clear, in a way, as the blue cows browsing in the shadow of a blue State House on Staffordshire plate, a scheme and design, an essence of living that has survived a long time into an age of streamlined trains to Providence and Gertrude Stein in Beacon Street with all the intact qualities it possessed, say, when the Bunch of Grapes tavern was standing. There are still the green tranquillity of the Common, the eroded slates of King's Chapel burying ground, the grim-statued visage of Daniel Webster, tempered by the recollection of his fondness for brandy and oysters, the colored evening waistcoats of the Tavern members as they smoke their churchwarden pipes after dinner, the serenity of a midnight Beacon Hill in winter, the church bells of the city on Sunday mornings in May, and it is from these and a hundred other characteristics, happy and homely things, that the entirety of Boston as it was and is is built.

In Boston the past is too immediate and too vital for any near oblivion, and the present seems to invite no impending doom. There have been mutations and there will still be change, but somewhere down the corridors of the years there must be a Boston, and, while the tides roll in from the Atlantic and the green uplands of Massachusetts slope down to meet the city and the sea, there inevitably must always be the Boston legend.

REFERENCES

Boston Evening Transcript: files
Brown, Abram English, *Faneuil Hall and Faneuil Hall Market*
Carter, Morris, *Isabella Stewart Gardner and Fenway Court*
Conwell, Col. Russell H., *History of the Great Fire of Boston*
Crawford, Mary Caroline, *Old Boston in Colonial Days*
———— *Romantic Days in Old Boston*
Drake, Samuel G., *History of Boston*
———— *Old Landmarks of Boston*
Fiske, John, *The Beginnings of New England*
Fortune, February, 1933
Frothingham, Jr., Richard, *History of the Siege of Boston*
Gaines Universal Register for 1776
Gilman, Arthur, *The Story of the City of Boston*
Howe and Matthews, *American Clipper Ships*
McKay, Richard C., *Some Famous Sailing Ships and Their Builders*
The Memorial History of Boston
Mitchell, Edward P., *Memoires of an Editor*
New York Daily Tribune: files
New York Herald: files
The Prince Society, *The Letters of John Dunton*
Regan, Mary Jane, *Echoes from the Past*
State Street Trust Company: Pamphlets
Suffolk County Deeds
Thwing, Annie Haven, *The Crooked and Narrow Streets of Boston*

INDEX

343

Index

Index

Beacon Hill, 5, 14, 62, 76-83, 106, 109, 111, 148, 152, 159, 164, 190, 196, 251, 253, 261, 267, 282, 297, 310, 341
  Bohemia on, 303-315
  Christmas Eve on, 230-233
  Hancock mansion on, 78
  Irish on, 245
  naming of, 31
  spared by fire, 147
Beacon Society, 317, 325
Beacon Street, 12, 91, 107, 112, 122, 138, 164, 174, 184, 185, 186, 226, 259, 261, 298, 313, 322, 341
  governor's house on, 77
Beal, Willis P., 326
Beal family, 261
Beaver, arrival of tea-laden, 53
"Beebe's Block," burning of, 146
Beecher, sermons by, 166
Beer, attempt to popularize, 21
Belcher, Governor Jonathan, first store on Long Wharf owned by, 224
Belknap, Jeremy, 199
Bellamy, Captain Samuel, hanging of, 33
  story of, 32-33
Bell and Everett procession, 124, 125
Bell in Hand, 114, 278
  Copeland at, 210
  history of, 299-302
  patrons of, 300
Bellows, Dr., sermon on Boston fire, 153
Bellows, George, 299
Bellringer, Harvard College, 200
Belmont, 339
Belmont, August, 332
Bellomont, Earl of, 32
Benchley, Robert, 211
  Copeland's readings from, 212
Benjamin Bangs and Co., 87
Bennett, on coach horses, 36
Bennett, James Gordon, 124, 129
Bennington, celebration of victory at, 44
Berenson, 178
Berlin Museum, 179

Berlin Opera, jailing of Dr. Muck of, 237
Betting, among ship-owners, 95
Beverly, 261
Beverly Farms, 176
Bible, Copeland's readings from, 212
Bigelow, Miss, 129
Bigelow family, home of, 261
Bigelow Papers, quoted, 104
Black, Viola, 306, 307, 315
Black April, ban on, 253
Blackstone, William, 3-5, 10, 13, 14, 151, 158, 258, 334
  Mather on, 5
  neighbors of, 4, 5
  orchard of, 4
  purchase of, 160
Blackstone's Point, 11
Blizzard of 1717, 340
"Blue Boy," 179
Blue Hill, 262
Blue Voyage, ban on, 252
Bode, Dr. Wilhelm, 179
Bohemians, 251, 303-315
Bolton, Larry, 306, 307, 315
Books, censorship of, 249, 251-253
Booth, Edwin, 257
Borden, Richard, 325
Border Street, 93
Boston, early commentators on, 25
  first character of, 4
  first citizen of, 4
  geography of, 13-14
  growth of, 15, 19
  naming of, 11
  population of, 19-20
  selection of site of, 6, 11
Boston Advertiser, 272
Boston and Albany railroad, 132, 326
Boston and Dedham railroad, 135
Boston and Lowell railroad, 135
Boston and Maine railroad, 132, 135, 176, 337
  Eastern Division of, 132
  progress of train in 1846, 136-137
  Western Division of, 132, 133
Boston and Providence railroad, 135
Boston and Revere Beach railroad, 140

345

Index

Index

347

Index

Index

349

Index

Index

Index

Index

353

Index

Galsworthy, 136
Game cocks, fighting, Boston center of, 327
Game Fowl News, 330
"Ganymede and Helen," 12
Gardner, John L., 174
Gardner, Mrs. Isabella Stewart, 173-183, 188, 262, 320
  admirers of, 175
  death of, 182
  exploits of, 176-182
  Sargent's portraits of, 182*f.*
Gardner family, 256, 323
Garrison, Mrs. William Lloyd, 118
Garrison, William Lloyd, 111, 112, 114, 116
  attacked by mob, 117
  inscription on jail cell by, 118
Garvin, Thomas J., 244
Gaston, Mayor William, 150, 154
Geese, dogs fed on, 3
General Court, Governor Endicott reprimanded by, 18
General Electric, 260
George III, 292
  Bostonian loyalty to, 259
Gerry, Elbridge, 61
Gerry the Chimney Man, 172
Gibbs' Wharf, 57
Giblin, 246
Gibson, Samuel, 200
Gilbert and Sullivan, popularity of, 257
Gill, 55
Ginseng, trade in, 90
Giorgione, at Fenway Court, 181
Girl from Rector's, The, 250
Glasgow, 67
  at Battle of Bunker Hill, 69
Globe, Boston. See Boston Globe
Glyn, Elinor, *Three Weeks* by, ban on, 252
Goats, on Boston Common, 16
Goddard, D. A., 190
Goodman, use of, 20
Goodspeed's book store, 252
Goodwife, use of, 20
Gore, Governor, 112
"Go to Halifax," origin of, 43

Gould, 137
Governor's Island, 228
Gramercy Park, New York, 125, 325
Granary Burying Ground, 13, 278, 336
  Woodbridge buried in, 162
Grand Banks, fish from, 223
Grant, General, at Revere House, 273
Grant, Robert, at Boston fire, 147-148
  on Sacco-Vanzetti commission of inquiry, 267
Grasshopper, on Faneuil Hall, 286
  inscription in, 286*f.*
Gratitude, Burke's rescue of passengers from, 95
Graves, Admiral, at Battle of Bunker Hill, 68
Gray, Captain, 128
Gray, Harrison, 54
Great Fire of 1872, 14
Great Spie-pond, 38
Greeley, Horace, 187
Gregory, Elinor, 320
  election of, as Athenaeum librarian, 321*f.*
Green Dragon Lane, 44
Green Dragon Lane Tavern, 169, 270
  Revolutionary activity in, 43
Green Shutters, The, 305, 309, 310
Greenwich Village, 306
  Beacon Hill as Boston's, 303
Greenwood, Isaac, 146
  dismissal of, 201
Griffin's Wharf, 53, 58
  Long Room members at, 56
Grinnell, Minturn and Co., *Flying Cloud* bought by, 93
Grinnell, Moses H., *New World* of, 92
Grit and Steel, 330
Grozier, Edwin, Copeland's employment by, 210
  editor-in-chief of *Post,* 191
Gustavus Adolphus, prayers of, 28
Guy Fawkes Day, celebration of, 39

354

Index

Index

Index

Ice, transportation from Boston to Orient of, 88
Indians, as servants, 20
 at Old South Meeting House mass meeting, 55
 Morton's harem of, 4
 punishment for fornication with, 27
India Wharf, 88
Individualism, at Harvard, 209
 Boston as home of, 24
Innkeeper, regard for, 42
Inns. *See* Taverns
Institute of 1770, 187, 202
Insurance companies, reorganization after fire, 157
Ipswich, 7
Ireland, famine in, 241
 immigration to Boston from, 241*f.*
Irish, cycle of, 248
 increase in population of, in Boston, 242
 reasons for decline of, 259
 rise of, in Boston, 243
 social progress of, 245
 supremacy of, in Boston politics, 245
Irving, 97
Isabella Stewart Gardner Museum, laying of cornerstone of, 179
Italy, little, on Copps Hill, 231
Ive, John, funeral of, 38

Jacimo, of Winter Place tavern, 281
Jackson, Andrew, 208
Jackson College, 219
Jagendorf, Prince Charles at, 70
Jamaica Pond, 318
James, Henry, 104
 novels of, 109
 on Emerson, 99
 on Mrs. Gardner, 173
James, William, writing of, 109
Jefferson, Thomas, 40
Jeffries, David, 47
Jehu, 96
Jewett, Henry, 312

Jewett, Sarah Orne, quoted, 108
"John Anderson, My Jo," Copeland's reading of, 212
Johnson, Isaac, 8, 9, 11
Johnson, Lady Arbella, 11
Johnson bar, 140
 Mrs. Gardner's skill at, 176
John the Orangeman, 204
Joinville, Prince de, at Tremont House, 273
Jones, College Bellringer, 200
Jones, Margaret, 164
Jones, Robert Edmond, 306
Jordan, Eben, 171, 278
Jordan, Effie, 313
Jordan Marsh, 262
Joshua Bates, building of, by McKay, 91
Journal, Boston, 239*f.*
Journal, Thoreau's, 100
Joy Street, 303, 311, 315
 Bohemians' purchase of real estate on, 307*f.*
 increased police force in, 304
Joy Street Station, 166, 314
Joyce, James, 303, 306
Julien, 160, 282, 283
 history of, 269*ff.*
 soup of, 269
Julien House, 272
Junior League, 253, 339

Keayne, Robert, 288
Keezer, Max, 204
Kelley, on Professor Copeland's mail, 213
Kenmore Square, 337
Keyserling, Count, *Twilight* by, ban on, 253
Kidd, Captain, hanging of, 32
King Philip, fishing parties on, 340
King's Arms, 42
King's Chapel, 275
King's Chapel burying ground, 341
Kingston Street, 143

Index

Index

Index

Index

Index

Index

Index

Index

Index

Index

Index

Stein, Gertrude, 306, 341
Stereoscope, 105
Stevenson, Marmaduke, 163
Stewart, Isabella. *See* Gardner, Mrs. Isabella Stewart
Stillman family, Delphic membership of, 216
Stockton family, 256
Stoddard, Thomas, 169
Stone ale, 12-13
Stone boat, 16
Stoneham, 64
Stone, Lucy, 113
Stoughton, William, 199
Stowe, Harriet Beecher, 118
Strachey, Lytton, 186
Strange Interlude, censor's rejection of, 250
Stratton, Dr. Samuel W., on Sacco-Vanzetti commission of inquiry, 267
Stravinsky, 236
  on Symphony programs, 238
Stuart, Gilbert, portrait of Washington by, in Faneuil Hall, 287
Stuhl, Nick, 280
Sturgis, Julian, 87
  Houqua's protest to, 90
Sturgis, Russell, 87
  agreement with Houqua, 90
Sturgis and Company, 87
Suffolk, 7
Sullivan, Deacon John, 301
Sullivan, John L., 284
Summer Street, 86, 114, 143, 164, 185
  fire in, 147, 156
  residential section, 87
Sumner, Charles, 118, 320
Sun, New York, Mitchell of, 189
Sun Also Rises, The, ban on, 252
Swan-boats, 230, 335
Swearing, punishment for, 27
Sweden, King of, 28
Swiftsure, Dabney's, 94
Swinburne, 311
Symmes, Rev. Z., 197
Symmetry, at Battle of Bunker Hill, 69
Symphony, 234-240, 256, 336

conductor of, 235
cultural legend upheld by, 257
first concert of, 236
Friday afternoon, 188
H. T. P. at, 187
importance of, to Bostonians, 234*f.*
musicians' strike, 237
Philip Hale on, 192
Symphony Hall, "Pops" in, 238*ff.*
"Symphony of Psalms," 236

Tabby the Wise, 108
Tales of a Wayside Inn, 59, 105
Tammany, 137
Taunton, locomotives from, 137
Taunton Branch Railroad, 137
Tavern Club, 341
  illuminating gas in, 323
  membership of, 323
  play produced by, 324
Taverns, 40-50
  function of, 41
  on Long Wharf, 224
  Revolution hatched in, 41, 50
  social life of, 45
Taylor, General, 192, 236, 300
Taylor, William, 192
Taylor family, *Globe* owned by, 191, 192
Tchapitoulas family, 255
Tea, Christian Science ban on, 263
  in Harvard Commons after Stamp Act, 201
  popular ban on, 52
  tax on, 52
  three-cent, at Athenaeum, 320
  trade in, with China, 90
Tea Party, 51-58
Telegram, 311*f.,* 315
Temple Place, 164, 338
  residential section, 87
Terrapin, 40, 223
Textbooks, early selling technic, 29
Thacher's, H. C., 95
Thackeray, at Mrs. James T. Fields', 107
  on oysters, 107

368

Index

Index

United Shoe Machinery Company, 260
United States Hotel, 273
United States Post Office, 87
United States Treasury building fire stopped by, 149
University Hall, Harvard, 203, 207
statue of Harvard before, 197
Upton, George, 129
Ursuline Convent, burning of, 243, 244
destruction of, 48
Usher, John, house of, 26
Utopia, Thoreau's, 100

Van Buren, President, at Tremont House, 273
Van Dyke, Henry, 213
Vane, Harry, elected governor, 19
Van Vechten, Carl, *Nigger Heaven* by, ban on, 253
Vanzetti, Bartolomeo, 266
See also Sacco-Vanzetti case
Vardy, Luke, 42
Varsovienne, 39
Vassall, William, 8, 9
Vendome Hotel, haircutting salon of, 39
incandescent lamps in, 235
Vestoff, 310
Vincent, Beth, 325
Vincent Club, 339
Victoria, Queen, 186
Vinal, Harold, 312
Virginia, opulence of, 78
Virginia Tidewater, 161
terrapin of, 223
Voices, 312

Wabash Avenue, 156
Wait, Gamaliel, death of, 38
Wakefield, firemen from, 146
Wakefield, Cyrus, 134
Walden, 100
Walden Pond, Thoreau's cottage on, 99

Wales, Prince of, 122, 123-130
at Revere House, 273
Walford, Thomas, forge of, 5, 10
Wallace, Alan, 305, 313
Walpole, 140
Walsh, David Ignatius, governor of Massachusetts, 245
Walter, Cornelia M., 188
Waltz, 39
Ward, Artemus, 213
Ward, James, 198
Ward, Thomas, 45
Ward Eight, 340
invention of, 279f.
Locke and Ober prosper on, 280
Wardell, Jonathan, 35
Warre, Mr., 128
Warren, Dr. John C., 112
Warren, Dr. Joseph, 43, 47, 60, 62
Copley portrait of, 287
death of, at Bunker Hill, 74
Washington, George, 60, 170
banquet for, in Hancock mansion, 80
entertained at Bunch of Grapes, 44
first LL.D. from Harvard, 201
help from, after fire, 155
library of, in Athenaeum, 320
Stuart portrait of, 287
Washington Irving, design of, 92
Washington Street, 26, 115, 116, 185, 186, 187, 191, 228, 236, 243, 266, 295, 298, 299, 300, 306
after the fire, 152
department stores on, 262
fire in, 147, 148, 149
residential section, 87
Watch and Ward Society, 9, 42, 249, 250
Longfellow approved by, 105
original purpose of, 251
Water fowl, 3
Water-front, 220-229
marketing along, 222
Water Street, 87
Watertown, 274, 308
Watson, Abraham, 61
Wayland, 268
Wayside Inn of, 105

Index

Index

[2]

372